MEN AND MASCULINITIES

MEN AND MASCULINITIES
Theory, research and social practice

Chris Haywood
and **Máirtín Mac an Ghaill**

Open University Press
Buckingham · Philadelphia

Open University Press
Celtic Court
22 Ballmoor
Buckingham
MK 18 1XW

email: enquiries@openup.co.uk
world wide web: www.openup.co.uk

and
325 Chestnut Street
Philadelphia, PA 19106, USA

First Published 2003

A catalogue record of this book is available from the British Library

ISBN   0 335 20891 6 (pb)   0 335 20892 4 (hb)

Library of Congress Cataloging-in-Publication Data
Haywood, Chris (Christian), 1970–
    Men and masculinities : theory, research, and social practice / Chris Haywood
and Maírtín Mac an Ghaill.
        p. cm.
    Includes bibliographical references and index.
    ISBN 0-335-20892-4 – ISBN 0-335-20891-6 (pbk.)
        1. Men   2. Men–Social conditions.   3. Masculinity.   I. Mac an Ghaill,
    Mairtin.   II. Title.

HQ1090 .H396 2003
305.32–dc21   2002066239

Typeset by Graphicraft Limited, Hong Kong
Printed in Great Britain by Biddles Ltd, Guildford and King's Lynn

For John Haywood
      Seosámh Mac an Ghaill

CONTENTS

ACKNOWLEDGEMENTS

A number of people have contributed to the writing of this book. Our thanks to those who have read through various chapters: Kathryn Ecclestone, Chris Skelton and Iestyn Williams. Thanks to the publishers of Open University Press, particularly Justin Vaughan for his support. We are particularly grateful to Richard Johnson, who provided us with critical comments on the text.

SOCIAL PRACTICES AND CULTURAL ARENAS: INSTITUTIONAL SITES

INTRODUCTION

Key concepts

Theoretical synthesis; second-wave feminism; patriarchy; materialist analysis; poststructuralism; sex role theory; gender identity; masculinism; hegemony; complex identity formation; multiple masculinities.

Introduction: masculinity in context

What is this book about?

Are all men the same? What do men want? What makes a real man? What about the boys? During the last decade such questions have been raised across the social spaces of state, family life, workplace and education. At the same time, masculinity has gained increasing popular interest with the 'football hooligan', the 'absent father', 'underachieving boys', 'Essex man' and the 'new man' being regular popular media features. Presently there is much talk across the western world about a crisis in masculinity. Such discussions provide unclear and unbalanced accounts of men and masculinity with simple and complex explanations being developed that fail to connect with individuals' experiences. The elusiveness, fluidity and complex interconnectedness of masculinity in modern societies add to the complexity of researching and writing in this area. Currently what is missing from the study of men and masculinity is an introductory sociology text that provides a systematic overview of the field (see Connell 1995). In response, *Men and Masculinities* attempts a synthesis of main theories and key concepts. While in no way simplifying its complexities or understating the challenges it presents, this book sets out to make the sociological study of men and masculinities more accessible to a wider readership.

Sociologically, we are in a privileged position. New frameworks have emerged that trouble common sense assumptions about gender. The second-wave feminist movement of the 1960s and 1970s provided a social vocabulary that included: sexual politics, patriarchy and sexual division of labour. More recently gay and lesbian writers, AIDS activism and the influence of queer theory have made popular a language around sexual regulation employing notions of homophobia, compulsory heterosexuality, the heterosexual matrix and transgendered identities.[1] In the book every effort is made to translate the abstractness of current theorizing of sex, gender and sexuality. Our use of case studies throughout the text is of particular importance in enabling us critically to examine the above questions.

These emerging conceptual frameworks with their social vocabularies have provided the context for a number of high quality theoretical accounts that offer fresh insights into the social importance of masculinity. Since the early 1990s we have been provided with theoretical frameworks that have enabled us to analyse systematically and document coherently the material, social and discursive production of masculinities within the broader context of gender relations (Cockburn 1983; Connell 1987, 1995; Kimmel 1987a; Weeks 1989; Hearn and Morgan 1990; Segal 1990; Middleton 1992; Mac an Ghaill 1996a; Collier 1998; Ervo and Johansson 1999). These texts reveal a tension between what are referred to as *materialist* and *poststructuralist* critiques of gender identity formation.[2] Materialist in this book refers to a broader philosophical perspective held by those who insist on the primacy of 'matter' as a source of meaning and experience. This means that social relations are based upon a 'fixed' source. For example, early feminist studies located the source of women's oppression in the male body. In contrast, poststructuralist theorists have emphasized the indeterminacy of meanings. As a result, meanings can not be simply 'read off' from an identifiable source. In terms of exploring men and masculinities, this means that the living of sexual/gender categories and divisions is more contradictory, fragmented, shifting and ambivalent than the dominant public definitions of these categories suggest. Sex/gender practices can be seen as being shaped by and shaping the processes of colonization, of racism, of class hegemony, of male domination, of heterosexism, of homophobia and other forms of oppression. In short, masculinity can be viewed as crucial points of intersection of different forms of power, stratification, desire and subjective identity formation (Fanon 1970; Hemphill 1991; Prieur and Taksdal 1993; Jefferson 1994; Mac an Ghaill 1994a; Haywood 1996).

A main argument of this book is the need to hold onto the productive tension between these different sociological explanations of men and masculinity (Haywood and Mac an Ghaill 1997a). At a time of the conceptual ascendancy of poststructuralism with its focus on the cultural, there is a need to return the social to critical theory, bringing together the categories of *social* and *cultural* as mutually constitutive elements, into a productive dialogue. We need to renew the social and cultural analysis of gendered social relations and identity formations, mapping out some of the more intricate positions as they articulate the shifting boundaries of class, sexuality, ethnicity and generation. In other words, we are not suggesting a return to a sociological reductionism, that either views minority groups as unitary social categories or a materialist account that reifies patriarchy as a monolithic state practice operating against women. There is a need to re-engage with earlier academic and political representations of women, alongside critical explorations of the suggested crisis in heterosexual men's lifestyles. This is particularly salient at a time when there is a lack of consensus in sociology concerning how we conceptualize our concern with commonalties of experience and specific experiences of the world in the context of rapid social and cultural transformations at global and local levels (Brah *et al.* 1999).

Aims of the book

Men and Masculinities has a number of interrelated aims in providing up-to-date accounts of research and writing on men and masculinity in key social and cultural arenas:

1 To explore the main sociological approaches to men and masculinities within the broader context of gender relations. This includes critically

examining theories of: sex role, gender and power, discourse analysis, multiple identities and relations.
2 To use these sociological perspectives to emphasize the social organization of masculinity and active cultural production of masculinities within institutional sites, including the state, family, workplace, education and media. This will enable us to understand masculinity as being central to more traditional sociological concerns with conceptions of power and stratification, alongside more recent questions of the body, desire and subjective identity formation.
3 To examine critically the suggested crisis of masculinity in relation to wider social and cultural transformations in late modernity. This draws upon a historical approach that makes links with earlier periods of structural change impacting on gender relations.
4 To trace the shift from earlier monocausal models of power to more inclusive forms of power, thus exploring the interplay between different social divisions – including sexuality, class, ethnicity, and generation, alongside the political question of how we live with difference.
5 To explore emerging forms of contemporary masculinity cross-culturally, highlighting multiple, collective and multilayered social practices at local and global levels (Connell 2000).

The book meets these aims by examining men and masculinities within broader sociological problems, including essentialism/social constructionism, structured action/subjectivity and categoricalism/deconstructionism (see Seidman 1996). We conduct this exploration of men and masculinities in the context of the following developing frameworks. These are not exhaustive, rather they are used to contextualize how sociological ways of seeing men and masculinity are developing.

Framing men and masculinities: towards a sociology

Every story needs an audience. Currently, accounts of men's lives are one of the most popular stories across advanced capitalist societies. Best-selling books on masculinity, experts on television shows discussing the difficulties of being a man and male confessional writing in magazines and tabloid newspapers attest to the suggested crisis in (western) masculinity. However, an interesting paradox immediately emerges. On the one hand, media representations suggest that this 'what about the boys?' narrative, which they have been central in projecting, is a late modern(ity) phenomenon. On the other hand, they draw upon rather atavistic ideas – an amalgam of common sense and scientific theories – making appeals to an earlier imaginary gendered social order, based on biological differences between men and women. These images are accompanied by a nostalgic remembering of a 'golden past', when men and women occupied established gender roles in a stable social system.

The popular media script follows a familiar format in which particular social issues are selected: the absent father, the violent football fan or the underachieving male student, for example. There is a description of the hard times that men are experiencing, which, in turn, seems to have wide popular resonance across social groups. This is followed by an explanation that the increase in these failed masculinities is caused by their inability to internalize appropriate models of masculinity. A major flaw in this approach is that it is tautological, with the high profile media attention to the crisis of masculinity producing a lot of information but little explanation. Part of the difficulty in discussing questions about men and women is that the terms of reference are already defined. There is a real sense in which we all feel that we *really know* what we mean by men and women, girls and boys, masculinity and femininity, heterosexuality and homosexuality. The potential for sociology, as illustrated in this book, to problematize, contest and interrogate these categories provides an antidote to implicit knowledges of men and masculinities.

Sex role theory

Current popular accounts of men's problems, particularly with reference to women, speak of a gender polarity of fixed notions of masculinity and femininity, in which gender identity is seen as an attribute of the individual. Earlier definitions of masculinity were closely connected to psychological paradigms that perceived masculinity as present in different behaviours and attitudes (Stoller 1968, Farrell 1974). There are a range of approaches drawing upon sex roles as a concept to understand masculinity that have tended to be closely developed with theories of socialization (Parsons and Bales 1955). Through socialization, sex role theorists argue, males and females are conditioned into appropriate roles of behaviour. Polarized norms and expectations between genders are central to the definition of masculinity. Consequently, attitude tests, according to one strand of sex role theory, can be used to measure levels of socialization by the amounts of masculinity that males possess (see Bem 1974). Within this perspective, masculinity is subject to objective and unproblematic measurement through an index of gender norms. According to Pleck (1981), living up to a gender role is more problematic for boys because of the level of social expectations that males experience. In particular, expectations of strength, power and sexual competence form the basis of male roles. Boys, he argues, are likely to experience failure because of the contradiction between the ideal 'role' and lived experience. For Pleck, this is the necessary basis for an understanding of masculine identity formation.

There is a tendency within sex role theory to assume that these ahistorical gender essences are quantifiable and measurable. Hence a wide range of individual men and male groups, such as effeminate boys and gays, are seen as *not having enough masculinity*, which is explained in terms of deficient levels of testosterone, inadequate role models, or overpowering mothers. In contrast, black boys and white working-class boys are seen as having *too much masculinity*. These texts serve to erase or underplay the significance of the social in the making of men and women. At the same time, the deployment of 'nature' as a key category is a common strategy among these writers. Scientific discourses, particularly spoken through psychological conceptions, have the effect of naturalizing gender relations, suggesting that they are determined by an underlying 'natural' force. This work, which can be linked to historical constructions of nature deriving from Enlightenment understandings, continues to be highly influential with considerable rhetorical and persuasive explanatory power.

For feminism: sociology, masculinity and oppression

It is a misnomer to suggest that early sociology wasn't interested in men. As Maynard (1990: 282) points out: 'It may seem strange to describe the study of men as a "new" area. This is particularly so when the current interest in gender arose partly in response to the fact that sociology had previously been concerned almost exclusively with men.' At the same time, a critical study of men and masculinity has tended to be absent from mainstream sociology textbooks. Initial studies of gender relations compensated for this sociological partiality by contributing much needed knowledge on the social worlds of women and girls. Such work opened up masculinity to critical scrutiny, employing a unitary notion (one style) of masculinity, with patriarchy attaining a universal status as the single cause of women's oppression. A central concern was to understand masculinity that is situated within a structure of gendered hierarchies, in which particular social practices are used to reproduce social divisions and inequality. A major success of early feminism is based upon its explanatory power (and its mobilizing force) in uncovering the logic behind the organization of social inequalities, named as patriarchy. It also provided a public language for women as a political minority to speak to each other and name their oppression.

From a pro-feminist position, Hearn (1992) has illustrated a more complex picture of male domination, examining the shift from private to public patriarchies (see also Walby 1990). These texts argue for the need to rethink categorical theories that suggest that gender/sexual relations are shaped by a single overarching factor. Rather, they point out that there is a need to disaggregate the overinflated concept of patriarchy, maintaining that these relations are multidimensional and differentially experienced and responded to within specific historical contexts and social locations. In other words, differentiated forms of male power can only be explained by an analysis which takes into consideration the specific conditions that give rise to these situations. It is the relationship between these social structures that determines how gender relations are lived out. One way of doing this has been to consider men and women as sexual classes, structurally located within the relationships of patriarchy and capitalism. Hearn's (1987) early work *The Gender of Oppression* is a useful and innovative example of exploring masculinity in this way. He considers 'sexual classes' in terms of structures and super structures, where masculinity is a structured ideology of males' biological relationship to reproduction. He notes that: 'While men persist in the base of reproduction, masculinities persist in the "ideology" of production' (Hearn 1987: 98). Masculinity in this way can be connected to an individual male's relationship to the economy. In short, collective masculinities result from men's shared structural location.

Holding on to the centrality of women's oppression in the study of masculinity has generated some of the most exciting work on men and masculinity. In *Gender and Power*, Connell (1987) identifies inequalities between males and females in relation to levels of income, levels of literacy, women's participation rates in government and their overwhelming experience of domestic violence. For him, these inequalities indicate a pervasive pattern of male oppression of females. Connell (1987: 183) suggests that: 'It is the global subordination of women to men that provides an essential basis of differentiation'. He anchors this global subordination into a perspective that identifies differentiated forms of masculinities and femininities existing relationally, at local levels. Methodologically, this has involved him in researching particular local arenas using in-depth interviews and life history research methods. Connell argues: 'structure is the pattern of constraint on practice inherent in a set of social relations' (1987: 97). In looking at particular social relations in localized contexts, we can map out the material, cultural, and psychic practices and constraints that produce formations of masculinity.

Turning to the internal dynamics of masculinity, Connell develops earlier cultural approaches to masculinity, like those of Tolson (1977: 12), who provides a definition of gender that:

> allows us to appreciate the highly particular ways in which 'masculinity' is commonly understood . . . 'masculinity' is not simply the opposite of 'femininity' but there are many different types of gender identity . . . and different expressions of masculinity within and between different cultures.

· In his highly influential text, *Masculinities*, Connell (1995) maintains that masculinities are not only differentiated, they stand against one another in relations of power. It is the internal relations of masculinities and femininities that are the significant dynamic of continued gender inequality. He makes use of Antonio Gramsci's (1971) notion of hegemony to describe the relationships in society's gender order. A hegemony of masculinity is established by the domination of one masculinity over another. Masculinities in

this way are 'not fixed character types but configurations of practice generated in particular situations in a changing structure of relationships' (Connell
1995: 81). Men occupying a hegemonic masculinity are asserting a position
of superiority. They do this by 'winning the consent' of other males and
females, in order to secure their (hegemonic) legitimacy. Men are able to position other men by way of their subordinated, complicit, or marginalized relationships. By considering gender meanings as relatively autonomous, a range
of masculinities can exist in the same institution. This range of masculinities is produced through individual life histories that involve family
background, peer groups and other social experiences. It is in this way,
Connell (1995: 736) argues that: 'Different masculinities are constituted
in relation to other masculinities and to femininities through the structure
of gender relations'.

Within broadly pro-feminist approaches to men and masculinity, Brittan
(1989) moves the frameworks of masculinity towards a notion of increased
contextual specificity by examining the historical constitution of masculinity. Firmly rejecting the universality of masculinity, Brittan suggests that we
need to take seriously the plurality of masculinity. Like Hearn and Connell,
by identifying *masculinities* rather than a masculinity, we are made aware of
a range of ways of becoming male. However, rather than simply considering masculinities as a range of masculine forms, or what Brittan calls 'male
signs', he retains a concept of masculinity that also deals with socially and
economically structured male behaviours. Brittan argues: 'While it is apparent
that styles of masculinity alter in relatively short time spans, the substance
of male power does not' (1989: 2). The apparent contradiction between
pluralistic styles of behaviour and the predictability of male domination is
resolved by attempting to redefine what is meant by masculinity. When we
talk of masculinity we are talking about different styles of self-presentation.
For instance, Brittan argues that we can talk about these styles of male
behaviours almost like fashions. In England, in the 1960s, males had different
hair styles which changed during the 1970s. Similarly, males experimented
with macho and androgynous forms of identity. At the present time, fatherhood is a popular masculine style.

To resolve this conceptual tension Brittan uses the term 'masculinism' as
an ideology that men use to justify and legitimate male positions of power.
'It is the ideology of patriarchy' (Brittan 1989: 4) which is much more fixed
than the signs of masculinity. Masculinism is an ideology that stresses the
natural and inherently superior position of males, while serving to justify
the oppression and subjugation of females. This ideology of males being
naturally more powerful, competent, successful and fundamentally different
from females is one that can be located in various historical periods. Easthope
(1990:56) reminds us that:

> The myth of masculinity certainly goes back to the ancient world of
> Greece and Rome; however, its present form is stamped indelibly by

the Renaissance and by the rise of capitalism. No attempt to analyse masculinity can ignore the way masculinity is defined by history.

In this way, masculinism transcends reproductive and productive relations, and from Brittan's position, ideology informs and forms the nature of those relations. In effect, Brittan inverts the classic Marxist tenet that the infrastructure determines the superstructure. In contrast, he emphasizes the transcendence of ideologies over class relations. This conceptual separation allows Brittan to consider the fluidity of male behaviours, while simultaneously allowing for the continuities of male oppression of females.

One of the major strengths of pro-feminist analyses is that they connect masculinity to wider social and economic forces. This link between the class relations of society and patriarchy illustrates a perspective on masculinity that remains close to feminist aims of reducing oppression (see Hearn and Morgan 1990). However, it could be argued that in emphasizing wider social structures of oppression that determine the position of men, these accounts tend to marginalize men's subjectivities. They draw upon a wider problematic in social sciences of 'structure' and 'agency' or in more recent terms 'subjectivity' and 'discourse' (Weedon 1987; Smith 1987). These divisions are resolved by holding onto continuous unchanging structures of capitalism and patriarchy, alongside a whole range of signs. From this perspective, new signs of 'maleness' or masculinities are seen merely as new mediations of oppression.

Beyond oppression

A specific feature of *Men and Masculinities*, in seeking a synthesis in the field, is to bring together recent historical and contemporary theoretical and empirical work. This allows a critical reflection on the relative adequacy of different perspectives on masculinities, while at the same time highlighting the different problematics about men and masculinities. Although providing a highly productive set of frameworks with which to analyse masculinities, profeminist perspectives are not without their problems. Middleton (1989, 1992) has problematized their notion of oppression. First, he argues that studies of masculinity have tended to see oppression itself as a structure, rather than consider that oppression is structural practice. Second, and what is more important, he suggests that male oppression of females refers not only to an infraction of a standard, but also an intention to infract. With this he points out that writers on gender politics suggest that men can change oppressions. However, this creates conceptual confusion. As he notes: 'oppression results in a double bind for those who are accused of being oppressors, because they are assumed to have intentionally violated rights which everyone can agree to, and to have constructed the system of those rights for their own aggrandizement' (Middleton 1989: 9).

Middleton suggests that we need to understand gender relations beyond oppression and domination. One way of doing this is to see gender relations as dynamic forms of regulation and control, both excluding and including social inequalities. An important aspect of this more complex view of power is a critical focus on the multidimensional social subject, involving an exploration of the interactions and the intersections within and between different sets of social relations. For example, Brah (1992: 136) has argued that: 'As a result of our location within diasporas formed by the history of slavery, colonialism and imperialism, black feminists have consistently argued against parochialism and stressed the need for a feminism sensitive to the international social relations of power'.

More recently, social psychologists have produced interesting poststructural texts, with psychoanalytic inflections, that address the limitations of sociology around issues of the self, subjectivity, the body and gender/sexual identity formations. Poststructuralism involves displacing hierarchies, destabilizing dominant meanings and deconstructing binary and oppositional thinking (Davies and Hunt 1994: 389). At the same time, psychoanalysis has developed highly productive accounts of the complex psychic investments that individuals have in dominant sexual and gendered discourses (Hollway 1989; Middleton 1992; Frosh 1994; Butler 1997). Masculinity is central to the modernity project with its emphasis on rationality, reason and scientific progress. With notable exceptions, studies on men and masculinity have tended to examine masculinity as part of a rationalist project. Work from other disciplines, such as psychoanalysis, has the potential to open up the soft underbelly of these masculinity studies. This illustrates the limits of overrationalist sociological explanations of sexual politics that fail to acknowledge that what we *feel* is as important as what we *know* in relation to the maintenance of dominant gendered and heterosexual discourses and social practices.

Men and masculinities in late modernity

If men's lives are intricately linked to social and cultural transformations, emerging forms of sexuality in late modernity have major significance for men, masculinity and gender relations. Social and cultural shifts such as the separation of sexual pleasure from reproduction and marriage (the sexual as plastic), the development of reproductive technologies, the increasing spatial visibility of lesbians and gays, the mass production of sexual products and pornography and the emergence of HIV/AIDS have had a major impact upon meanings of manhood (Giddens 1993; Hawkes 1996). The cultural possibilities of sexual violence against men, alongside a new set of media representations such as 'absent fathers', 'child abusers' and 'laddism' have emerged through these sexual fractures. Social and cultural transformations are making tears in the social fabric of sexual meanings, leading to frayed understandings of what it means to be a man. For instance, the emergence of 'hard gays' with tough masculinities in multipartner sexual cultures interrogates a traditional understanding of manhood that fuses tough masculinities and heterosexuality. This book, through commentaries on contemporary research on men and masculinities, alongside our own grounded material will provide sociological understandings on the interconnections between sexualities and masculinities.

During the last two decades, as a result of feminist, gay and lesbian writing and AIDS activism, the changing nature of men's lives and their experiences have been much debated within a range of literatures, drawing upon sex role, gender identity, psychoanalysis, and gender and power relations (Weeks 1981, 1989; Watney and Carter 1989; Dollimore 1991; Sedgwick 1990; Plummer 1992; Sinfield 1994). *Men and Masculinities* reflects an engagement with these theoretical influences. Sociological debates on masculinity are explored with reference to disciplinary developments in criminology, social psychology, psychoanalysis, anthropology, history and cultural studies (Easthope 1990; Hall 1992; Collier 1998). For example, historically the relationship between sociology and psychology has been important, with the sociology of gender being developed against psychological accounts, resulting in inadequate explanations for both fields of study. As Connell (1987: 193–4) points out with reference to the development of an understanding of socialization within the context of Australia:

> The popularity of socialization notions in academic research has been supported by two occupational blindnesses, the inability of sociologists to recognize the complexities of the person and the unwillingness of psychologists to recognize the dimension of social power. Both groups have been willing to settle for a consensual model of intergenerational transfer – playing down conflict and ignoring violence – and for a consensual model of the psychological structure produced.

Men and Masculinities suggests that masculinity is intimately linked to wider social and cultural transformations within the British nation-state and other western countries and that the assumed crisis of masculinity can be read as an effect of the wider crisis of late modernity. The question of identity has emerged as one of the key dynamic concepts in the context of rethinking social and cultural change. It is suggested that sociocultural change is marked by the disintegration of older social collectivities – such as social class – and increased fluidity of social relationships, with an accompanying interest in identity and subjectivity (Bradley 1996). More specifically, there has been a focus on the pluralization of identities involving processes of fragmentation and dislocation (Giddens 1991; Hall 1992). The concept of identity is a highly resonant term that is used in a wide variety of ways in different contexts. Brittan (1989: 17) illustrates the usefulness of the concept of identity, examining three emphases, which are relevant to the theorization of masculinity, namely, the socialization case, masculine crisis theory, and the reality construction model. Sociologically, the high conceptual value of identity emerges from its contribution to new frameworks, which open up innovative ways of exploring the relationship between individuals and society.

Most importantly, as Mercer (1990: 43) argues with reference to social change: 'Identity only becomes an issue when it is in crisis, when something assumed to be fixed, coherent and stable is displaced by the experience of doubt and uncertainty'. This doubt and uncertainty is experienced at individual, social and psychic levels, circumscribed by the local–global nexus of cultural transformations. Within this context at the start of the new century, masculinity has come to speak a wider sense of social dislocation in a postcolonial, deindustrializing, Disunit(ing) Kingdom (Kinealy 1999). The process of social change has thrown up an unexplored set of questions about the Anglo-gender majority (male) identity location, concerning a collective national past and future. Who are 'we' (English men)? Who were 'we'? Who have 'we' become? Who can 'we' become? As a result there is a need to begin to develop a sociology that explores the changing collective self-representations of dominant forms of Anglo-masculinity around questions of Englishness, whiteness, social location and cultural belonging, alongside the material and symbolic systems and practices that produce this ethnicized gender position that is not named as such (Mac an Ghaill 1999). This is part of a more general trend whereby the ascendant social category in established binaries (for example, men, heterosexuals and whites) are becoming the new objects of critical appraisal. In other words, masculinity is central to an understanding of the new politics of race and nation in the west and the accompanying new ethnicities, marked by a new cultural condition of diaspora (movement of people – cultural dispersal), hybridity (mixing cultures), syncretism (pluralistic forms of cultural belonging) and transnationalism (Mac an Ghaill 2000).

Another innovative way of sociologically exploring the relationship between the individual and society, which is underplayed by cultural theorists, is the question of social class. More specifically, the changing dynamics of class formations with the shift from industrial capitalism to global consumer capitalism has made a major impact on working-class men's and women's lives. Locating earlier materialist representations of patriarchy, class domination and social change within their sociohistorical context enables us to see how they resonated with wider social concerns and anxieties of their period. These 'Old Times' explanations were once 'New Times'. Presently, it is easy to dismiss these accounts by concentrating on their limitations, such as their essentialism, functionalism and overdeterminism. However, a main strength of this position has been to place on the sociological agenda such issues as the social reproduction of sexist ideology, state regulation of patriarchy, and institutionalized sexual discrimination. At the present time, it is important to hold onto the theoretical and political achievements of this work, which raised questions of the state's control of women's bodies, violence against women, and women's exclusive responsibility for childcare and housework in the sexual division of labour (Dobash *et al.* 1998; Hearn and Parkin 2001). Doing so serves as a useful reminder of the historical amnesia that characterizes many contemporary contributions in the field. There is a strong tendency in postmodern work to downplay or erase such issues as that of the patriarchal state power, social class divisions, institutional structures and hegemonic cultural capital. In such texts, there is a suggestion that discourses and practices of representation have displaced the conceptual necessity of such terms as ideology and social reproduction.

Moving beyond the body: thinking globally

A recent conceptual framework has emerged that focuses on uncoupling masculinity from male bodies, that is, uncoupling *what men do* from *what men are*. Halberstam (1998) suggests that Butler's (1990) contemporary theorizing on gender as performative has opened up ways of understanding gender categories. The emphasis on gender as performative has problematized the cultural formation of sex and the interconnections between sex and gender. As a result, Halberstam argues that we need to develop this idea and in particular disconnect masculinity from male bodies. Masculinity and femininity in this way should be understood as something that cannot simply be equated with biological sex. The implications of this is that, at particular historical junctures, female bodies are able to take on and live out particular masculinities. Drawing upon a range of historical, archival and literary sources, Halberstam outlines a number of case studies.

For example, one of the more striking cases that she outlines surrounds the story of Colonel Barker (1895). Raised as a tomboy by her father, Lillian Barker joined the Canadian army. During that time, an unsuccessful marriage broke up and she had two children by another man. After leaving him she adopted the lifestyle of a man. S/he then married a woman claiming s/he was really a man before suffering war injuries. Eventually Colonel Victor Barker joined the British Expeditionary Force and won medals. Only years later through charges of bankruptcy was Colonel Barker taken to jail where upon he was examined and named as 'really' female. Colonel Barker sustained a masculinity for over 30 years. Halberstam argues that such cases are widespread and continuities can be found in particular sexual subcultures such as (although not exclusively) Stone Butches[3] and female to male transsexuals. In particular, this highlights the inadequacy of contemporary theories of gender to accommodate female masculinities. Disconnecting masculinities from bodies, while continuing to hold onto a sociological notion of maleness, is a challenging project that is engaged with at various times throughout this book. At the same time, such work enables us to consider the more problematical status of masculinity. Hearn (1996) points out that a diversity of masculinity/*ies* is a central facet of its limitations. By disconnecting masculinity from the body we are problematizing the suggested nature of power relations between men and women. However, an exploration of masculinities creates the possibilities for other forms of social power to constitute the body.

The conceptual development of masculinity in the context of western academia has tended to construct a set of insular concepts and reified types that inadequately describe gender relations in other cultures (Cornwall and Lindisfarne 1994). Work on masculinities has tended to concentrate on the localized production of men's meanings and experiences. However, more recent studies suggest the need to understand masculinities within a broader social and cultural framework that includes issues of globalization and transnationalism (see Sweetman 1997). Taking seriously the concept of masculinities, we begin to acknowledge that: 'it is important to capture the diversity of these signs and forms of behaviour by understanding that masculinity can not be treated as something fixed and universal' (Archetti 1999: 113). Competing representations and performances of masculinity are taking shape within the context of the growth of western capitalism, with cultural imperialism, articulated in and through hegemonic masculinities, traversing international boundaries (Shire 1994; Mirandé 1997).

The structure of the book

As mentioned above, *Men and Masculinities* is written in an attempt to capture different sociological answers to the questions: Are all men the same? What do men want? What makes a real man? What about the boys? It is located within the context of what often seems to many women to be nothing but the same old 'patriarchal story', alongside new responses to questions of gender/sexual differences among men. One response in answering such questions has been to explore these accounts in terms of their 'situatedness' at a specific moment, when notions of multiple masculinities, emerging (hetero)sexualities and new definitions of processes of identity formation are helping to provide fresh sociological frameworks. With the explosion of texts in the field, we have had to be selective. Areas of inquiry, including health, sport and crime are well represented in the sociological literature. In contrast, fatherhood, globalization and methodology are underdeveloped. Also, given our preference for theory-led ethnographic work, we have included areas with which we are familiar: work, education and politics.

Part I: Social practices and cultural arenas: institutional sites consists of four chapters. The introduction provides a theoretical and conceptual context to begin our exploration of men and masculinities. The next three chapters use these sociological perspectives to explore the social organization of masculinity and active cultural production of masculinities within institutional sites.

Chapter 1 examines the arena of work and draws upon a growing number of studies that have used the concept of masculinity to make sense of men's practices. In this chapter various ways of working are explored from managing to engineering. It also examines the interrelationship between masculinity and unemployment.

In Chapter 2, we suggest that sociologists have outlined the changing significance of the family in pre- to late modern societies. This chapter connects with a main sociological concern to examine the issue of men's participation in family life. There are few studies that explore men and the family through masculinities. We address the invisibility of masculinity in family studies, arguing for the need to establish a sociology of fatherhood.

Chapter 3 provides a wide range of investigations of school-based masculinities. We identify some of the salient features of these studies such as teachers, the curriculum and peer groups. It also seeks to locate masculinity within the social relations of age, sexuality and ethnicity.

Part II: Mapping, researching and practising masculinities illustrates why, within contemporary conditions, studying masculinity as an object of knowledge is both so interesting and so very difficult.

Chapter 4 addresses questions that have tended to be underplayed in sociological textbooks. It is concerned with global masculinities. This cross-cultural analysis illustrates the limitations of generalizing from a western model of masculinity about what it means to be a man. The chapter enables us to understand masculinity as being central to conventional sociological concerns that denote masculinity as embodied. Alongside an exploration of more traditional cross-cultural approaches to masculinity, the chapter suggests that masculinity may also be articulated through international politics, intranational economic relations and globalized desires.

A main concern of Chapter 5 is to indicate the major significance of gender in social research methodologies. While illustrating the key contributions that feminism has historically made to this field and male researchers' critical engagement with different strands of feminist theory, we explore the conceptual development of research frameworks. In light of the emergence of post-structuralism and postmodernism, we consider the possibilities that more recent epistemologies, methodologies and methods might begin to open up.

Finally Chapter 6 examines the politics of masculinity and locates it within the long history of sexual politics. This includes: the new social movements of feminism, gay and lesbian mobilization and the more recent HIV/AIDS activism and queer interventions. As a result, this puts us in a position to explore the question of the future of masculinity politics and the search for a postidentity politics position (Pease 2000). Our conclusion summarizing the aims of the book, re-examines the notion of synthesis and the specificities of *our* sociology of men and masculinities, namely a concern with social relations, practices and organization.

Questions for your reflection

1 Why has the issue of masculinity attracted so much discussion across western societies?

2 What are the main differences between materialist and post-structuralist approaches to gender analysis?

3 What are the main explanations of masculinity?

4 When studying men and masculinities, what are the advantages of models of inclusive power?

5 What do institutional based and cross-cultural analyses of masculinity offer us in trying to understand the complexity of male–female relations?

Suggested further reading

Brittan, A. (1989) *Masculinity and Power*. New York: Blackwell.
Connell, R.W. (1995) *Masculinities*. Berkeley, CA: University of California Press.
Dunphy, R. (2000) *Sexual Politics: An Introduction*. Edinburgh: Edinburgh University Press.
Segal, L. (1990) *Slow Motion: Changing Masculinities, Changing Men*. London: Virago.
Sinfield, A. (1994) *Cultural Politics: Queer Reader*. London: Routledge.

Notes

1 These terms are defined and explored in the book.
2 A diversity of terms are used to pin down new sociological approaches. In discussion of other authors' perspectives, we use postmodernism and poststructuralism as they do. When conveying our own position we use poststructuralism.
3 'Stone Butch' usually refers to lesbians who identify with and articulate a hyper-masculinity.

CHAPTER I

WORKING MEN'S WAY? EXPLORING MASCULINITY AT WORK

Key concepts

Family wage; feminization; compensatory masculinities; product fetishism; masculine schizophrenia; technologies of the self; discourse analysis; protest masculinity.

Introduction

The main aim of this chapter is to catalogue how social change is impacting on men and their masculinities and to explore how these changes are being mediated through different occupations in local contexts. In so doing, we interrogate *masculinity at work* through the use of empirical examples. By using these examples, the chapter focuses on a number of themes. In the first part we draw out the links between masculinity and work, with a quantitative focus on men's employment patterns. The second part of the chapter adopts a more qualitative approach, exploring the experiential interconnections between masculinity and class by focusing on different occupations. Finally, we suggest that a conceptual shift from working *with* the body to working *on* the body is a productive way forward in analysing the ways that men work.

The sociology of work: a 'man's world?'

During the last two centuries highly influential studies of 'men at work' have made available frameworks to explain industrial relations (see for example Mayo 1933; Taylor 1947; Weber 1958; Marx 1972). More recently, sociologists have developed a sociology of work that makes gender a central feature of analysis. As with other institutional sites explored in this book, feminism plays a crucial part in highlighting the discriminative perspective embedded in social studies on work, which often unproblematically assumes that men are the key object of inquiry (Delphy 1984; Beechey 1987; Kim 1997; see methodology chapter on empiricism). Collinson and Hearn (1996: 3) capture this paradox:

> A critical analysis of men and masculinities is particularly important in the study of work, organisation and management. Yet an examination of the available literature reveals a recurring paradox. The categories of men and masculinities are frequently central to analyses, yet remain taken for granted, hidden and unexamined; men are both talked about and ignored.

This resulting critical analysis sits uneasily alongside the confusions and contradictions that are present when holding on to rigid distinctions that circulate through categories such as work and non-work, employment and unemployment and the corresponding sphere of leisure time and free time (Pahl 1984; Grint 1998; Roberts 1999). Indeed, feminist perspectives outline how women have been excluded from analyses of work and offer important criticism of studies of work as a public exchange of labour power for payment. Highlighting the semblance between domestic labour and public labour, feminism makes an invaluable contribution by demonstrating the significance of gender and work. This is in the context of studies that have made connections between the history of gender relations and its changing social and cultural significances, embedded in economic rationalizations, managerialist ideologies, technological changes, political justifications and social policies (Pollert 1981; Walby 1986; Phizacklea 1990; Bradley 1999). In light of these analyses we need to understand 'men' and 'work' as a gendered interrelationship, through which diverse meanings of manhood are established and sustained.

Making connections: work as masculine

Importantly, what we understand as masculinity impacts on what we classify or typify as work. Historically, changes in England over the course of the eighteenth, nineteenth and twentieth centuries gave rise to gendered spatial divisions between domestic and public spheres. The gendered nature of small scale domestic units of production that characterized early industrialization gave way to a redefinition of men's and women's relationship to the public and the private. Hollway (1996) suggests that this distinction helped to establish and sustain middle-class ideologies of femininity and masculinity. The interrelationship between middle-class ideologies and industrialization produced a reordering of the gendered landscape of work. One effect of this reordering was to place work within a breadwinner/homemaker dichotomy. The notion of the family wage, earned by the man to support the home, both resonated with Christian doctrine and provided a rationale for English trade unions' justification for inflation-linked wage rises.[1] During the twentieth century the notion of the breadwinner bringing in the 'family wage' had a major impact on employment strategies. Women's employment was frequently deemed as supplemental, often sustained through low pay and poor working conditions (Walby 1997). As a result, work and men became synonymous, as Acker (1992: 257) suggests:

> The abstract worker transformed into a concrete worker turns out to be a man whose work is his life and whose wife takes care of everything else. Thus the concept of a job is gendered, in spite of its presentation as gender neutral, because only a male worker can begin to meet its implicit demands. Hidden within the concept of a job are assumptions about separations between the public and private spheres and the gendered organisation of reproduction and production.

At the same time, men have been understood through the notion of being a worker, with which they have closely identified and invested. Alvesson and Billing (1997), when discussing the relationship between masculinity and work, operate a gender symbolism framework. They argue that gendered work is 'deeper than sex typing, meaning that not only is a job openly viewed as women's or men's work, but that it refers also to non-explicit meanings, unconscious fantasies and associations' (1997: 90). Importantly, this goes beyond overrationalistic accounts and places work within the context of desire, fear, and imagination. Morgan (1992) also uses a notion of gender symbolism. He suggests that we should begin to make sense of masculinities and work by identifying a range of 'polarities', 'tendencies' or 'oppositions' that include: skilled/unskilled, heavy/light, dangerous/less dangerous, dirty/clean, interesting/boring, mobile/immobile. These oppositions work together in a number of complex ways to establish the gendered nature of work and its symbolic value.

Finally, connections between masculinity and work are inflected by other social categories. For example, for many western societies work has traditionally been understood as an important moment in the passage from childhood to adulthood. Another example of this inflection is illustrated through the separation of the private sphere of family life from the public sphere, from values of dependence to independence. In short, to become a man is to become a worker. Historically, many processes involved in becoming a worker simultaneously interconnect with becoming a man. In this way the meanings of men and work are not understood as static or fixed. Rather, they are part of a constant negotiation at a number of political, economic, social and cultural levels.

Mapping men's employment patterns: identifying social change

It is a key aim of this book to document how social change – historically and presently – is impacting upon men and their masculinities. One way to do this is to examine the changing patterns of men's participation in work. We identify two considerations. First, by accounting for participation rates we can gain a relatively accurate picture of where men are located within the labour market and how their positions may be changing. Second, we are wary of identifying men's participation rates as constituting a gendering of work. As we pointed out in the introduction to the book, the biological characteristics of male and female do not necessarily equate to masculinities and femininities. For example, in some education sectors the workforce is predominantly female. At the same time, recent changes in education policies have directed school organization towards more masculine working styles in western societies, such as 'managerialism' etc. (Haywood and Mac an Ghaill 2001). As a result, we need to be conceptually open to accommodate the masculine cultures that females may work within, identify with and sustain. In other words, we need to track male participation in the workforce, as well as to consider the processes involved in becoming a man.

The majority of the world's manufacturing is concentrated in the northern hemisphere, with four-fifths of it being distributed between the US, western Europe and Japan. However, since the 1970s developing countries have quadrupled their manufacturing output (Dicken 1998). In contrast, the northern hemisphere has experienced a slower growth rate. Some of those countries, such as the United Kingdom and Germany, have experienced a contraction of traditional industries. For example, coal mining, ship building, engineering, car production, fishing and agriculture are experiencing collapse, fragmentation and contraction (World Trade Organization 2000). It has been argued that the declining economic importance of these industries is creating a 'crisis for men', as key material resources used to forge masculinities are becoming scarce (Willis 2000).

By using Britain as a local case study we wish to explore this suggested crisis. Our starting point is an examination of men's participation rates. It is important to note that at the beginning of the twenty-first century, over 70 per cent of men compared to under 54 per cent of women are involved in the British labour force (see Table 1.1).

For some, this reads as 'nothing but the same old story' (Walby 1997). However, this story has an interesting new theme. In real terms, men's participation in the labour force is increasing at a very slow rate, whereas women's participation is increasing at a much faster rate. The percentage of men involved in the labour force is on a downward trend, however, for women the trend is upward (see Table 1.1). These statistics illustrate that over the last 30 years the sex-based constitution of the labour force is changing. It must be added that this 'participation' obscures the fact that many women experience relatively lower pay, and insecure, poor working conditions. However, this story has another interesting twist.

Labour market changes in the United Kingdom are taking place against a context of industrial restructuring. Service sector employment has increased, whereas employment in the manufacturing industry is decreasing. From 1971 to 2000, jobs in the service sector have increased by 36 per cent, from 15.6 million to 21.2 million. In contrast, manufacturing work has fallen from 7.0 million to 4.2 million (see Tables 1.2. and 1.3). This has implications for cultural representations of men's work. Recent empirical evidence

Table 1.1 British labour force (aged 16 and over) by gender

Year	Males (%)	Females (%)	All 16+ (000s)
1971	80.5	43.9	24,900
1976	78.9	46.8	25,700
1981	76.5	47.6	26,200
1986	75.2	50	27,566
1991	73.4	53.1	28,185
1996	72.2	53.7	28,717

Source: reconstructed from Central Statistical Office (2001).

Table 1.2   All male employment by industry sector (thousands – not seasonally adjusted)

Year	Agriculture and Fishing	Manufacturing	Banking and Finance	Administration
1984	448	3938	1350	1859
1986	396	3955	1510	1891
1988	431	3999	1648	1920
1990	411	4006	1845	1928
1992	404	3656	1774	1966
1994	402	3505	1833	1996
1996	375	3654	1935	2050
1998	354	3656	2182	2042
2000	330	3511	2392	2141

Source: reconstructed from OPCS (1999, 2001).

Table 1.3   All female employment by industry sector (thousands – not seasonally adjusted)

Year	Agriculture and Fishing	Manufacturing	Banking and Finance	Administration
1984	124	1579	1136	3202
1986	111	1594	1282	3472
1988	130	1617	1456	3595
1990	131	1606	1663	3791
1992	131	1469	1577	4044
1994	133	1370	1635	4224
1996	137	1382	1657	4398
1998	111	1331	1771	4526
2000	96	1228	1880	4788

Source: reconstructed from OPCS (1999, 2001).

challenges pervasive images of men facing harsh work in creating wealth. The British man in the twenty-first century is more likely to be a service sector worker.

These changes have led Goodwin (1999: 44) to argue that the nature and content of men's employment has changed and is continuing to be transformed: 'that men's identification with work in western society, has become a function of (and is maintained by) a social sex-ordered division resulting from both capitalist and patriarchal relationships as developed in Western civilisation'. One of the key features, according to Goodwin, has been the fluctuation of men's work, in terms of nature, type and amount. For instance, at the turn of the twentieth century, men were concentrated in engineering and heavy manufacturing with the majority working full time. At the end of the twentieth century, as suggested above, the decline in heavy industry and the rise of new technology made men main participants in the service sector.

Men's full time employment has severely declined at the same time as the number of males eligible to work has increased from 24,900,000 in 1971 to a projected 30,092,00 by 2006 (CSO 2001). In contrast to women's participation in the labour force, men's participation has reduced. This has led some commentators to suggest that work is now becoming feminized.

Feminization I: sexing the crisis

The sociological concept of feminization can be used as a device to explain changing employment participation. Breugal (2000) maintains that women constitute the majority labour group in the public spheres of health and education. On the other hand, men dominate the private spheres of manufacturing, electricity, gas, water, construction, transport and communication, constituting more than half of the workforce in these arenas. Feminization therefore is a term used to capture historical changes that are taking place in specific labour markets. Using Breugal's concept of feminization, we can describe men's changing participation in specific occupations as men consolidating male employments. One example of this is the agriculture and fishing industry in which female participation has decreased, consolidating its position as a male occupation. In contrast, Breugal suggests that feminization is taking place in hotel, banking and catering occupations. Here, men's work is becoming casualized, as they experience high levels of labour turnover and undergo organizational restructuring. We explore the evidence that supports these trends in Table 1.4 and Table 1.5.

Tables 1.4 and 1.5 show selected employment participation rates for men and women. Over the last decade a partial increase in women's manual

Table 1.4 All male employment by occupation (thousands – not seasonally adjusted)

	Manual	Non-manual	Clerical and Related	Craft and Related	Selling
1992	7034	7013	969	3188	750
1994	6861	7092	952	3045	732
1996	6919	7314	976	2924	743
1998	7146	7611	1026	2996	762
2000	7133	8063	1056	3026	819

Source: reconstructed from OPCS (1999, 2001).

Table 1.5 All female employment by occupation (thousands – not seasonally adjusted)

	Manual	Non-manual	Clerical and Related	Craft and Related	Selling
1992	3485	7914	3018	397	1298
1994	3437	8024	2929	332	1267
1996	3514	8201	2913	321	1336
1998	3576	8447	3009	296	1349
2000	3529	9016	3040	232	1483

Source: reconstructed from OPCS (1999, 2001).

work has been offset by the stabilizing of male participation in the same sector. However, craft and related work shows a downward trend for men and women but increasing male participation rates in clerical and retail occupations. An increase of women in particular labour markets with a corresponding decreasing participation and recruitment of men appears to support the claim that feminization is taking place. Another way of examining feminization may be to consider analytically how the meanings surrounding men's and women's work have changed, with some areas of work coming to be understood as 'women's work'. Finally, the feminization of work can be described as resulting from employers increasingly targeting and employing women. In this way costs are kept low by employing female cheap labour, with men priced out of the market. Historically, similar processes were involved in the racialization of ethnic minority groups, who were perceived as a cheap replacement labour force for indigenous workers (Mac an Ghaill 1999).

These material changes, including an increase in part-time, temporary and casual work, home-working and self-employment, may suggest that men's and women's work is becoming blurred. If work is men's traditional source of power and status, with the changing nature of work, men's position in society may also be changing. However, it is important to be aware, as Bradley (1999) points out, that statistics can often obfuscate local and regional variations and it is unwise to attempt to read off local specificities from large scale data, particularly at a time of rapid global transformations. Rather, we need to explore how these indicators of social change are being lived out at the local level.

Feminization II: new ways of working with men

An alternative way of conceptualizing the feminization of work shifts the focus away from rates of participation based upon sex, to a consideration of gendered styles. For example, in the U.S., Douglas (1977) developed the notion of sentimentalization to explain feminization. She argued that men in the US were increasingly adopting traditionally ascribed feminine values of emotionality, intimacy and sentimentality. This resulted in a controversy over whether American men were becoming more like women and the implications of this for the nation. From another perspective, Lee (2000) also moves away from a descriptive account of feminization. Grounded in interviews with 50 male workers, her research seeks to establish whether or not men can experience sexual harassment. She argues that feminization results from men being positioned in traditional 'female' locations. For example, she suggests that men who exhibit caring and emotional attributes at work are not consonant with dominant definitions of masculinity. When men do not correspond to the perceptions of dominant occupational masculinities, other workers 'feminize' them and they are described as 'women'. Hence, taking up different styles within the workplace may be understood in gender-specific ways and assigned gender attributes. Importantly, these notions of feminization suggest a more complex analytical understanding that goes beyond the simpler framework of male and female employment participation rates.

We use this understanding of feminization to consider how we might make sense of recent structural changes in the labour market. Roper (1994) in his study of British organizational life, captures managers' anxieties working in engineering that accompanied this restructuring. Importantly, in his research, industrial arenas are not seen simply in economic terms but as containing classed and gendered dimensions. One managing director of an automotive company explains:

> I never discovered anybody from Oxford actually making, actually creating, any economic wealth. And I think in this country the people who are best regarded, get the benefit of the honours system – if that is a good thing anyway – socially are better regarded, are what I would call the consumers of wealth . . . You know the army, the civil service, solicitors, educationalists . . . The guys who actually create it are not particularly well regarded.
>
> (Roper 1994: 138)

From this perspective, workers in manufacturing are a nation's breadwinners, while service sector workers 'consume' the wealth. The masculinities of these sectors intersect with national identities. For example, in nineteenth-century America there was much anxiety that men working in newly established service occupations might lose their 'manhood'. What was named as 'overcivilization' had a specific effect on men working in the cities. Mumford (1993) succinctly outlines how medical professionals at the time connected overcivilization with sexual impotence among men working within white-collar occupations. Drawing upon a Social Darwinist notion that theoretically connects social behaviours with physical traits, she suggests that the U.S. faced a crisis of masculinity (see Kimmel 1996). The crisis centred on the distinction between 'muscle worker' and 'brain worker', with the latter being disconnected from their 'natural' self, where overcivilization has had an impact on their ability to become men. Mumford (1993: 44) outlines how medical professionals argued that: 'white middle class men were highly susceptible to sexual neurasthenia [nervous exhaustion], that working class men were largely immune from the disorder, and black men represented what might be called hyperpotency'.

As Mumford points out, class position articulated through labour market sectors becomes an articulation of a racial position that at the same time sustains a sexual identity. Not only were middle-class men becoming sexually impotent because they were becoming disconnected from nature, they were as a consequence losing their manhood. A similar argument has been popularized by Bly (1993), who argues that men need to get back in touch with their true spiritual selves that have been alienated by industrialization (see Chapter 6, this volume). With assumptions of natural vigour and energy surrounding manufacturing work, the current shift can be understood as a reworking of masculinities. As Adkins (1998) suggests, the move to different managerial strategies such as 'just in time working' or 'flexible specialization' does not necessarily result in the take up of different masculine values. It is suggested here that current restructuring is a process that is resignifying at a broader cultural level representations of men, masculinity and work.

Holding onto real men: exploring men's working experience

So far, this chapter has focused on the need to understand men's work as a gendered practice, to consider men and masculinity as mutually informing and to explore social change, work and masculinity through the concept of feminization. The next section of this chapter explores men's working experience by examining the interconnections between class and masculinity in different occupations. We begin with one of the most pervasive representations of working men: traditional manual workers.

Working with the body: exploring manual working-class masculinities

The traditional manual worker is located lower down the occupational hierarchy and generally experiences lower pay and poor working conditions. Tolson (1977) makes direct connections between the types of work that men *do* with the types of men that they *are*. His text provides an entry point for a discussion of work and masculinity, as it highlights how different occupations may envelop different male identities. This structuralist Marxist approach maintains that different societal locations generate specific masculinity dynamics. Furthermore, it suggests that work sustains particular masculine beliefs and values, while underlying men's work is the operation of a fundamental contradiction. This contradiction is exacerbated by men who occupy working-class positions. According to Tolson, the latter's relationship to work is one of deep alienation but is also characterized by dependence. Alienation at work can take on a heroic character as men, by virtue of the capitalist system, become forced to endure its vicissitudes. He expands upon this theme, suggesting that a capitalist society fractures male identity as the division of labour collapses a psychological unity of home and work. This is further destabilized by the expansion of capitalism in reducing patriarchal privilege; a historically grounded dominance of masculine beliefs and values that support capitalism. Important in this analysis is the need to connect capitalist relations of organization with class positions. In a classic Marxist understanding of surplus value, the more the 'male' manual worker exercises his right to work, the more he becomes an alienated and objectified worker. The wage itself for working-class men compensates for their alienating and objectifying experiences. The notion of 'false need' generated in capitalism and sustained by the wage compensates for men's alienated position; such needs creating a tolerance of work. From this perspective, the very phenomenon that creates and substantiates a masculine identity, the wage, constitutes the very phenomenon that disrupts and fractures masculine self-identities.

Tolson makes a connection between working-class masculinities and capitalist work practices. For him, it is the logic of capitalism and the history of gender relations that produces masculinities. In a similar way, Willis (1979) also sees male working-class culture as an alienating effect of work. He suggests that:

> There is an infusion of assertive masculine style and meaning into the primitive, mythologized elements of confrontation with the task. It is also a masculine expressivity which often delivers or makes possible some of the concrete revelatory or oppositional cultural practices . . . resistance to authority; control of the group; humour and language; distrust of theory.
>
> (Willis 1979: 196)

The hard, physically demanding labour of manual work is understood and reinterpreted by working-class men as being heroic and as requiring physical and mental bravery. The wage packet, according to Willis, becomes a 'prize' of masculinity at work, a symbol of strength and endurance.

Importantly, Willis's work illustrates that the higher the wage, the greater the masculinity. Masculinities, in this sense, are produced through the work in which bodies are involved; masculinities are made through work *by* the body and what the body does. Harsh work becomes the symbol of masculinity. However, the higher wages provided by non-manual occupations do not equate to 'better men'. On the contrary, while manual workers perceive white-collar workers as possessing a lower masculine status – understood as weak and effeminate – the latter have greater relative control and autonomy over the production process. The position of manual workers is further complicated by the fact that much mentally orientated work revolves around intelligence and competence, aspects of masculinity that have traditionally been used to partition and exclude women from employment.

Crafting masculinities

Cockburn (1983, 1985) also explores the impact of control and autonomy on workplace masculinities. Her analysis focuses on male craft and technical workers in the printing industry and like both Tolson and Willis, she understands masculinities as a result of contradictions and syntheses between patriarchal and capitalist practices. From a feminist dual systems theory, Cockburn suggests that capitalism and patriarchy both complement and contradict one another as male interests interact with the capitalist quest for greater profits. Unlike other writers, who use patriarchy as an analytic tool, Cockburn usefully suggests that *men* as well as *women* have their social worlds constructed through patriarchal practices. Hence it is masculinity that forges the types of working relationships that emerge in a particular occupation.

   Importantly, this analysis which is closely connected to a notion of social change also informs broader debates addressing the deskilling of work. Setting the scene, Cockburn suggests that the history of printing is marked by gender struggles. The inception of capitalism resulted in the industrialized production of printing, thus removing the local familial nature of the work and placing it under the control of factory owners. However, with this shift in control, men sought to consolidate their position through various strategies, excluding women and children from the labour process. Cockburn provides a good example of the logic of capitalist production, the searching for cheap labour, in order to increase profit. For print workers, an underlying justification for relatively high wage levels involved a masculine familial identity of the breadwinner and the family wage. The introduction of 'foreigners' – meaning non-skilled apprentice workers (cheap labour) – was a threat not only to their position as workers but also as men. Another interesting aspect of the craftsperson was the nature of their work. Cockburn describes work in the printing industry as dirty, noisy and odorous but also providing various amounts of freedom and self-expressiveness. In contrast to manual workers, these men understood themselves as part of the labour process rather than its object. Their work often involved control over production and subjectively was experienced as fulfilling and satisfying. Like manual workers, masculinities were established through the nature of the work. However, rather than have masculinities forged against brutal alienation, these craftsmen were connected to the potential control and management of some part of the labour process.

From Cockburn's account, there appeared to be little change in the nature of printing work from the late 1800s to the 1960s. As indicated above, the men in her study operated large machines that were noisy and dirty. They identified with their machines and their work process, investing them with pride and self-respect. Apart from the cyclical negotiation of wage levels, the labour process of the craftsmen changed very little. It was the development of technology that had a major impact on the form and content of the print workers' labour. The impact of technological innovation, according to Cockburn, left many of them confused not only about their class status but also about their masculine identities. Such insecurities were exacerbated by the move from a printing compositors' keyboard to that of the QWERTY keyboard of the modern typewriter or computer. The shift was understood by many of the men as a move from compository printing work to that of typing. One of the key implications of printing work becoming aligned with typing work was that it generated a gendered significance. The introduction of the QWERTY keyboard meant that women could not only be seen as potential workers in the new system, their ascribed 'naturalized' affinity potentially made them better suited to the work. At the same time, there was a whole range of labour process implications for men in adapting to the typewriter. For the male print workers, changes in the control and pace of the work, the keyboard layout, and the size of the installation, was experienced as move towards 'women's work'. Another aspect of change was captured in the movement from metal to paper as their primary working material. The metal that men had traditionally used required more physical labour and time had to be spent crafting it to make it workable. This was combined with a move from the shop floor to office space. As one worker from Cockburn's study explains: 'I think it may make softies of us – I feel it may make us, I don't know if this is the word, "effete". Less manly, somehow' (1983: 108). Thus, changes in the labour force were understood through a gender-based perspective.

In the work of Tolson, Willis and Cockburn, we are provided with examples of what might be called compensatory masculinities. This is where gendered identities stand in opposition to capitalist relations of production. Within this realist philosophical framework (see Chapter 5 on methodology) we are able to talk about uncovering what 'real' or 'true' masculinities might look like, away from the influence of distorting and alienating relations of production. In contrast, Knights (1990) suggests that theorists tend to conflate subjectivity with creativity, autonomy and control.

Workplace relationships can be understood as a struggle to maintain autonomy and thus become a struggle for subjectivity itself. In this way, the loss of subjectivity becomes the loss of masculinity. Hence workers in Cockburn's study become emasculated. Such an analysis is uneasily positioned within capitalism and patriarchy, where capitalism is bad and 'true' masculinity is good. Masculinity becomes a consequence of, and form of resistance to, the labour process. Knights' analysis, situated within the debate on deskilling in the labour process questions the success of organizations in producing functional worker identities. Although a number of work-based identities are made available, worker responses to those identities are not predictable. Knights suggests closer examination of subjectivication (the experience of identity). Rather than focusing upon organizational identity positions, we need to concentrate on the meanings that workers ascribe to them.

Engineering masculinities: working through identities

Knights' understanding of the dynamic nature of subjectivity is further developed by Collinson (1992). He studied an engineering firm in the north of England that employed over 1000 workers, highlighting that class distinctions were critical to how gendered identities were being understood. However, instead of locating workplace gendered identities in terms of products of contradictions of class or patriarchy, he develops a view that work masculinities are a:

> condition and a consequence of the widespread pre-occupation with the search to maintain material and symbolic security in a sometimes precarious, usually competitive and ever changing social and organisational world that is deeply hierarchical and divided by class, gender and age (to name a few dimensions).
>
> (Collinson 1992: 29)

He draws upon Henriques *et al.* (1984), where subjectivity becomes a key dynamic in social practices. By bringing in subjectivity as a key dynamic in the formation of masculinities, he explicitly inserts men's intentions into the formation of masculinity. For Knights, intentions are part of a technology of the self; a technology that is engineered by institutional practices that generate gendered and classed selves. However, Collinson argues that rather than a dual analysis of men's selves, gender and class should be examined as interconnecting categories.

Some of the men in Collinson's study appear similar to those researched by Willis. These shop-floor men were performing the most alienating tasks in the company, involving the longest hours, highest job insecurity, least job control, and worst canteen and car parking facilities. In short, their work within the company was the least valued and the most vulnerable. It is within this context that Collinson asserts that masculinity crucially shapes men's relationship to the work process. His research identified two main responses to the workplace. One was based on indifference, with workers seeing their job as a means to an end; a teleology. Another response was their aligning and working with management. For Collinson, whether men related to the workplace through compliance or resistance, fundamentally, the form and content of masculine identifications circulated through anxieties generated by their occupational status.

Masculinity in the engineering workplace was seen as a resource to manage the hidden injuries of manual work and the securing of subjectivity. This could either be done formally, for example through the trade union, or informally through shop-floor social relations. Collinson developed a concept of critical narcissism, involving men using other men to consolidate their own identities, often through the operation of culturally shared social practices. McLean *et al.* (1997: 6) suggest that: 'the culture of engineering is a clear example of a dominant masculinity – white, heterosexual, middle class'. However, Collinson suggests that in this arena masculinities are much more fragmented. He found marked divisions between those men who worked in the offices and those who worked on the shop-floor, with critical narcissism operating through this division. Other divisions on the shop-floor were based upon workers' social evaluation of different factory departments. While workers in certain parts of the plant were deemed as lazy and non-political, others could be understood as more militant.

Alongside these spatial differentiations, divisions occurred between men in the same department. One division centred around generation, where younger workers displayed their masculinities by 'winding up' (making fun of) older workers. Closely related to this division were those who held on to a strong division between family and work and invested in a notion of the male breadwinner. In contrast, other workers often boasted about frequent sexual encounters with different women. These different masculine styles were captured through the practice of 'tipping', whereby workers handed over their wages to their wives. In contrast, Bert, an engineer, perceived his ownership of the wage packet as an important aspect of his masculinity; to give the wage to a wife was viewed as a form of emasculation. Collinson suggests that these divisions may be subjectively bridged through what he calls 'masculine schizophrenia', with men taking up both positions, having domestic responsibilities at one moment, while in another, adopting a heterosexuality disconnected from the domestic arena. Therefore masculinity dynamics in engineering were far from predictable and there was much more heterogeneity than traditional class distinctions would presume.

The main purpose in the above discussion is to highlight how masculinities can be understood as subjectively constituted. However, what has been underplayed in the use of Collinson's work in this section is the importance of managerialist ideology. In the next section, the question of subjectivity and managerialist ideologies and practices are discussed in greater depth.

Managing to be male

At the beginning of the twenty-first century, identifying and targeting the middle-class continues to generate particular problems, especially in light of the ascendancy of service sector work. It is important to acknowledge that the effects of social and economic change have impacted upon management practices as well as upon employees. Managers are not simply agents of social change but also subject to it and in this process they reconstruct their masculinities.

Returning to Tolson's analysis of the middle class, he argues that, as a result of their being confronted by particular rules and conventions that cannot be avoided, they are also subjected to forms of alienation in their work. He maintains that these institutional rules resonate with their own personal experience. For Tolson, such masculinities are mediated through a notion of professionalism that is encapsulated by individualistic expertise and an identification with work; what he calls a 'self-discipline'. He also recognizes the fractured nature of the middle class and the breadth of occupations that constitute this social group. According to Tolson, middle-class masculinity is facing a crisis as career structures become viewed as unavailable. The traditional, pre-Second World War moral authority of the middle class was traditionally embedded in British imperialism. The expansion of capitalism has created a crisis of professionalism, as specialization has dissolved structures of individual merit, and segmented and diversified company career paths. As a result, middle-class occupations are no longer necessarily part of a career progression infused with company identification, but are now producing similar forms of alienation and objectification that working-class men experience, albeit in new ways.

The impact of social change on management is identified in a study by Roper (1994). He examines 30 senior managers' life stories (25 male and five female), in exploring the notion of the 'organizational man'. Roper suggests that popular representations of managers often take the form of 'faceless middle men'. Using their life stories, he highlights the impact of capitalist economies on how men and women manage businesses and how they make sense of it subjectively. A key dynamic in how they understand social change is to analyse it as gendered. For example, men, in his account, experience their management practices as masculinity processes. He suggests that we need to understand what 'organizational man' means, by linking him to economies of change and that management masculinities are closely worked out in relation to the demands of the capitalist market. Roper found that one characteristic of a management masculinity involved an intense attachment and emotional investment in the company product or *product fetishism*. In the offices where Roper interviewed these men he noticed that they adorned their surroundings with pictures or miniature models of company products. Interestingly, Roper explains that looking back on his study, the particular men were indistinct; their products came to represent them. He reports:

The symbiosis between men and goods suffuses both the organisation, man's individual identity and management cultures as a whole. Yet changes in capitalist demands become a catalyst for the significance of the product in the market. The result can be a structuring of the manager's masculinity'.

(Roper 1994: 138–9)

For these managers, the company appeared to be a device in perfecting the product and generating product quality. Investing in the product was a common managerialist strategy. These men intrinsically linked quality products to increased profit margins. This way of managing the company was related to the familial nature of many of the firms that were often set up by themselves and other family members. In a metaphorical sense, the manager became the 'father' of the firm with the product often viewed as 'their baby'. A process of protective strategies could be identified in these men, including keeping secret aspects of the product or maintaining a controlling interest in the company. Another example of this can be found in Messerschmidt's (1995) analysis of the Challenger space-shuttle disaster, in which higher management's concern with the consolidation of the company and its long term future overrode concern for the safety of the shuttle crew.

In Roper's study, with the reorganization of capitalist economic relations and the rise of corporatism, the managers' identifications and investments became problematic. For most of the men, the company tended to concentrate on selling the product rather than an image of a product. The rise of corporatism produced a large number of company mergers, accompanying a shift from product identification to a strategy of asset stripping. This meant that a company would be bought up, have non-profitable elements discarded and often be streamlined and sold on, without any investment in the product.

Corporate management strategies contain some interesting language. Themes of warfare and sexuality emerged to describe particular management practices: ambush marketing; aggressive quoting; drilling down; granularity; hired gun; getting hot; jettison employees; on target; sacrifice and strategic decisions. The emergence of corporate capitalism also signals a shift from producer to consumer needs. In the last three decades this has involved a specific focus on consumer culture, where the process of selling is as, if not more, important than the product. Managers, as fathers of the firm, experience 'takeovers' as a break-up of the family, with their products as the children being violated and defaced by uninterested companies that aim to strip their assets. Roper (1994: 150–1), for whom corporatism is a feminine practice, summarizes the managers' perspective as follows:

The young wimps of my age gain no inherent pleasure from objects, but instead adopt a feminine stance, offering up body and soul for money. They model themselves instead of dressing up the product. At least their fathers refused to be bought and sold, and so will go out like men, will 'die hard', dreaming of the perfect product.

There is an important generational aspect to Roper's account, where masculinities are closely linked to the psychic investments that are specific to different sectors in different generations. In many ways the careers of these older men mirrored broader economic cycles. For example, the economic growth of the 1960s and early 1970s were now part of the general downturn, and recession was mirrored by the men's imminent retirement.

Before concluding this section, it should be added that a range of themes could have been taken up and explored in relation to workplace masculinities. For instance, one might have focused more on the content and style of masculinities rather than the specific ways in which masculinities are constituted. Clothes and uniforms become important devices not only to codify hierarchies but also as styles of masculinities. One of the striking things to emerge from the literature is that workers are categorized as either *white collar* ('shirts') or *blue collar* ('overalls'). Alongside this, middle managers are often portrayed as 'suits', something that in Roper's study made the men somewhat faceless. Du Gay (1996) usefully highlights the importance that uniforms have on worker identities. In one of his case studies, he reports how the introduction by the company of a standardized uniform to shore up their collective image made the workers feel like schoolchildren. As Addleston and Stirratt (1996) in their examination of public schooling argue, the uniform is a key aspect of male solidarity. Stripping bodies of their individuality, uniforms are used to provide collective solidarity. Citing Morgan (1992: 6), they note that: 'The uniform absorbs individualities into a generalised and timeless masculinity while also connoting a control of emotion and subordination to a higher rationality.' The men in Roper's study wore suits and he suggests that the suit hid the male body, reorienting focus towards the company and its merchandise *as* the male body. Furthermore, he argues that the suit not only seeks to objectify others, but it keeps their own sexualities out of view. Alternatively, it may be that sexuality is not so much kept out of view but that a different representation of sexuality is on offer.

Unemployment: the others

With the current impact of global social changes upon men's work suggesting a 'crisis of masculinity', a different crisis might be claimed by those men who are unemployed. A cautious note needs to be made about unemployment, with the issue of unemployed women remaining an academically underexplored area of inquiry across western Europe. Examining the impact of unemployment on masculinity can unintentionally reinforce the notion that unemployment is simply a problem for men. In fact, as research on women and work makes clear, women tend to be used more expediently in a range of labour markets. Often the old modernist ideology of women earning 'pin money' or 'a little extra cash' is reasserted in the context of flexible labour markets or 'just in time management' strategies (Adkins 1998). However, women's systematic absence from the literature should not necessarily preclude an exploration of the impact of unemployment on men. We have noted earlier that in the last 30 years unemployment is a growing feature of men's labour. Yet there are very few studies that systematically examine unemployment as a masculinity issue. Morgan (1992) suggests that one strategy for understanding masculinity would be to study men whose identities are 'put on the line', with unemployed men representing such a group.

A popular understanding of unemployment is to suggest that it is antithetical to wage labour and that men experiencing it are emasculated. In relation to Italian men, Gheradi (1995) maintains that work is constitutive of masculinity and hence that unemployment threatens the identity of men. There is little doubt that unemployment does have a specific impact on men's lifestyles. Russell (1999) interviewed nearly 400 English men and women in six different labour markets. She argues that unemployed women utilized and intensified existing social networks that were closely aligned to the home. In contrast, unemployed men found it more difficult to replicate their existing social networks, often premised upon formal leisure patterns that were generally not home-centred. The spatial partitions between home and work in this study had particular gendered impacts on how unemployment was experienced.

Willott and Griffin (1997) suggest that the disruption of employment creates a spatial convergence between men and the domestic sphere. However, it is not predictable what this convergence means. For instance, they ask whether men taking up a domestic role creates more equitable relationships between women and men. From their data it appears that simply occupying domestic spaces does not change men's masculinities. The starting point for Willott and Griffin is that in the current social and historical context 'white, middle-class, heterosexual, employed males are considered the "norm"'. They argue that such groups occupy hegemonic space and therefore it is important to recognize how the unemployed position themselves against this norm. From this location, unemployed men are involved in a process of recovering their masculine identities. Willott and Griffin adopt a discourse analysis approach that maps out patterns of meanings and semantic resonances in people's speech. In this way, Willott and Griffin identify two important discourses around the private and the public, that long-term unemployed men appear to acknowledge and negotiate within the context of economic and social deprivation, as well as poor local travel, shopping and leisure facilities.

A key aspect of these men's identity was the performance of a public masculinity. Segal (1990: 202) suggests that the convergence of home and work acts as a challenge to masculinity. In this arena, she argues that men have to reassert their masculinity through a domestic refusal, an active dissociation from the private sphere.

As workers, their flight from fatherhood was mediated by their pay packet: men's quest to purge women from the world of work, and their struggle to gain privilege for their own pay packet, at the expense of women, was expressed symbolically in the notions of 'breadwinner' and the 'family wage'.

In Willott and Griffin's study, this involved being out of the house, with 'escape' from the domestic sphere a key aspect of the men's identities. The pub became an important resource within which to maintain a spatial division of public and domestic spheres, though the impact of unemployment did not simply cause a reconstruction of masculine identity.

However, unemployment did produce a range of personal anxieties. Some of the men voiced concerns that the loss of employment made them feel less attractive to their female partners, by placing them in direct competition with men who were working. Such anxieties were also expressed through the domestic provision discourse, with men arguing that they should be in a position to provide for their families. In this way their inability to provide was experienced as disempowerment and emasculation, feelings of shame and inadequacy in relation to the cultural expectations that surrounded them. This domestic provision discourse was also connected to the idea of respectability, with some men arguing that those who adopted a public masculinity lacked respect. Skeggs (1997) in her study of working-class females points out that a key element of their feminine identity was premised on establishing a notion of respect. A similar idea can been traced here, with working-class men holding on to a concept of respectability which is highly gendered. Willott and Griffin conclude that unemployment had the potential to disrupt the hegemonic ideal and the associated discourses of public and domestic provision. However some men adopted alternative discourses drawn from the hidden economy, although they did little to reconstruct this as a viable alternative masculinity.

Campbell (1993), in her account of English urban riots in the early 1990s, also highlights the significance of unemployed masculinities. For her, unemployment is not necessarily a crisis of masculinity but rather the assertion of a different mode of masculinity. Hence civil unrest is understood as a masculine response to an economic crisis. At the time of the riots, a representation of masculinity and unemployment had emerged based on the notion of the underclass. Murray's (1989, 1994) popular American representation of unemployed men as gravitating towards a value system of non-socially conscious morals, that is, socially feckless, captures a dominant perspective of the underclass in England. For these men, irresponsibility can be ascribed as a way of life, disidentifying with a notion of respectability.

As Campbell suggests, in relation to the underclass thesis, young, white working-class men are some of the most powerless in society, continuing to leave school with few qualifications and limited likelihood of geographical and social mobility. Yet, at the same time, their class-based spectacular performances create social practices that the rest of society can identify and target, re-presenting their powerlessness as a threat to the social order and stability. Alongside this, however, the aggression and violence in which some men and a few working-class women engage is experienced as highly threatening to other social groups. As explored above, sociological studies of masculinities have addressed these aspects from a materialist position. However, we need also to explore the reported masculine subjectivities and their claim that being violent and aggressive feels good; it is exciting. More sociological studies are required which examine critically not only emotional and economic deprivation but the reasons why certain forms of behaviour have some pay-off for some young men (Connell 1995).

Connell (1995) suggests that it is useful, in making sense of the dynamics of masculinity, to understand males on the periphery of the labour market. In a similar fashion to Campbell, Connell argues that masculinities are constructed in relation to specific labour markets. For Connell, young unemployed, or under-employed men take up a 'protest masculinity'. This style is developed in relation to a position of powerlessness where the existing cultural resources for a gendered claim to power are no longer available. In response, men exaggerate, through the pressure of existing masculine conventions, their claims to masculinity. As a result, individuals exhibit spectacular masculinities centred around sexuality, violence and bohemianism. Connell (1995: 111) suggests that: 'Through interaction in this milieu, the growing boy puts together a tense freak façade, making a claim to power where there are no real resources to power'. Protest in this way is the observance, or the exaggerated observance of a male role. As a marginalized gender, protest masculinity develops themes of hegemonic masculinity, reconstituting them in the context of a marginalized labour market. We can see evidence of this notion of the use of hegemonic masculinity in Campbell's study. One of the striking aspects of civil unrest was the continuities between young unemployed men and the masculinities of the police. Therefore, rather than unemployment generating a counter-culture, she suggests that unemployed men reinforce a shared gendered hegemony.

Conclusion

A specific difficulty in writing this chapter is an awareness of the changing relations of social class (Savage 2000). First, what we understand as class is mediated through other social categories such as masculinity. At the same time, we need to be aware that we can not simply 'read off' a masculinity from its relationship to the economic sector. The previous section on unemployment highlights that work-based masculinities reflect broader aspects of men in the wider culture. Studies on masculinity and class might be more fruitful if they moved away from privileging workplace practices as defining men to broader cultural practices that men take up. For example, studies of the formation of class identities have traditionally been understood as based upon working *with* the body. In the twenty-first century, manhood can be acquired through work *on* the body.

Evidence of this was apparent in a study of young unemployed men from the West Midlands in England (Haywood and Mac an Ghaill 1997c). Themes of real and authentic maleness were key points of discussion for the young men, who were experiencing dramatic and condensed disenfranchisement from the local labour market. Consequently the option of making masculinities by working with the body was not available. Not even alternative forms of 'fiddlin' (criminal activities) appeared available or were not taken up by them. Rather, forms of masculine validation centred around 'makeovers'. A makeover in England has become a popular phenomenon, especially on daytime television, with which these young men were well acquainted. At the beginning of these programmes, individuals (usually women), appear in their normal attire and by the end, they are transformed with new hairstyles, new clothes, new outlook on life – thus becoming new people. Usually, the end effect is a more glamorous or chic presentation. What is important is that by simply working on the body, young unemployed men (in our own study) had the potential to gain social status without working in the labour market.

The young men offered explanations of where the best makeovers could be obtained. 'Best' in this context meant the more convincing transformation of self. They engaged in a range of cultural practices that they insisted could validate and display their masculinities. For them, a real, authentic masculinity could be achieved by working on the body, thus, transforming their identity. It may be argued that unemployment did not matter as masculine identity was based upon what they looked like, rather than where they worked. Masculinities in this sense could be articulated through a consumerism that could be written onto the body. However, the instability of the masculinities was often voiced in terms of 'fooling other people':

> When you got a girl you need a job. Do you know what I mean? I mean, I have been out with a girl, yeah and she has got a job, and she had a car . . . and she has got her big wages, wads and all that and I used to go out with her in town, yeah? And she'd wear all these different Armani jeans, all different Armani jeans and I thought , 'What am I doin' with that?' and my friends used to say to me, 'What are you doing with that? You're on the dole, she's workin', she's got this nice car and look at the jeans, the jeans, Jeromiah, man' . . . 'Cos you think, if I get a job yeah, you wouldn't have to worry about impressin' her . . . but because you are on the dole you have got to try your best to say 'Look I have got this money and I have got that money', when you haven't.
>
> (Jeromiah; Haywood and Mac an Ghaill 1997c: 12–13)

As Hearn (1992) suggests, linking economic class with masculinities is problematic. One inadequacy he identifies that seems fitting for our analysis of work and masculinity here is that economic class cultures tend to be assumed to be the class cultures of men. When studying manual workers' or craft workers' masculinities, this chapter has focused on occupational-based class cultures. By situating masculinities within this location, an emphasis on the exploration of the constitution of workplace masculinities is given priority, while recognizing the overwhelming salience of class analysis. Hearn makes another interesting point about how far we can assume workplace masculinities as overriding domestic-based masculinities. He maintains that: 'The emphasis on public domain and economic class dimensions of men's lives as the prime basis of masculinities neglects these contradictory inter-relations of the private and the public' (Hearn 1992: 246). These tensions are further explored in Chapter 2 on fathers.

Questions for your reflection

1 Is men's work changing?

2 Does belonging to the working class produce a specific kind of male worker?

3 If ways of working are changing, are gender relations?

4 What characteristics make up a management masculinity?

5 Do unemployed men have masculinities?

Suggested further reading

Bradley, H. (1999) *Gender and Power in the Workplace: Analyzing the Impact of Industrial Change*. Basingstoke: Macmillan.

Campbell, B. (1993) *Goliath: Britain's Dangerous Places*. London: Methuen.

Hamada, T. (1996) Unwrapping Euro-American masculinity in a Japanese multinational corporation, in C. Cheng (ed.) *Masculinities in Organization*. Thousand Oaks: Sage Publications.

Morgan, D. (1992) *Discovering Men*. London: Routledge.

Note

1 I Timothy 5:8 'But if anyone does not provide for his own, and especially for those of his household, he has denied the faith and is worse than an unbeliever'.

CHAPTER 2

MEN IN THE FAMILY WAY: REMAKING FATHERHOOD

Key concepts

Male breadwinner/female homemaker; paternal masculinities; new father; paternal rights; sex-role segregation; patriarchal and heterosexual state; private/public masculinities; 'feckless fathers'; gay fathers.

Introduction

Pervasive media representations of family life portraying men and women as trading places, are a defining feature of late modernity. Images of increasing numbers of women entering the public domain of paid labour contrast with increasing numbers of men talking about their experiences of the private domain of the home. This chapter complements the exploration in the last chapter of the blurring of men's and women's work and its impact upon men's position in society. From a sociological perspective, these experiences are socially structured and differentiated with, for example, western governments actively persuading women to (re)enter the labour market. At the same time, while some groups of men, such as the unemployed, are being coerced into taking up increased domestic and paternal responsibilities, other men are asserting claims about the pleasures of fathering. Such accounts challenge traditional sociological explanations of the structure and meaning of parental responsibilities presented in terms of the functional needs of capital in industrial societies (Parsons and Bales 1955; Morgan 1992). Two main models of the relationship between the home and workplace that mediated men's domestic experiences as husbands and fathers emerged from this earlier work. First, that a subordinated work masculinity produced a patriarchal, authoritarian masculinity within the home. Second, that the private arena of the home provided men with a space, a haven from enforced instrumentalism and alienation, within which to develop expressive qualities. Earlier feminist studies, using patriarchy as an analytical tool, challenged limitations in these models, emphasizing the undertheorization of gender identity formation, the false dichotomy of the private (home) and the public (work), the demonization of mothering and the social invisibility of women's involvement in paid labour.

Within this wider context of the changing family, including the emergence of what Stacey (1996) refers to as the 'postmodern family', recent years have seen increasing research and writing on men's experience of families, and the personal, social and political representations of those experiences. More specifically, there now exists a large body of studies, as well as a wide range of popular cultural texts, focusing upon fathers and fatherhood (McKee and O'Brien 1982; Russell 1983; Pleck 1987; Burgess 1997). Much of this work has been developed by psychologists and social policy analysts, with their attendant conceptual frameworks, methodologies and core substantive concerns. Moving beyond a mother-focused paradigm, it has addressed a broad set of issues: What does it mean to be a good father? Historically, how has the role of fathers changed within the context of family and wider kinship networks? What is the effect of father absence from the family? Do we need fathers? This chapter uses a number of sociological strategies to re-examine these questions, while developing others. First, the chapter establishes fatherhood as part of the sociology of masculinity. Second, it provides a sociohistorical consideration of fatherhood, including its reconstitution across different periods. Third, it concentrates on the relationship between the state and the formation of familial masculinities and the accompanying production of paternal subjectivities. Finally, it considers the future of fatherhood, examining the emergence of families of choice and the growing visibility of gay fathers.

Establishing fatherhood as a masculinity issue

This chapter establishes fatherhood as part of a sociology of masculinity, highlighting the need to understand the concepts of men and family life as a gendered interrelationship, through which diverse meanings of both paternal masculinities and manhood itself are mutually constructed and maintained. This enables us to rethink the dominant modernist gendered dualism of *male breadwinner/female homemaker*, tracing the multiple ways of being a father, by desegregating specific origins, causes and effects of gender structures in particular periods and in particular geographical spaces. We begin to read through the ideological gender work that surrounds the rigid distinctions that circulate through notions of an active mothering and a passive fathering. Culturally, this is most clearly captured in the concept of mothering, understood as a biological and a social relationship. In contrast, fathering is popularly understood simply as a biological category. A key issue is to address this reductionist position, by conceptualizing fathering as a social category within the sociology of masculinity. The history of the reconfiguration of fatherhood and the attendant changing meanings of fathering within the wider context of a shifting sex/gender social structure enables us to trace the development of sociology itself. A shift from a structuralist position, (in which fatherhood remains conceptually underdeveloped, via a feminist intervention naming paternal masculinity as a power relation), to a postmodern position (with its emphasis on different styles of being a father), allows fatherhood to be understood as a key cultural and discursive resource in the making of contemporary heterosexual male identities.

Earlier constructions of fathers relied upon concepts such as 'traditional' and 'nuclear families', 'socialization' and 'role models'. These conceptual tools, developed in a wide range of diverse areas of sociology and psychology during the 1960s and 1970s, were important in reconsidering domestic and sexual lifestyles as socially constructed rather than biologically determined (see Introduction, this volume). In other words, gender differences were seen to derive from social and cultural processes that created systems of ideas and practices about gender, rather than natural characteristics, such as chromosomal differences (for example, XXY chromosomes) or hormonal differences (for example, testosterone). Such a perspective continues to be prominent in contemporary accounts of fatherhood (Ku *et al.* 1993; Moss 1995). These studies tend to understand fathers as asymmetrically positioned within absent/present, powerless/powerful, good/bad typologies. More recently, there has been a conceptual shift from *simple models of sex role reproduction* to the *active production of complex identity formations*. This enables us to understand fathers as occupying, at the *same time*, contradictory social and emotional subject positions. The latter approach provides a more complex analytic framework that brings together multiple levels of fathers' experiences (Weeks *et al.* 2001). In turn, this allows a shift away from an overrationalist account of sex role theory that fails to acknowledge that what fathers *emotionally* feel and desire is as important as what they *rationally* think in shaping paternal behaviour. Such a shift places at its centre a more complex analysis of power that allows an interrelation between the social, psychological and interpersonal, alongside emotional histories and future lifestyle aspirations. At the same time, it encourages a view that takes into account the shifting patterns of gender relations and conceptualizes fatherhood as a multifaceted lived out experience of classed, racialized and generationally located dynamics.

A major element of establishing fatherhood within a sociology of masculinity is that it is characterized by a number of social divisions or inclusions and exclusions. These can be articulated through cultural representations of familial masculinity and men's participation in family life. Social theorists have outlined the changing significance of representations of the family in pre- to late modern societies. Burgess (1997: 19–20) highlights the range of negative contemporary images of fathers, who are seen as: 'absurd, pitiable, marginal, violent, abusive, uncaring and delinquent'. As she points out, this devaluing of fatherhood in late twentieth century Europe is a remarkable shift from an earlier position in which the authoritarian father was portrayed as central to the moral and political maintenance of western civilisation. The legitimization of the father figure and his authority was seen as deriving from God the father and was reflected in the position and accompanying hierarchical social relations associated with the monarch, the lord, the master and the husband (Seidler 1988). For example, until the middle of the nineteenth century, it was assumed that American fathers would have custody over children where marital breakdown occurred (Furstenberg 1988). In late modern societies, maternal instinct and children's rights rather than paternal authority are central to discussion of modern families. The legislative demands on fathers, as exemplified in the Child Support Agency (CSA) in Britain, explored below, highlights the historical move from paternal *rights* to paternal *duties*.

Cultural remembering and forgetting fathers and fatherhood

Novelists, playwrights and poets such as James Baldwin, Seamus Heaney and J. M. Synge appear to be better placed than sociologists to record the central importance of cultural memory for how we live our lives. They are particularly good at capturing the way that cultural memory mediates the complex interweaving of individual (paternal) biography and wider social practices, marked by institutional constraints (Heward 1988). A sociohistorical approach makes explicit the act of remembering. Sociology theorists of gender, with their tendency to search out general patterns, need to pay special attention to holding on to the significance of the historically and geographically specific.

Current understandings of fatherhood are shaped by the legacy of a past that consists both of fatherhood stories remembered and forgotten. For example, Burgess (1997: 4) considers how recently mythologists have begun investigating fatherhood imagery, 'and guess what they have found: an alternative paternal archetype, who like the "ruler father" can be found in many cultures. This archetype is an "earth father", a nurturer . . .' She adds that its relevance for contemporary conditions is that:

> in our culture, the ancient association of males with birth and rebirth has been severed. For societies that retain earth fathers in their my-thologies tend to accept nurturing behaviour by men towards children as the norm, while societies which disown earth father imagery perceive such involvement by men as deviant.

Hewlett (1991) in *Intimate Fathers: The Nature and Content of Aka Pygmy Paternal Infant Care*, finely illustrates this alternative concept of fatherhood. Such work is highly relevant at a time when fatherhood in Britain is associated with *dangerous men*, with statistics indicating that most child abuse takes place within the home – involving, fathers, stepfathers and brothers (Kincaid 1992).

This sociohistorical approach resonates with diverse representations of men, masculinity and family life generated and circulated through the media and changing patterns of cultural production and consumption. As Westwood (1996: 25) argues, this can be seen, for example, in relation to one of the major cultural signifiers of masculinity, fatherhood,

> which was seized upon by advertisers following the photograph of the great Caribbean cricketer Viv Richardson with a baby on his back. The suggestion was, and is, that fatherhood is 'back in fashion' and it will sell products as diverse as Flora Margarine and Armani suits and cologne.

More recently, media speculation about whether the British Prime Minister, Tony Blair, would take paternity leave projected a normative image of a major role model for how modern fathers *should* behave within the context of the moral management of family life, displaying responsibility, tenderness and expressiveness. Mobilizing such images of the contemporary co-parenting, childcaring, family man offers the promise of social change in politically pessimistic times. At the same time, the media, as a highly influential space of modern iconography, has projected notions of the *new man*, the *new lad* and the *new father*. Implicit within these cultural representations and the attendant resignification of paternal masculinity is the assumption that men are in crisis and consequently are being coerced into processes of change.[1] This suggests that current restructuring of the home, with a diverse range of fathering styles emerging, is one of the main arenas in which this crisis is located.

The accounts embedded in the shifting semantics of fatherhood are historically specific in producing gendered subjects. We can trace the shift from a narrative of the premodern (Christian-based father figure), through the modern (economic breadwinner), to the postmodern (ambiguous, domestic identity). Within a British context, it has been suggested that fatherhood is becoming feminized (Burgess and Ruxton 1996). The latter argue that historically, men's position in the family has been subject to radical change. In the nineteenth century, men held exclusive rights over their children. At the start of the twenty-first century, women have displaced men as legal guardians. This has been consolidated by recent moves giving children the legal status of citizens (Collier 1995). Similarly, Pleck (1987: 84–5), examining the changing historical representations of fatherhood in the United States, describes how in the colonial era, fathers were the major source of moral teaching, adding that: 'notions of the "duty" of fathers to their children, and of children to their fathers, were central to father–child relationships'. By the mid-twentieth century, the father was removed from the home as exemplified in the primary image of the distant breadwinner.

Richards (1987: 33–4) has suggested that: 'as our historical understanding of fatherhood increases, so will our ability to understand the present'. Perhaps the major contribution of this approach to interpreting contemporary issues around fathering is to explore the general tenets that have emerged from historical data. Within a British context, McKee and O'Brien (1982: 14) summarize these as follows:

> the concept of 'the family' is not static throughout history but subject to definitional and structural modifications in terms of co-residence and kinship . . . and consequently that the 'family' as equalling father–mother–child(ren) is a relatively recent configuration; that social change is not necessarily linear or continuous . . . that change in social behaviour and values is not coterminous . . . that regional, occupation, ecological and social class factors influence family structures; that it is not enough simply to know about the size or composition of the 'domestic cell': we need to know about the nature of intra-familial as well as structural relations, and relations between the family unit and the wider society.

Finally, an historical account suggests that there is a potential for the transformation of shifting forms of fathering and mothering. There emerges a clearer understanding that different material conditions and attendant symbolic signs produce different effects in local geographical spaces. For example, regional meanings of fatherhood differ in East Anglia (agricultural), Newcastle-upon-Tyne (deindustrializing) and London (cosmopolitan). This enables us to place the contemporary micropolitical realities of male domesticity and child nurturing in the bigger picture and on a longer time-scale. Such an approach challenges the determinist notion of history without individual actors as active agents, while at the same time rescuing accounts of subordinated paternal social practices, including that of non-cohabiting dads, granddads, disabled fathers, ethnic minority dads and gay dads (Shakespeare *et al.* 1996; Weeks *et al.* 2001).

Embourgoisement, and the symmetrical family: the reconstituted father I

Sociology texts report the postwar period in Britain as a time of fundamental social change in relation to social class and gender structures. The economic sphere was marked by a suggested classlessness as economic growth and Keynesian demand management helped produce full employment and an accompanying sense of rising standards for all. Segal (1990) captures the suggested achievement of sexual equality by naming the period as *Man About the House*, with the old deprivations associated with early death, ill health and mass poverty being contrasted with the new era of 'child benefit, family planning and other forms of welfare provision for mothers and their children' (1990: 2). These economic changes provided the context for the suggested emergence of a modernized nuclear family. A defining feature of the assumed universal democratization of family life was a more equal distribution of household tasks between wives and husbands. For example, sociological studies of the period detailed the brave new world of domesticated husbands. Studies carried out from the 1950s through to the 1970s had shown the tight boundary gender classifications of married couples (Young and Willmott 1957). By the early 1970s, Young and Willmott (1973) maintain that a process of cultural diffusion led the middle-class egalitarian family lifestyle to trickle down to working-class couples. A new picture showed a younger generation of men as husbands and 'androgynous fathers' represented as active within the home and having a close relationship with their children (Robinson and Barret 1986). This was compared to a more traditional image of absent, authoritarian fathers. Horna and Lupri (1987) describe a similar patterning of marital role enactments within Canada, providing two polar 'ideal types' of complementary marriages and symmetrical marriages, in order empirically to assess social trends, that is, a search for the 'typical' father. They found that the transition between the two types of marital relationships was far from complete with the dialectic interplay of parental role enactments inside and outside the household being both varied and complex (Horna and Lupri 1987: 71).

As Segal (1990) points out, British studies that pointed out the flaws of this limited comparison would later become evidence of how patriarchal ideology continued to operate on and within family life. For example, Dennis *et al.* (1969: 196) examined the social structure of family life in a Yorkshire mining community in Britain, and noted the continuation of separate spheres for husbands and wives in relation to childcare and house-work. They write:

> If the husband's duty to his family goes little if at all further than delivering part of his wage each Friday, here the duty and the respons-ibilities of his partner begin. It is for him to earn the money and for her to administer it wisely. In actual fact, this means that the wife takes virtually all the responsibility for the household and the family.

At this time, the ideology of domesticity and the notion of separate spheres underpinned the main frameworks within sociological, psycholo-gical and popular commentaries that created a familial myth in which women were assumed to be the main benefactors.

Early work on the sociology of the family examined social processes that shaped gender relations within the domestic arena. More specifically, there was a concern with the social position of women in institutional areas, such as the sexual division of labour and the social organization of repro-duction and childcare. Parsons' (1955) elaboration of structural functional theory explained how sex-role segregation, in which the father/husband is projected as provider/protector, within the context of the nuclear family as a socializing agency met the complex needs of an industrial society. As Cheal (1991: 6) points out:

> The particular tasks assigned to the sexes are, in Parsons' opinion, due the primacy of the relationship between small child and its mother. The special nature of that relationship, he claimed, is a consequence of the unique capacities of women for bearing and nursing children.

The *visibility* of women in these sociological texts can be contrasted with the *invisibility* of men as a gendered social group. Much of this work in Britain and the U.S. operated within a role model approach, projecting an oppositional structure of male *breadwinner* and female *homemaker*. Feminist accounts of the family from the 1960s through to the early 1980s empha-sized the need to see gender as primarily not a property of the individual but rather of social institutions and cultural practices. These accounts were important in critiquing this dominant sex-role perspective. Feminists were primarily concerned with critically exploring the social positioning of women as wives and mothers within marital and domestic arenas, thereby challenging the social polarization involved in women's ascribed naturalized affinity for such domestic work. In her classic text, *The Sociology of Housework*, Oakley (1974: 17–18) pointed out:

> By far the largest segment of sociological literature concerning women is focused upon their roles as wives, mothers and housewives . . . Possibly family and marriage are areas in which [women's] sociological visibility exceeds social presence.

She argues that a major reason for the subordination of women in the labour market is the institutionalization of the mother–housewife role as 'the primary role for all women'. Early feminist work in this area remains integral to maintaining a high profile on sociological and political agendas of such controversial questions as the redistribution of housework, child-rearing, domestic violence and child abuse (see Walby 1999).

Understanding modern family life: the reconstituted father II

Contemporary theorists of gender relations suggest that the family is undergoing significant changes with a wide range of family formations now being commonplace. This includes non-married cohabiting partners, non-cohabiting fathers, the increasing number of non-blood-related children, ethnic minority extended families and the visibility of gay/lesbian partnerships, all emerging alongside the traditional extended family and the modern nuclear family (Weeks *et al.* 1999). Across Europe, Australia and North America there is more diversity in family life (Russell 1983; Kimmel 1987b; Bjornberg 1992). In the early 1980s, Rapoport *et al.* (1982: 476) suggest that: 'Families in Britain today are in transition in a society in which there was a single overriding norm of what family life should be like to a society in which a plurality of norms are recognised as legitimate and, indeed, desirable'. This diversity of family life is located within structural changes of late modernity, including mass male unemployment, the increased dependency of young people on their family and the feminization of paid work that are making an important impact on the shifting meaning of the family in the new century (Haywood and Mac an Ghaill 1997b).

The ontological question of whether men and fatherhood have *really changed* is one of the most highly contested issues in this field of study. A range of accounts have emerged in response to the ambiguities as to whether men now have greater investments and involvement in parenting and childcare. Within a context of rapid social change, Pleck (1987: 93) examines the characteristics of the 'new father' and how he differs from older images of fatherhood: 'he is present at the birth; he is involved with his children as infants, not just when they are older; he participates in the actual day-to-day work of child care, and not just play; he is involved with his daughters as well as his sons'. Early cultural analysis of masculinity was highly sceptical of notions of the 'new man' and the 'new father' (Chapman and Rutherford 1988). This critical questioning permeated much of the social scientific literature on masculinity. In contrast, researchers working with fathers were more optimistic, noting that they had 'been struck by the very involvement of men in their paternal relationships' (Lewis and O'Brien 1987: 9). From a traditional feminist position, accounts of a reconstructed fatherhood needed to be placed within a wider patriarchal framework. Any forms of personal paternal involvement in the home would have to be set within the specific context of the social institution of fatherhood and the accompanying gendered domination of women by men in both private and public spheres. Other feminists welcomed the limited change. One of the most innovative studies of British masculinity is Segal's (1990) *Slow Motion: Changing Masculinities, Changing Men*. She comments that, by the mid-1980s, disillusioned feminists had produced a number of surveys which challenged the optimism of much recent literature on fathers, claiming greater involvement in parenting and childcare. Segal (1990: 36) argues that:

> The pre-women's liberation rhetoric of the eternal sex-war has crept back to replace what was, for a while in the seventies, a feminist-inspired, more confident rhetoric on the need and possibility for change in men. It almost seems as if, for some, things which are not completely different, are not different at all.

Yet there are limitations in the way in which this discussion about the new father was framed. First, much research and writing with its implicit positivist methodology, operated with the assumption of a unitary model of the father and attempted to set up a simple classification of what in fact are complex and contradictory paternal attitudes and behaviour. Social historians of family life highlight the flaws in this search for a uniform model of the father figure. For example, Hood (1993: xi) writing of the contemporary American situation, suggests that:

> the image of the workaholic upper middle-class husband has splintered into myriad images of husbands and fathers. Now, in addition to . . . early examples of family-orientated middle-class men, we have research on working-class fathers who put their families first . . . and on men who avoid the provider role . . . as well as those who are trapped by it.

Lewis and O'Brien (1987: 6) chart a path through the inherent contradictions contained within the social institution of fatherhood at structural (domination) and personal (individual close reciprocal relationships with women and children) levels. They suggest that:

When the collected mass data on paternal involvement is examined, two contrasting, yet compatible, conclusions can be drawn. On the social level, men perform a far less important nurturing role then women in all societies despite a few exceptional families . . . However, close examination of paternal involvement suggests that the variations between individual fathers can themselves be considerable.

Hence, they conclude that the very heterogeneity of styles of fathering invalidates any general claims about *the father*.

Second, the range of perspectives on the emergence of the new father illustrates a gap between attitudes and behaviour, image and reality, or ideology and action. The resulting confusion has intensified the ontological question of whether the new father *really exists*. One of the main difficulties of this approach is that the object of enquiry is reified, translated into a reductionist dual model of bad (traditional) and good (new) categories of paternal behaviour. In response, it may be useful to draw upon a sociological distinction between identity (who fathers *are*) and behaviour (what fathers *do*). Presently, there is little empirical evidence of men's participation in domestic responsibilities and childcare (that is, behaviour) matching up to the projected notion of active fathers. Cultural theorists have suggested that the context of postmodern conditions has seen a shift from work as the primary site in which to establish a collective identity to a complex, more open society with multiple sources of potential identification and an accompanying choice of diverse social identities.

More specifically, there has been a focus on the pluralization of identities involving processes of fragmentation, fluidity and dislocation. These identities are translated into lifestyles. Currently, various individual men and men's groups, such as profeminist men, invoke the identity of fatherhood as a dynamic element of their lifestyle. This shift projects a contemporary version of manhood through a move from cultivating a *public masculinity* around *work* to the forging of a *private masculinity* around *fathering*. This may be linked to wider social and cultural change and more specifically, to an implied transformation in intimacy (Giddens 1992). Intimate father–son/daughter relationships as a visible mode of masculinity appear to be deployed by younger men as a means of distancing themselves from an older male generation's gender order which was translated into distant fathering. Perhaps a key point to emphasize here is that descriptions and prescriptions of men's behaviour are conflated. The notion of the new father is probably best thought of as a cultural ideal: normative claims are being made about how contemporary men as fathers *should* behave. Hence, the current methodological difficulty of carrying out empirical work to gauge shifts in everyday interaction between fathers and their children.

Third, questions about the new father are clouded by a tendency to undertheorize an understanding of social and cultural change. In their discussion of the idea of change, Lewis and O'Brien (1987: 3) question whether the assumption that men are now more involved in family life is justified. Importantly, they point to 'the methodological difficulties in measuring couples' division of labour in child-care and housework', that is a key element of the acclaimed new fatherhood. Building on the work of Lewis (1986), they argue that: 'implicit in the notion of the "new father" are assumptions that fathers have only recently been discovered by researchers and that in previous generations fathers were not involved in child-rearing'. Yet discussion above suggests that a range of fathering styles coexisted historically, including the paternal nurturant role. Within much contemporary discussion of changing fathers, there is an implicit assumption of social change occurring in a universal and uniform way. In reality, as comparative international studies, including those from Sweden, Denmark and Ireland illustrate, social transformations involve fundamentally complex issues that are deeply embedded in social structures and cultural practices (Carlsen 1993; McKeown *et al.* 2000). They produce changes that are uneven, chequered and gradual across generations, regions and individual households (McKee and O'Brien 1982).

Many of the studies cited above are located within *simple models of sex role reproduction*, whose understanding emphasizes an individualized paternal masculinity. As indicated in the introduction, there is a recent conceptual shift to a notion of the *active production of complex identity formations* that sees fathers as occupying, at the same time, contradictory social and emotional subject positions. This latter approach provides an analytic framework that brings together multiple levels of fathers' experiences, and is sensitive to complexity and differentiation. We illustrate this by examining two substantive areas of inquiry, that of the state, and gay fathers.

The state: producing legislative gendered categories

There is a long history to the articulation of masculinity and the state, involving images of the military, imperial invasion and colonial expansion linked to national identity, cultural belonging and citizenship. More recently, the media has popularized global images of men's involvement in fundamentalisms, ethno-nationalisms and ethnic cleansing (Mac an Ghaill 1999). However one of the main sociological conceptions of the state has been the liberal view. This view has presented it as an impartial adjudicator between competing interests, for example, between men and women, and hence as a legitimate source of power and means of violence. During the 1970s and 1980s, Marxist and feminist accounts challenged this notion of the benign state. The former emphasized the state as an agent of ruling class interests, defending domination and exploitation of working-class people. In turn, feminist analysis challenged the degendering of existing theories, both liberal and Marxist, constructing the term 'patriarchal state' to signal the close relationship between masculine domination and the state (McKinnon 1989;

Walby 1990). Importantly, feminists demonstrated the interconnection between the state, masculinity and violence (Miedzian 1991; Biron 2000). Drawing upon this work, Brittan (1989: 129–30) makes clear the normative function of the state. He writes:

> State enacted legislation on prostitution, on child labour, on divorce, on abortion, legitimated a particular version of the family in which the father was both breadwinner and upholder of heterosexual values. What had previously been a fusion between church and state was now an alliance between the state and the medical and biological sciences, of which psychiatry and sexology were constituent parts.

Earlier Marxist and feminist views implicitly suggested an image of the state as an overly determining unitary entity. Drawing on Foucault (1977), more recent accounts have understood the state in a desegregated way as a complex of discourses and practices infused with power relations that are not located within one place but are suffused throughout social formations (Westwood 1996). However, there are limitations in conceptions of a non-unitary state that focus upon the diffusion of power and power-knowledges. One limitation is to underplay the cumulative effect of diverse discourses in different state agencies that impose gender, sexual and national divisions in society. These limitations have been made clear in recent research on sexual politics. As Ballard (1992: 106) points out in his paper 'Sexuality and the state in time of epidemic', in which he argues for a non-determinative approach:

> The state has a prominent role to play through law, which reifies dominant social values by their enforcement through the coercive apparatus of the state, and through the services and controls of the welfare state. The modes of state influence lie first, in labelling categories; second, in explicitly and implicitly encouraging or discouraging identities and behaviour; and third, in effectively institutionalising various forms of discourse and practice.

Through its command of the apparatus of enforcement, the state sets limits on nationality and citizenship, defining who is 'national' and who is 'alien'. Therefore there is a need to acknowledge the power of the patriarchal and heterosexual state and its central functions of sexual regulation and order to produce categories of inclusion and exclusion. For example, traditional legislative racial categories have included the early twentieth-century 'Jewish alien' and the post-war 'New Commonwealth immigrant' and, more recently, the 'ethnic minority' and 'asylum seeker'. The degendering and desexualization of these racial categories have tended to be underplayed in the sociological literature. However, as Walter (1999: 77), examining Irish women's experiences of the British state makes clear: 'Images of Irishness are not gender-neutral. Their representations are inscribed on bodies whose gender is integral to processes of construction of national identities'. Connell (1987) has written extensively on the patriarchal state and its key functions of sexual regulation and the generation of sexual order through the legislative production of categories. Traditional categories have included 'the prostitute' and the 'homosexual' and more recently there has been focus upon the 'one-parent family', alongside that of lesbian and gay 'pretended families' (Goss and Strongheart 1997; Weeks *et al.* 2001). There is a long history of state generated discourses about 'bad mothers', including that of maternal deprivation (1950s), latchkey kids (1970s), and dual workers (1980s). A common theme linking these discourses is a claim that women fail to manage men (Campbell 1993). By the late 1980s, with the emergence of the absent father as a major moral panic, 'bad fathers' were placed along-side 'bad mothers'. Current concerns about absent fathers resonate with post-war panics surrounding evacuees, working mothers and absent fathers in the army (Winnicott 1993).

Enemies of the state: the production of 'feckless fathers'

We noted above that the state has played an important part in normalizing certain familial masculinities in various historical eras. Taking up the themes developed throughout this chapter on exclusion and inclusion, these normalizing practices produce categories of difference that are used to justify particular state administered economic and social policies. For instance, the 1980s moral panic about absent fathers was part of a wider political anxiety concerning one of the most significant aspects of the changing demography of Britain – that of the rapid increase in the number of lone parents (see Table 2.1).

The late 1980s through to the 1990s brought British lone parents under increased state scrutiny, projected by the Conservative government as a major financial burden on public expenditure that needed reducing. With the state as the main supporter of families, social policies were designed to combat the 'nationalization of fatherhood'. As a result the state created the Child Support Agency, through the Child Support Act (1991), to make absent fathers economically responsible for their children.[2] Westwood (1996: 28) describes this strategy as a classic example of the Foucauldian notion of governability and power of surveillance in postmodern societies. She writes:

Table 2.1 The estimated numbers of lone parents in Great Britain

	1971	1981	1999
Lone parents	570	900	1,700

Source: Reconstructed from Stationery Office cm199900; cited in Hansard (2001).

It was constructed out of a series of discourses that generated a specific subject/object, one of which was the 'feckless father', who was to be the subject/object of surveillance, tracking and intervention at both the economic and moral moments. The feckless father had already forfeited his rights as a moral person to engage in self-regulation. Instead a refashioned state agency would regulate him and the woman and children to whom he was to be forcibly attached.

Under the threat of reducing their personal benefit, lone mothers were obliged to disclose details about the father of their children. As a consequence, women continued to be seen as the primary cause of the problem. In short, the state was not responding to father absenteeism per se, but rather to mother's dependence upon benefits.

However, this concern with the 'feckless father' was never simply a financial question. A government which projected itself as defender of 'family values' was committed to an ideological intervention against what it saw as a 'dependency culture' 'in which the notion of the individual and citizen as responsible for their own welfare replaced an earlier settlement based on welfare as part of a collective responsibility and social wage' (Westwood 1996: 26–7). In fact, this post-war British settlement was underpinned by three assumptions: that of full employment, male breadwinners and stable families (Millar 1994). Each of these assumptions had collapsed by the 1980s. It was argued that, unlike those children with active fathers, the children of absent fathers were likely to be depressed, were more likely to take part in criminal activity, to be involved in violence, to suffer educationally and experience prolonged periods of unemployment. This cycle of deprivation was consolidated by the suggestion that the sons of absent fathers were in turn likely to become absent fathers. While acknowledging the social construction of sex roles as an important factor in absent men's behaviour, these accounts tended to pathologize men generally, and more specifically groups of working-class and black fathers.

Writing from a sociology of law perspective, Collier (1995: 203–4) makes a telling point in suggesting that the construction of the absent father as problematic in legal discourse involved establishing fatherhood as a desirable presence during marriage (the economic provider discourse). As he argues, the irony is that, given the logic of economic rationality in advanced capitalism, the breadwinner masculinity of the 'good father' entails many men being absent from their families. He suggests that evidence from divorce reveals that the presence of paternal masculinity was always open-ended. However he makes clear what paternal masculinity, presumed by law to be desirable, actually entails. Hence for Collier the absent father really signifies something else, namely the desirability of masculinity within the family embodying the three axes of authority, economic responsibility and heterosexuality, which constitute the idea of the 'good father' in law.

Families of choice: gay fathers

A main concern of this book is to locate our understanding of masculinity within the institutional processes and practices that make up the wider social structure of contemporary gender relations. A major limitation of most writing on paternal masculinities is its failure to place the changing nature of fatherhood and accompanying diverse modes of fathering within the bigger picture of the changing family, a shifting emotional landscape and the complex transformations of intimate life (Sedgwick 1994; Van Every 1995). In what she refers to as the optimistic story of the postmodern period, Jamieson (1998: 19) captures this changing sensibility, arguing that:

> The good relationship is a relationship of disclosing intimacy, a mutual relationship of close association between equals in which really know-ing and understanding each other are the crux of the relationship rather than more practical forms of 'love and care'.

In the final chapter, we explore how gay men are one of the most dynamic constituent elements of recent sexual politics in destabilizing common-sense and sociological meanings of men and masculinity. Same-sex marriages and parenting are two of the most visible spaces in which this has been publicly played out. Reading through the literature on gay fathers, one is immediately struck by a comparison with divorced heterosexual men's campaigns for legal rights to their children. Whereas the latter often appear to be driven by a principle of maintaining/reclaiming an old patriarchal masculinity, gay men's (and lesbians') campaigning for relational rights resonates with wider historical changes – in personal relationships, identity formations, biological and social parenting, cultural belonging and citizen-ship. Shifting beyond an earlier political stance on community identity recognition and validation, gay men are now operating on the traditional terrain of family values. As Castells (1997: 219) writing of San Francisco's gay community points out:

> The yearning for same-sex families became one of the most powerful cultural trends among gays and, even more so, among lesbians . . . furthermore, the legalization of same-sex marriages became a major demand of the movement, taking conservatives at their word in pro-moting family values, and extending the value of the family to non-traditional, non-heterosexual forms of love, sharing and child rearing. What started as a movement for sexual liberation came full circle to haunt the patriarchal family by attacking its heterosexual roots, and subverting its exclusive appropriation of family values.

In so doing, they are actively 'rethinking family values in the postmodern age' (Stacey 1996). In short, gay and lesbian communities are at the cutting edge of producing one version of 'the "new" family' (Silva and Smart 1999a) within postindustrial societies.

Social and political discussion of sexual minorities' domestic, sexual and emotional arrangements has gained an international media profile (Ali 1996; Velu 1999). Much theoretical and empirical work on gay fathers and lesbian mothers is carried out in the USA (Goss and Strongheart 1997; Sullivan 1997). However, an increasing number of European countries, at national or local government level, are instituting some form of gay partnership recognition, including Holland, Germany, France, Denmark, Iceland, Norway, Sweden and England (Fox 2000).[3] Two recent important British texts are: Weeks *et al.*'s (2001) *Same Sex Intimacies: Families of Choice and Other Life Experiments* and Dunne's (2001) *The Lady Vanishes? Reflections on the Experiences of Married and Divorced Gay Fathers*. They explore a fascinatingly diverse range of sexual stories of how everyday experience is reordered with new meanings emerging that serve to open up discussion of masculinity politics (Plummer 1995). These stories are being lived out within the specific context of a number of critical developments: the changing age profile of non-heterosexuals; the gay community's creative response to the AIDS epidemics, including safe sex practices, new reproductive technological advances and state legislation (see Chapter 6, this volume). The research participants vividly recall their experiences of the current dominant sex/gender system, in which gay men are represented in the media and social commentary as having too *little* masculinity. At the same time, within these narratives, gay men are also ascribed a perverse, promiscuous maleness, a myth with a long history of naming 'homosexuals as corrupters of young boys' which currently manifests itself in producing gays as the dangerous men of paedophilia. In contrast, lesbian relationships are conceived as having too *much* masculinity. In turn, this is translated into a major moral panic about the twin social problems of boys being emasculated within all-women spaces (for example in primary schools) and the absent father, both of which are seen as a central contribution to what is assumed to be a crisis in the traditional family.

This book argues for the need to combine contemporary social and cultural theory with empirical studies that may test out what often appear as rather grand abstract visions of the future of gender relations, while making little connection with the way that we live our lives. A major criticism of sociological theorists such as Giddens (1992), with his notions of 'the transformation of intimacy' and 'of parent–child relationships veering towards the pure relationship', is that there is little empirical evidence to substantiate the generalized claims of his theoretical model (Jamieson 1998). In contrast, Weeks *et al.*'s (2001) and Dunne's (2001) theory-led empirical work captures wonderfully the emergence of new ways of conceiving family and intimate life. They emphasize the location of the individual as a central reference point with accompanying needs and meanings, the prioritization of intimacy as the focus of domestic arrangements, and the negotiated nature of caring, commitment and responsibility. At a time of fluid and changeable relationships, this results in the return of the family as the main site of emotional growth for children and adults (see Silva and Smart 1999b).

Until the late twentieth century, the traditional patriarchal family has functioned as a main container of the dominant sex/gender order, the central social agency for the making of young femininities and masculinities and a central institution for the affirmation of gender difference. Especially within this site, '"real" women and "real" men are always heterosexual' (Dunne 1999: 69). Hence, as suggested above, dominant media images of gay fathers and lesbian mothers are projected as a threat to mainstream society. However, as research cited here finely illustrates, there are alternative understandings. First, given the rapidity of current social and cultural change and its impact on heterosexual families, where high divorce rates, absent fathers and stepchildren indicate a rejection of traditional forms of family life, same-sex partnerships may be seen as a cultural resource for the (hetero)sexual majority. In a shifting society, this is an example where that which is socially marginal becomes culturally central. As Stacey (1996: 15) suggests, lesbian and gay families are not marginal or exceptional:

> but rather a paradigmatic illustration of the 'queer' postmodern conditions of kinship that we all now inhabit. Gays and lesbians who self-consciously form families are forced to confront the challenges, opportunities and dilemmas of the postmodern condition with much lower levels of denial, resistance, displacement or bad faith than most others can indulge.

Different-sex couples' current marital and parenting anxieties may find a resolution within lesbians' and gays' constructions of new ways of mothering and fathering as part of the latter's longer history of having to invent a self, a social identity and a wider community. Second, both conceptually and practically, gay fathering makes clear that masculinity is not something that one is born with or an inherent individual possession, but rather an active process of achievement, performance and enactment. Gay fathering provides an example of Weeks *et al.*'s (2001) life experiments, in doing gender beyond the confines of heterosexual romance and the traditional nuclear family (Dunne 2001). Reminiscent of earlier gay stories of 'coming out', the above studies report accounts of gay paternal masculinities as marked by a highly reflective self, illustrating the creative possibilities of fathering being constituted by egalitarian partnerships, active co-parenting, shared willingness to nurture children, involvement in shared domestic responsibilities and a revisioning of intimacy with and between adults and children.

Conclusion

Current exclusions or underrepresentation of different kinds of fathers include: young fathers, older fathers, lone fathers, widowed fathers, ethnic minority fathers, disabled fathers, gay fathers, unmarried fathers and grandfathers. Contemporary theories have begun to make visible this diversity of fathering. They also establish a clearer framework to explore the complex geographies of fathering involved in a regionally-based politics of location. In turn, this allows us to identify continuities alongside discontinuities in challenging what seems to be the inevitable logic of fathering and mothering as natural biological or cultural forces. Currently, this is of particular significance when cultural theorists tend to overemphasize change, difference and diversity in western nation-states. This is also important when there is a sense that no single theory can give the whole picture of an increasingly complex global arena experiencing rapid transformations. With reference to the reconfiguration of fathering and wider social and cultural transformations, parenting is experienced and negotiated in quite complex ways within contemporary western societies, and it is difficult to offer a generalized sociological perspective on sex/gender relations that characterizes these societies as a whole. Fundamentally, while holding on to a notion of fatherhood as masculinity, we need to recognize that social change is shaped by and is shaping the social organization of fathering with its own inclusions and exclusions.

Questions for your reflection

1 Why is it so difficult to find out if there is a new type of father?

2 What are the methodological issues involved in exploring paternal childcare?

3 What are the main historical forces that have helped reshape fatherhood?

4 How does the state impact on family life?

5 How might gay fathers provide a cultural resource for heterosexual couples?

Suggested further reading

Bjornberg, U. (ed.) (1992) *European Parents in the 1990s: Contradictions and Comparisons*. New Brunswick, NJ: Transcation Publication.
Jamieson, L. (1998) *Intimacy: Personal Relationships in Modern Society*. Cambridge: Polity Press.

Lewis, C. and O'Brien, M. (1987) (eds) *Reassessing Fatherhood: New Observations on Fathers and the Modern Family*. London: Sage.

McKee, L. and O'Brien, M. (eds) (1982) *The Father Figure*. London: Tavistock.

Moss, P. (1995) *Father Figures: Fathers in the Families of the 1990s*. Edinburgh: HMSO.

Westwood, S. (1996) 'Feckless fathers': Masculinities and the British state, in M. Mac an Ghaill (ed.) *Understanding Masculinities: Social Relations and Cultural Arenas*. Buckingham: Open University Press.

Notes

1 See Kimmel (1996) who locates the contemporary 'crisis' of masculinity in historical perspective.

2 Similar schemes have been introduced in Australia (Harrison *et al.* 1990) and in the USA (Kahn and Kamerman 1988).

3 In September 2001 the new London Partnership Register was launched, providing official civil recognition of gay and lesbian unions. In the USA official recognition of gay civil unions varies from state to state.

CHAPTER 3

TROUBLING SCHOOL BOYS: MAKING YOUNG MASCULINITIES

Key concepts

Remasculinization of teacher work; melancholic boys; working-class resistance; gendered regime; hegemonic masculinity; teacher/student cultures; 'boyness'; heterosexual matrix; compulsory heterosexuality; homophobia.

Introduction

This chapter highlights schooling processes and practices that are important in making young masculinities in schools. Within the school there are
particular spaces where 'masculinity making' appears more visible. Therefore, we focus on teacher identities and practice, the curricula, peer group
networks and the formation of male student subjectivity that includes an
exploration of the interconnections of masculinity with age, ethnicity and
sexuality. Internationally, the sociology of education is highly productive
in illustrating how education and training institutions are strategically significant in shaping young men and masculinities (Connell 1989; Thorne
1993; Mac an Ghaill 1994a). The school is a social process, a set of social
relations charged with formal and informal meanings. All aspects of schooling are subject to these meanings and they are deployed across a diversity
of areas including discipline and control, the formal and hidden curriculum, streaming and prefectorial systems, teaching staff appointments, and
auxiliary staff. Research on masculinities suggests that schools through these
meanings offer interpretations about what it means to be 'male' or 'female'.
More specifically, schooling processes form gendered identities, marking
out 'correct' or 'appropriate' styles of being (Butler 1993).

Teacher culture and the making of masculine styles

We begin with a commentary on teacher relationships (micropolitics) and
suggest that the formation of teacher identities provides a salient context
for how students respond to education institutions. During the twentieth
century, teaching in many western societies has been professionalized and
has periodically undergone reconstruction, involving specialization, deskilling
and reskilling (Foster *et al.* 2001). The reconstruction of teachers' labour
process (work) closely corresponds with state definitions of 'proper' schooling. There is a continual adjustment of schooling practices to meet the
needs of industry, in order to generate national economic competitiveness.
A number of education practices that include the reorganization of the
curriculum have been developed with the intention of producing the right
kind of worker (Haywood and Mac an Ghaill 1997b). Within this changing
context, teaching styles are an important space for the production of young
masculinities.

In England, Mac an Ghaill (1994a) identified a range of male teacher
styles that emerged in response to neo-liberal ideologies of teacher labour.
These styles not only embodied assumptions and expectations about the
labour process, they were also closely connected to personal desires, fears
and investments. In the secondary school in which Mac an Ghaill carried
out his study, three particular groups of teachers became visible – the
Professionals, the Old Collectivists and the New Entrepreneurs – that could

be identified by conflicting responses to the political organization of schooling and educational reforms. Each group's strategic political positioning
was underpinned by their collective impressions of what constitutes the
labour process or 'proper teaching'. At another level, gender politics are
also at work here as masculine styles become contested. These styles are not
totally cohesive, but rather contain multiple and contradictory elements.
Nevertheless, the Professionals tended to advocate a masculine style that
revolved around authority, discipline and control, which appeared to draw
on themes of paternalism. The Old Collectivists attached significance to an
education system which emphasized equality, meritocracy, anti-sexist and
anti-racist practices. This can be seen as a masculine style that was drawing
on liberal pluralist and feminist ideas. The third group, the New Entrepreneurs were in favour of neo-liberal government interventions and welcomed
a labour process which was redefining teachers' work in terms of appraisal,
accountability and effective management. It is suggested that teaching practices have the potential to reinforce a sense of 'normal' masculinity.

The New Entrepreneurial teaching style in the above study connects with
contemporary representations of an upwardly mobile business like masculinity. It is argued that this remasculinization of teaching practice is characterized by emotional detachment. Gewirtz (1997) suggests that due to longer
classes, increased paperwork and an emphasis on performance levels rather
than teaching craft, the social relations between teacher and students have
been reshaped. As a consequence, she maintains that such ascendancy cultivates less sociability between teacher and students as contemporary teaching appears more formalized, dissolving the intimacy and complexity of
their interaction. Importantly, this ideological reconstruction of education
is generating specific responses and resistances to changes in school organization. The potential for conflict becomes heightened as teachers are not
only acting out their micropolitical interests in response to curriculum
changes, they are simultaneously acting out their gender politics through
the identification and performance of particular masculine subjectivities. In
short, micropolitical relations between teachers become a formative constitution of students' masculine practices.

Another aspect of teaching style that provides the context for the
emergence of young male identity formations is classroom discipline.
Heward (1991) has contextualized how historically, disciplinary regimes of
schools create specific kinds of men. For example, the public schools that
she examined ascribed to a teaching ideology that: 'tough teachers make
tough boys'. Similarly, for Connell (1989), schools that adopt violent teaching practices generate schoolboy masculinities based upon a competitive
machismo. These studies lead us to suggest that in educational sites,
masculinities tend to operate through mechanisms of official power and
authority (Brittan 1989). An inability to be powerful and authoritative
corresponds closely with a culturally ascribed inability to be a 'proper man'.
A lack of competence at a particular practice is also associated with signs of

'weakness' that are closely aligned with popular assumptions of femininity. In Robinson's (1992) school a competent teacher could keep a class quiet. A quiet class was deemed a class that could be managed, therefore learning could be achieved. The most common way of keeping a class quiet was through the use of discipline and force.

Making boys emotionally tough highlights the interrelated features of adulthood and manhood. Currently, a key element of institutional masculinities in western societies circulates through the controlled and disciplined use or mastery of physical force. Where violence in schools has been abolished (in terms of corporal punishment), other forms of physical force are often used to control male (and female) students. Beynon's (1989) ethnography of Lower School, in South Wales, highlights how coercive methods used in the classroom come to represent 'good' teaching. Physical coercion through shaking, cuffing and pushing were seen as acceptable everyday forms of discipline. This discipline complemented the ethos of a 'school for boys and men'. As he (1989: 194) points out, the principal believed that there was no place for women and children:

> Men and boys were expected to behave in a certain kind of way, put in a certain kind of manly performance, if they were to win the accolade of being a 'good teacher' or a 'good lad', whether that was a praiseworthy 'rough diamond' or 'playground hard'.

Teachers' awareness of other teachers' pedagogical styles, informed by notions of gender, created 'good' or 'bad' teachers. As a result 'good teachers' were 'real men' and 'bad teachers' had 'problems' (Wolpe 1988).

Capitalism, schooling and masculinity

If teacher identities provide an important context for the formation of masculine subjectivities, one area that is strategic to the veneration of particular masculine codes is the curriculum. Hierarchically organized knowledges legitimate particular spaces for masculinities to exist. It is important to stress that schools proscribe and prescribe specific kinds of knowledges. Furthermore, the spaces available to occupy certain masculinities do not necessarily hinge upon the acceptance of the hierarchy of knowledges, but can also be shaped through a range of responses, including resistance. The curriculum alongside disciplinary procedures, normalizing judgements and the examination represents an institutionalized gendered regime or a patterning of gender relations (Foucault 1977; Connell 2000).

During the 1970s, Marxist theorists such as Bowles and Gintis (1976) argued that schools reproduce the social relations of wider society. They suggested that schools have little impact on the social mobility of working-class children, with their statistical analysis indicating an institutional structuring of failure. Willis (1977) presents a more complex picture, arguing that male working-class students, in actively resisting the schooling process, placed themselves unequally inside social class relations. He provides a detailed analysis of academic failure by representing students' meanings and understandings as crucial dynamics. In his ethnography of a secondary school, Willis suggests that schools not only represent a middle-class view of the world, they also project a version of middle-class manhood. Working-class young men resist this institutional version of manhood and thus resist the schools' expectations and normative judgements. Such resistances involve practices including: 'havin' a laff', 'dossing', and 'blagging'. Willis argues that a process of differentiation occurs where the school's institutional interests are separated from working-class interests. A central feature of 'the Lads'' rejection of learning is that it is associated with mental work. According to Willis, enveloped in male working-class culture is a perception that 'real work' is manual labour. Significantly, 'the Lads'' rejection of school knowledges is not solely defined in terms of class but also exists along gendered lines, with mental work deemed 'effeminate'. Hence, mental work is juxtaposed to manual work, with the latter representing for this sector of working-class males legitimate forms of masculinity.

Therefore the curriculum has little to offer, as school subjects have no relevance for the type of jobs that 'the Lads' want/expect to get. This resistance to schooling is paralleled by the 'Earoles', a group of conformist students, who accepted the legitimacy of schooling and the importance of academic work. Understandings about being a real man become key to negotiating their relationship to schooling, with masculinity being the dynamic through which class relations are being worked out. In this way, institutional resistance to the curriculum takes on particular masculine forms of physical toughness, hedonism and rejection of school processes. As a result, young working-class masculinities can attach value to their own identities.

Critics of the above study suggest that Willis romanticizes the position of the working-class; celebrates a coercive form of masculinity as a response to a middle class schooling system, with apparently little indication that 'the Lads'' sexual domination results from their privileged position in an oppressive masculine regime and that in overemphasizing 'the Lads'' responses, he limits the range of masculine identities that are occupied across the school. Others suggest that Willis assumes that the processes that boys go through will also be experienced by girls. Evidence indicates that female students' oppression is reproduced in different ways (McRobbie 1991). However, Willis's *Learning to Labour* remains one of the most incisive texts on the capitalist organization of schooling and the formation of young masculinities. It provides a highly generative starting point, including our own, for the exploration of other forms of counter-school cultures in conditions of late modernity.

Similarly, work in Australia, carried out by Connell (1989), argues that an important dynamic in the formation of young masculinities is the class-based curriculum and the accompanying sorting of students into academic hierarchies. He undertakes a series of life histories with what he calls young 'unrespectable working-class' men and older affluent men. By exploring their lives and their experiences of schooling, Connell argues that school is an authority structure that formally distributes social power by authorizing access to higher education, entry to professions and command of communication processes. As schools actively fail students, these students are deprived of a certain source of power and status and take up alternative resources to validate their masculine identities.

Connell's association of social power with the middle class provides a useful way of reconsidering the position of sectors of the working class that goes beyond the economic dynamics of identity formation. He suggests a more tenuous causal link between masculinities and class positions. For example institutional values, which are both classed and racialized, promote particular masculine cultures. Importantly, Connell maintains that the differentiation of masculinities in schools is a collective process that involves the institutional sanctioning of 'correct' masculine styles and values. He sees the curriculum as an important shaper of masculinities: 'Some masculinities are formed by battering against the school's authority structure, others by smooth insertion into its academic pathways' (1989: 300). The alternative resources that young men take up in response to being failed by schools may involve sporting prowess, physical aggression and sexual conquests. In contrast, middle-class men to whom he talked tended to constitute their masculinities through rationality and responsibility. In sum, by moving young men's formation of masculinities away from an overly determining economic status, the dynamics of masculinity formation become more situational, as local schooling processes and practices institutionalize legitimate masculine values.

Curriculum and student cultures

The above accounts concentrate on the articulation of existing economic relations through masculinity in the context of education. This work provides an important insight into how economic relations exist as masculinized practices. However, other studies have contextualized schooling, and more specifically, the curriculum within changing cultural dynamics. For example, Willis's work was undertaken in a historically specific moment in the British economy, when manufacturing work was the main occupation of the working class. Combined with state legislation that has restricted benefits to school leavers and the explosion of post-16 schooling, more working-class young men are currently entering the field of further education than the manufacturing sector.[1] Importantly, the shifting economic organization of society has provided a context for the reorganization of the curriculum. English education systems have witnessed a continual reconstruction in order to meet economic/industrial needs. This ideological project has led to the revaluing of curriculum subjects and in response, sociological analysis places the formation of school-based masculinities in the context of ascendant (political) cultural agendas (Skelton 2001).

Student cultures emerge as a direct response to the school curriculum. Gilbert and Gilbert's (1998) exploration of the formation of young Australian masculinities highlights how sport is an important index of masculinity that is both valued by the school and taken up by working-class students. Interviews carried out within primary and secondary schools uncovered polarized masculine peer group cultures that were differentiated by their investment in sporting activities. Their research illustrates how anti-school cultures are not simply generated from working-class backgrounds. Similarly, the male students who participated in a 'cool masculinity' in Martino's (1999: 253) study of a secondary school were not academic failures but were involved in a middle-class protest masculinity that rejected school work and high academic achievement. In contrast, courting a high sporting and social profile gave access to and constituted a particular 'cool masculinity' that was institutionally sanctioned, sport being a highly valued aspect of the school curriculum. Earlier research by Aggleton (1987) suggests that a new kind of middle class has emerged whose values are not necessarily consonant with education and training career pathways. Generationally specific class fractions are responding to emerging politicized schooling agendas in differentiated ways. Students from a social justice inspired middle-class background reject traditional academic routes; they hold middle-class values but operate with anti-schooling responses (Redman 2001).

Such work provides clarity on how the interplay between the curriculum and masculinity does not work in deterministic ways; students can effectively renegotiate curriculum agendas (Davies and Hunt 1994). However, if the curriculum operates as a resource through which masculinities are produced, it follows that as the curriculum changes so will masculinities. The curriculum can be understood as a structure that closes off and opens up spaces for the formation of masculine subjectivities. Mac an Ghaill (1994a) has illustrated the reconstruction of the curriculum and subject hierarchies and its impact upon the formation of young masculinities. He argued that until recently, English schools were divided along a high status/academic and low status/vocational binary. Mac an Ghaill suggested that more recently this division was challenged and is in the process of being reconstructed. An impetus for this was increased funding for vocationally directed projects, marking a shift from a liberal-humanist schooling paradigm to a technical training paradigm. New resources for the fulfilment of career aspiration emerged as students entered subjects such as business studies, technology and computer studies. For Mac an Ghaill, the emergence of vocationalism as a legitimate academic subject signalled a change in the constitution of stratified knowledge.

In turn, as a result of the restratification of knowledges, male student identities take on new dimensions. Rather than seeing male groups in terms of a simple pro-school or anti-school dichotomy, Mac an Ghaill proposes a more nuanced approach in order to capture these new dimensions. In his study he identifies four groups of male student types representing styles of masculinity in the secondary school: the Macho Lads, the Academic Achievers, the New Entrepreneurs and the Real Englishmen. The student groups positioned their masculinities in relation to the school organization and in particular in relation to a shifting curriculum. The working-class Macho Lads rejected formal schooling, while the Academic Achievers legitimized and affirmed the schooling process, locating themselves within academic subjects. In contrast, the working-class New Entrepreneurs located themselves within the newly high status technical and vocational subjects as a resource to develop their masculinities. The Real Englishmen represented a group of middle-class students who, like the Macho Lads, rejected schooling but the former remained ambivalent to its significance. Key elements of their masculinity included honesty, being different, individuality and autonomy, which they claimed were absent from the school's middle-class culture. Significantly, it is within these peer group networks that masculinities were collectively regulated, maintained and contested. Each group attempted to impose its own definition of masculinity, thus reinforcing their own social position. This provided the context for the mediation of the students' schooling experiences. For instance, Redman and Mac an Ghaill (1996) highlight in an English context that to be a 'real' boy in schools is to be in opposition to the feminine and to 'feminized' versions of masculinity. At an institutional level, boys' identities are formed in relation to the formal curriculum and the categories it makes available, including the academic/vocational, arts/science, and the academic/sporting polarities. For example, the 'hard' scientific version of cleverness that is validated in school exists in opposition to supposedly 'soft' subjects, like art, music and literature, which are seen as easy options, as essentially frivolous, or somehow lacking in due rigour and seriousness. They are in effect girlish subjects and not for 'real' boys. Similarly to be 'bad at games' can be read as a cultural index, implying a suspect lack of manly vigour and hinted at effeminacy, while to be uninterested in the core aspects of 'laddishness' (in particular school opposition, a certain level of working-class credibility, football and the 'pub') is to be a 'bit of a poof'.

Male peer group networks are generative of many different masculinities in the sphere of education. Using ideas about what it means to be male and informed by school processes, male and female students legitimize and regulate meanings of masculinity. As schools create the conditions for the emergence of masculinities, differing meanings of maleness compete for ascendancy. Schools provide a range of resources for students to develop masculinities. At the same time, some boys are able to define their meaning of masculinity over others. These definitions create boundaries which serve to delineate what appropriate maleness should be within this social arena. Transgression of these boundaries activates techniques of normalization, ranging from labelling through to physical violence, that ultimately act to maintain differences embedded in the ascendant definitions of masculinity.

Understanding the formation of young men's identities at an institutional level suggests that changes in the administration, organization and delivery of the curriculum have some impact on how masculinities are shaped. It is by analysing the constitution of subjectivities that we begin to explore masculine identity processes.

Constituting schoolboy subjectivity: age, ethnicity and sexuality

The second part of this chapter explores young men's masculine subject-ivities. It is important to conceptualize subjectivity as a process of becoming, characterized by fluidity, oppositions and alliances between particular narrative positions that speak identities (see Davies 1993). This allows a simultaneous relationship between analytic concepts such as age, race/ethnicity, gender, sexuality, disability and class (Thorne 1993). In emphasizing the need for an inclusive account of multiple forms of social power, we are particularly focusing upon three dynamics of subjectivity that the sociology of education has addressed: age, ethnicity and sexuality.[2] In placing this view of power at the centre of analysis of male students' identity formation, it is important to comprehend fully the complexity of its dynamic within different institutional sites. The conceptual difficulties involved in moving beyond earlier monocausal explanations that employed 'simple' models of power are highlighted in our attempt throughout this book to hold onto the tension between materialist and poststructuralist accounts of male identity formation. Poststructuralist theories have been important in moving beyond role model, structuralist and resistance theories that often assume that young men and women are unitary, rational subjects occupying predictable power positions. The suggestion that there is a range of subject positions that may be occupied within different contradictory discourses is useful; it helps in understanding the local specificity in the cultural production and reproduction of young men's schooling formations (Henriques *et al.* 1984; Walkerdine 1990). On the other hand, the development of male student identities takes place within the continuing materially structured asymmetrical relations of power that constitute the state's hegemonic class divisions and gender/heterosexual arrangements (Walby 1990; Mac an Ghaill 1996a). This suggests that in order to understand identities in educational sites, researchers need to move away from the singular 'role' based on 'sex' to examine the simultaneous articulations of a dispersed and localized shifting nexus of social power.

This has led to the theorizing of masculinity in terms of multiple masculinities (Hearn 1996). As this book concentrates on the salient elements of manhood, it is easy to assume that masculinity is a one-dimensional aspect of maleness. Rather, we are suggesting that masculinities embody multiple social categories. An important question in theorizing masculinities and schooling is to see how the interconnections between social locations and social categories create the conditions for relations of power. Thus different men and women have differentiated access to power and practices of power that mediate differentiated effects. An argument emerges from this work that in order to understand the complex articulation between schooling and young people's identity formations, it is necessary to rethink masculinities as situational, relational and dynamic, being constituted by and constituting various arenas within this institutional space.

Age: searching for the gendered meaning of boyhood

In contemporary western schools, notions of adulthood and childhood have emerged as important devices to organize and administer educational processes and practices, with age having a variety of significances in a range of different educational sectors (Connolly 1998; Renold 2000). For example, primary school work can be closely aligned with parenting, as teaching practices are often articulated through maternal and paternal responsibilities. Schools, it is argued, depend upon the positioning of its members within age categories in order for them to run smoothly. Such is the mutually informing relationships between age and education philosophy, that disruptions and contestations to the adult–child binary are often interpreted not only as in direct opposition to institutional regimes, but to the education process itself (Riseborough 1993). However, the imposition of age-related categories is not unproblematic. Age contains a range of cultural codes that impact upon ideals of manliness. The positioning as a child often means a disqualification from dominant cultural ascriptions of masculinity, while feminist analyses have illustrated that the concept of the child carries similar values as that of femininity (Burman 1995). Currently, there is an interesting paradox emerging in English schools, which can be understood as promoting ascendant notions of English masculinity, while at the same time enforcing a devalued femininity onto the bodies of boys.

We need to develop ways of exploring schooling and the formation of masculinities that acknowledge the importance of these age dynamics. An important issue emerges here: the cultural formation of young men's identities generates specific masculine subjectivities that cannot be reduced to a singular notion of maleness. Yet much analysis of masculinity and schooling tends to be generationally unspecific, assuming that younger men operate through similar cultural dynamics as older men. Popular concerns have focused on schools moulding boys into the wrong type of man and developing 'emotional straitjackets' in boys (Askew and Ross 1988; Salisbury and Jackson 1996; Pollack 1998). However, it may be argued that this is not a simple one-dimensional transmission. In western schools, boys' identities may be worked out in age-specific ways that may not correspond to society's manly ideals. For instance, in research with younger children in a primary school, we found that many of the young boys were not interested in (hetero)sexual relationships (Haywood 2003). It was intriguing that not only did many of these boys find sexual relationships with girls boring but that expressing an interest in girls was itself a sign of femininity. Instead 'boyness' was often demonstrated through 'playing', in the classroom, playground or at home. Fascination with cartoons, computer games and board games that contained a high content of violence, aggression and toughness were juxtaposed but carried with it a 'benign boyness' that was inclusive of girls and other boys. Furthermore, real life expressions of aggressiveness and toughness in schools were despised by nearly all of the boys and girls. As a result, it could be argued that ascendant codes of adult masculinity stood in opposition to 'boyness'. Therefore 'boyness' may not be necessarily captured by the adult-defined and applied category of 'masculinity'. The symbolic (read also as physical and economic) resources and cultural texts used to forge masculinity, such as work, family and leisure may not be available in the same way to younger boys, and the limitations of using (adult-defined) masculinity as a heuristic (meaning making) device come into sharper focus.

In the same school, there were boys and girls who took up violent and aggressive practices that were emotionally and physically damaging to other students. For these boys, who also tended to be isolated from other peer groups, 'boyness' was demonstrated by highly exaggerated masculine practices. One way to make sense of 'boyness' is to use a notion of melancholy (Rose 1996). We may begin to look at exhibitions of masculinity by some children as demonstrating what cannot be obtained. In other words, young boys may be understood as melancholic – they are attempting to reconstruct (adult) masculinities to which they have limited access. As a result, boys' exaggerated displays of masculine traits become hyperbolic, through the performative re-creation of signs of adult masculinity that simultaneously expose their social ascriptions as boys. Such an understanding highlights the need for analyses of male schooling identities that enable us to engage with the specificities of masculinities *and* age relations.

Haywood (1993) provides an example of how *age* became an important aspect of older male students' policing of sexuality. The lack of heterosexual experience by a middle-class group of hard working students, the Academic Achievers, became a resource for other males in the school to impose legitimate definitions of masculinity. The other groups of males included the Dominant Heterosexuals, a group who believed in schooling but also that heterosexual relationships were equally important, and the Hyper-Heterosexuals, who tended to reject schooling and concentrated on developing their heterosexual career. These groups interpreted and represented the Academic Achievers' heterosexual inexperience as illustrating childlike behaviour. In a school where education strategies depended on the existence of normalized assumptions of childhood subjectivities, taking on codes of adult masculinity through heterosexuality became a significant dynamic in intrastudent relationships. The use of the term 'wankers' and terms of homophobic abuse such as 'bum bandits', 'gays' and 'poofs' became themes to produce Academic Achievers' identities as underdeveloped and thus abnormal. These terms were usually spoken outside the classroom in a public arena such as the student common room. In doing so, male students consolidated their masculine identities by making alternative/contradictory masculinities problematic. Terms of abuse were intensive and repeatedly distanced 'other' students. Interestingly, nearly all of the young men in the study had never met a 'homosexual' (male gay). However, the perpetual imposition of the label onto other boys forced into existence a sexualized masculinity. Across the adult/child divide, the young men had to imagine difference in order to incorporate it, thus consolidating their identities.

This process of making masculine identities is also evident in the terms of abuse used by the Academic Achievers. Such terms as 'cripple', 'cabbage', and 'spanner' were employed to describe other male students' inadequacy, representing something inanimate, inarticulate and stupid. They were commonly used when male students, particularly the Dominant Heterosexuals and the Hyper-Heterosexuals, answered teachers' questions incorrectly within the context of the classroom. For the Academic Achievers, these terms were a method of validating a masculinity based on educational competence, while serving to ridicule other masculine styles. Yet the Academic Achievers' language generally failed to position the other groups as subjects in their abuse and legitimate their own masculinities. This was mainly because the terms of abuse used by the Academic Achievers corresponded to the Hyper-Heterosexuals' and the Dominant Heterosexuals' perception that the Academic Achievers were 'childlike', reinforcing and amplifying their own inferiority. The latter's use of language colluded with a schooling system which desexualized students, emphasizing their immaturity, a schooling system which restricted their access to certain masculine subjectivities.

Ethnicity: a cultural resource to live out young male subjectivities

As with analyses of age, ethnicity in schooling is often understood as a simple binary social system. At the same time, there is a tendency in much social science to conflate ethnicity with colour that is composed of a juxtaposed white superiority and a black inferiority. The formation of young masculinities through the dynamics of ethnicity is not simply about exploring the intersubjective dimensions of 'blackness' and 'whiteness' but is also contained within lived and imagined ethnic (national) histories. In the schooling arena it is possible to identify different masculinities as constitutive of racialized/ethnic identities. As a result, masculinity may become the dynamic through which race/ethnicity is circumscribed (Mac an Ghaill 1999).

Fanon, in *Black Skins, White Masks* (1970) lucidly captures how the racialized black 'other' operates as a central dynamic in white identity formations. For Haywood (1993) in his ethnographic study of a sixth form college (postcompulsory), race created a number of complexities for white English males in their articulation of particular masculine heterosexualities. These male students conflated notions of Englishness and whiteness that became key components in circuits of desire. Those males who were part of a heterosexual culture that was premised on sexual athleticism experienced a range of psychic and microcultural contradictions because of their racist and homophobic disidentifications with black men and women. Englishness from their perspective, was about being 'not black and not gay'. Through the demonstration of their masculinities, these young men were simultaneously articulating a racialized politics. At the same time, such disidentifications limited, restricted and thus contested their claims to a sexual desire that was 'uncontrollable' – a mainstay of their heterosexual masculinities. The relations between them also involved a psychic structure, including such elements as: desire, attraction, repression, transference and projection in relation to a racialized 'sexual other' (Pajaczkowska and Young 1992). There is much work to be done in this area in order to understand the ambivalent structure of feeling and desire embedded within social institutions, such as schools (Fanon 1970; Bingham 2001).[3]

At the same time, among the Anglo-ethnic majority and ethnic minority young men living in England there has developed much emotional investment and cultural attachment to American black popular cultural forms such as music and sport. These cultural forms act as significant resources in their creative explorations of the shifting contours of cultural and political identities among and between ethnic majority and minority young people. It is particularly important to consider subjectivity not as a product, not as something possessed but rather as a complex and multifaceted process – the focus shifts from an emphasis on *being* (Anglo) ethnic to an emphasis on *becoming* ethnic. For young people living in multicultural urban settings, we have moved beyond the era of post-war colonial migration to that of English-born ethnic minorities. This marks a shift from the old certainties of colour as the primary signifier of social exclusion to more complex processes of regionally and institutionally-based inclusions and exclusions. However, at conceptual, political and policy levels, the ongoing narrative of the post-war immigration of Asians and African-Caribbeans is still being told in an older language of race and empire that is not able to grasp the generational specificities of emerging interethnic social relationships and their engagement with a different racial semantics. In short, we cannot simply read off social relations from fixed oppositional categories of black and white young men, which fail to capture formations of identity, subjectivity and cultural belonging.

In earlier work, Mac an Ghaill (1989), set out to reconceptualize African-Caribbean and Asian students' experience of schooling within a framework that moved beyond monocausal explanations and examined the multifaceted dimensions of racially structured English schooling. The African-Caribbean and Asian young men in this study, all of whom were academically successful, recall schooling biographies that have significant convergences and differences. What emerges is how racialized social and discursive configurations with their own local histories are grounded in specific material cultures at classroom and playground levels. For the students, the white teachers' racial and gender/sexual typifications did not take a unitary form but rather were differentially structured and experienced, mediated by the specificity of different school cultures and individual and collective student responses. In particular, the racial and gender composition of each school was a significant variable in the construction of teacher typifications. So, for example, in working-class schools where there was a majority Asian student population with a mainly white minority, the dominant representations of Asian youths tended to be negative, with caricatures of them as being 'sly' and 'not real men'. However, in working-class schools which included significant numbers of African-Caribbeans, students felt that Asians were caricatured in a more positive way in relation to African-Caribbeans, who were perceived as of 'low ability', 'aggressive' and 'anti-authority'. In contrast, in middle-class grammar schools (selective) with predominantly white student populations, such attributes as 'hard-working' and 'ambitious' were assigned to Asian students (Rattansi 1992).

At the time when the research was carried out – the mid-1980s – a racist practice called 'Paki bashing' had emerged, which involved white students physically and verbally attacking Asian students. A research question emerged, why was there no African-Caribbean bashing? The research originally framed social behaviour exclusively in terms of racial interaction, and hence could not resolve this absence in these terms. It became apparent that racial politics was simultaneously a sexual and gender politics and the research began to highlight how in the white imagination Asian boys were constructed as a weak masculinity, in relation to the tough masculinity of the African-Caribbean boys. The usefulness of exploring school boyhoods as cultural differences, spoken through each other, began to link 'Paki bashing' with 'poofter-bashing', that is physical and verbal attacks by straight people on gays – another soft masculinity. To be a 'Paki' is to be a 'poof' is to be a 'non-proper' boy. The notion of multiplicity offers a frame for understanding how boys policed themselves, particularly within informal peer group cultures/subcultures. In the following accounts, the Asian and African-Caribbean young men discuss the centrality of sexuality as a critical component in the constitution of masculinities (Brittan 1989).

Rajinder: Thinking about it, it's very complex. Straight men don't really have a problem with gays, they have a problem with themselves. Straight men seem to fear and love women but fear and hate gay men. Then whites, especially white men, have that fear and hatred for Asians and African-Caribbeans. So, black gay men are a real threat to white straight men. Like James Baldwin says, they act out their fears on us, on our bodies . . . But then there's other complications. Like at our school, you could see some of the white teachers, the men, they really admired the Caribbeans and not just in sport and music, where it was really homoerotic, though of course they could never admit it to themselves. I think for a lot of teachers there, who felt trapped in their jobs, the macho black kids represented freedom from the system. There were anti-school macho whites and Asians but the teachers with their stereotypes fantasised about the Caribbean kids, who they saw as anti-authority, more physical and athletic, everything they couldn't be but greatly admired.

Denton: It's true what Stephen was saying, most white teachers they would be afraid to live in the same areas as us. But at night they creep out to live it up among the black folk. You see a lot of whites fear us, especially 'big black men' but they also fantasise that black folk aren't as repressed as the whites. There are some real mixed up people about around the sexual and race thing.

(Mac an Ghaill 1994b: 159–60)

Here, Rajinder and Denton point to the range of split responses from white males to themselves, that were manifested in terms of the interplay between racial and sexual fear and desire and the accompanying contradictory elements of repulsion, fascination and misrecognition (Klein 1964; Mac an Ghaill 1994c).

Sexuality: forging 'proper' forms of young masculinity through a (hetero)sexual identity

In the above sections we have clarified the connections between schooling, 'proper' gender designations and the formation of young masculinities (Haywood and Mac an Ghaill 1995). Several studies have identified some of the ways in which inhabiting particular forms of heterosexual masculinity enables male students to negotiate wider gender relations and the formal/informal culture of schooling (Epstein and Johnson 1998). However, it does not immediately explain why these 'proper' forms of masculinity are heterosexual. A question arises: what is it about occupying 'proper' forms of masculinity that almost inevitably implies a heterosexual identity? The answer to this seems to lie in the fact that, in mainstream contemporary Anglo-American cultures at least, heterosexuality and gender are profoundly imbricated (overlapping). For example, Butler (1993) argues that gender is routinely spoken through a 'heterosexual matrix' in which heterosexuality is presupposed in the expression of 'real' forms of masculinity or femininity. Thus she (1993: 238) writes:

> Although forms of sexuality do not unilaterally determine gender, a non-causal and non-reductive connection between sexuality and gender is nevertheless crucial to maintain. Precisely because homophobia often operates through the attribution of a damaged, failed, or otherwise abject gender to homosexuals, that is, calling gay men 'feminine' or calling lesbians 'masculine', and because the homophobic terror over performing homosexual acts, where it exists, is often also a terror over losing proper gender ('no longer being a real or proper man' or 'no longer being a real or proper woman'), it seems crucial to retain a theoretical apparatus that will account for how sexuality is regulated through the policing and the shaming of gender.

Sedgwick's (1991) work on changes in Anglo-American male–male relations has begun to fill in some of the historical background to this imbrication of gender and sexuality. She argues that the current exclusion of male–male erotic contact from 'proper' forms of masculinity has its origins in an eighteenth-century shift from the religious to the secular discursive construction of sexuality, and that an important consequence of this 'endemic and ineradicable state of homosexual panic' has been the fact that homophobia is used to police the boundaries of acceptable heterosexual male behaviour and identity as well as more overtly (and often violently) being used to police homosexual behaviour and identity.

We have examined the constitutive cultural elements of heterosexual male students' subjectivity within secondary schools (Mac an Ghaill 1994b; Haywood and Mac an Ghaill 1995; see also Kehily 2001). These elements, which consist of contradictory forms of compulsory heterosexuality (automatic prescription of heterosexuality), misogyny (hatred of women) and homophobia (the fear of homosexuality in oneself or others), were marked by contextual ambivalence and contingency. The focus was the complex interplay of these cultural elements as institutionally specific forms of gendered and sexual power. More particularly, we have explored how they were operationalized as key defining processes in sexual boundary maintenance, policing and legitimization of male heterosexual identities. In order to understand how students attempted to learn the sexual/gender codes that conferred hegemonic masculinity, it was necessary to bring together social and psychic structures. What emerged as of particular salience was the way in which heterosexual male students were involved in a double relationship, of traducing the 'other', including women and gays (external relations), at the same time as expelling femininity and homosexuality from within themselves (internal relations). These were the complex and contradictory processes within which heterosexual male student apprentice- ships were developed within a secondary school context. Hence in structur- ing the attributes of maleness, the various forms of masculinity that are hegemonic in English schools can all be argued to be crucially involved in policing the boundaries of heterosexuality as much as the boundaries of 'proper' masculinity.

Arnot (1984: 145), examining the links between male compulsory hetero- sexuality, misogyny and the masculine processes of dissociation from femininity, argues that in a male dominated society femininity is ascribed; in contrast masculinity and manhood has to be 'achieved in a permanent process of struggle and confirmation'. Externally and internally males attempt to re-produce themselves as powerful within social circumstances which remain out their of control. This is illustrated within an English context by Redman and Mac an Ghaill (1996) in 'Schooling sexualities: Heterosexual, schooling, and the unconscious', in which they discuss a student's experi- ence (Peter Redman) of 'becoming heterosexual' in an all-boys grammar school in the late 1970s and early 1980s. Using an auto/biographical method- ology, they explore the meaning of Peter's investment in a particular form of heterosexual masculinity, named as 'muscular intellectualness'. They argue that Peter's fascination with the muscular intellectualness he identi- fied in his teacher, Mr Lefevre, can be understood in terms of the access it promised to give him to the entitlements of conventional masculinity. The world of ideas and knowledge that Mr Lefevre inhabited no longer seemed effeminately middle-class and thus the object of ridicule or embarrassment, but powerfully middle-class, a source of personal strength and a means to exercise control over others. Thus, as a source of 'real' masculinity, muscular intellectualness 'defeminized' academic work in the humanities and refused the label 'bit of a poof'.

In earlier work we have reported on young gay students' experiences of growing up in English schools, where there were no positive images of gay or lesbian people, nor acknowledgement of gay and lesbian history, sensib- ility, achievement, lifestyle and community. The students spoke of the fact that when texts written by gays or lesbians were used in schools, no reference is made to the authors' sexual orientation. In fact, in lessons homosexuality was rarely discussed and on the few occasions when it was introduced, it was presented in a negative way; most recently in relation to HIV/AIDS. For gay students this silence, reflecting that in the wider society, pervades the whole of the formal curriculum, serving to reproduce and legitimate dominant heterosexual hierarchies. From this perspective, hetero- sexuality is presented as natural, normal and universal, simply because there are no alternative ways of being. Gay students emphasize the personal isolation, confusion, marginalization and alienation that this engenders. Most significantly, without a positive reference group, they tend to internalize ambivalent negative messages about themselves as young gay men. A similar situation was found in curriculum analysis in North America (see Warren 1984; Epstein 1994; Trotter 1999).

However, the gay student accounts became more complex because their dissonant institutional location also contained a positive and creative experience. In particular, gay and lesbian students had an insight into the contradictory constitution of a naturalized heterosexuality that was structured through ambivalent misogyny and homophobia. In this way, gay and lesbian students were able to occupy social locations that allowed the contestation and inversion of heterosexual power. As Matthew, a young gay man illustrated (see Mac an Ghaill 1994a):

> The RE teacher said one day in class that teenagers go through a homosexual phase just like earlier on they go through an anti-girls phase . . . I told him, I did not think that boys go through phases. I said that if boys go through an anti-girls phase, it was a long phase because men were abusing women all of their lives . . . The teacher went mad. It was gays that were supposed to be the problem and I turned it round to show the way that it really is.

Importantly, we have found it productive to make sense of young gay and lesbians' experience of marginalization and disempowerment without *necessarily* reverting to a conventional understanding of power, where responses to a naturalized heterosexuality are read off as forms of 'resistance'. An unintended effect of this conventional approach (often called an anti-oppressive framework) is that experience is compressed within a powerful/powerless couplet (see Chapter 5 on methodology). In other words, there is no empirical, analytical or theoretical space beyond domination and subordination. In our own work with young people, we have found that social relations are in a continual constitutive process. As Foucault (1981: 99) suggests: 'Relations of power-knowledge are not static forms of distribution, they are "matrices of transformations"'. In this way, we have to move towards understanding structures and hierarchies as not completely stable and not completely forceful as well as engaging in a process where outcomes are not entirely secured.

Conclusion: rethinking the sex/gender system and schooling

Throughout this chapter we illustrated that schools act as 'masculinity making devices'. By theoretically examining masculinity and offering empirical examples of the way masculinities are shaped in the context of schools, an attempt has been made to address the notion of the 'schooling of masculinities'. It has to be emphasized that schools do not exist on their own as locations for the creation and contestation of masculinities but rather in complex interrelationships with other social and cultural sites, including the family, labour markets, media representations, cultural technologies and the legal system. However, perhaps contemporary schooling is the most strategic site, as it offers a condensed range of experiences in a sustained and mandatory fashion. It is also necessary to emphasize that schools do not produce masculinities in a direct, overly deterministic way, but that the construction of student identities is a process of negotiation, rejection, acceptance and ambivalence. It is hoped that this chapter contributes to generating fresh insights into what constitutes masculinities. More specifically, the chapter has argued for the need to examine critically heterosexual masculinities and in the process to destabilize the assumed naturalness and inevitability of sex/gender schooling regimes.

Questions for your reflection

1 How do teacher styles influence schoolboy masculinities?

2 What is the relationship between capitalism and the formation of young working-class masculinities?

3 How does the curriculum impact on student peer group cultures?

4 How does age, ethnicity and sexuality constitute male students' subjectivity?

Suggested further reading

Davies, B. (1993) *Shards of Glass: Children, Reading and Writing beyond Gendered Identities*. Sydney, NSW: Allen & Unwin.
Mac an Ghaill, M. (1994) *The Making of Men: Masculinities, Sexualities and Schooling*. Buckingham: Open University Press.
Thorne, B. (1993) *Gender Play: Girls and Boys in School*. Buckingham: Open University Press.

Notes

1 Post–16 refers to postcompulsory schooling.
2 Social class and masculinity is usually explored in the literature from a materialist position, with a focus upon political economy, as illustrated above. For a post-structuralist examination of social class and masculinity, see Easthope (1990) and Mort (1996).
3 For another example of the ambivalent structure of feeling and desire between social groups, see Mac an Ghaill (1996b) on Irish diasporic masculinities and sexualities.

MAPPING, RESEARCHING AND PRACTISING MASCULINITIES

CHAPTER 4

A MAN OF THE WORLD: EMERGING REPRESENTATIONS OF GLOBAL MASCULINITIES

Key concepts

Globalization; gendered nation; postcolonialism; 'machismo'; cross-cultural analysis; ubiquitous male; structural functionalism; rites of passage; diaspora; transnational genders; hyper-masculinity; global masculinities; disembodied masculinity.

Introduction

From the seemingly 'brutal' male circumcision in non-western cultures to the 'compassionate' killings in Inuit culture, cross-cultural analyses have provided sociologists with understandings of the underlying dynamics of social processes and practices. This chapter employs a similar approach. The first section adopts a more familiar understanding of the study of masculinities by examining men and masculinities in different international contexts. It uses a concept of the 'gendered nation' to identify salient aspects of national regimes of masculinity. In doing so, the chapter emphasizes the local arrangements of meanings of masculinities – in their exoticized and eroticized particularities. In short, the first section reflects a more traditional, mainstream cross-cultural analysis of men and masculinities. In contrast, the second section focuses on how we might begin to imagine masculinities as disembodied transnational gender regimes. Here we take a more postmodern approach and shift from examining men and masculinities in the local context, to analysing gender relations as articulated through global processes that are travelling beyond national boundaries. As a result, the chapter is located within the main current conceptual confusions/tensions in this field of inquiry. In other words, the notion of globalized masculinities is highly contested.

Operating within these two positions, we find ourselves presented with a particular conceptual confusion. At a general level, globalization may be understood as referring to the processes, procedures and technologies – political, economic and cultural – underpinning the current 'time–space' compression which produces a sense of immediacy and simultaneity about the world (Brah *et al.* 1999). However, this emphasis on transnational phenomena often eclipses the significance of local voices, issues and histories (Taylor *et al.* 1996). It also tends to neglect the power of imagined national communities that reconfigure and localize global processes. Hall (1991: 33) describes two forms of globalization that are still struggling with one another:

> an older, corporate enclosed, increasingly defensive one which has to go back to nationalism and national cultural identity in a highly defensive way, and to try to build barriers around it before it is eroded. And then this other form of the global post-modern which is trying to live with, and at the same moment, overcome, sublate, get hold of, and incorporate difference.

Locating the chapter within these two approaches, we suggest a broader definition of globalization that contains a conceptual tension of both localized difference as well as shared transnational sameness *at the same time*. This means that we perceive the world as a series of heterogeneous differentiated cultural contexts that contain and include homogenizing global processes. One of the problems associated with reconceptualizing certain social behaviours and practices is that the latter can become merely re-described without offering any further explanations or alternative under-standings (White 1997). As White (1997: 20) suggests:

> Different styles of masculinity are developed historically, not given for all times and places. Those now dominant are therefore integrally interwoven with 'development' – through colonialism, the movement towards modernity, and now globalization. To explore masculinities therefore represents not only a challenge to gender analysis, but to the power and culture of the development enterprise as a whole.

Men of the world: in search of the 'ubiquitous male'

Cross-cultural investigations provide sociologists with much information on the socially constructed nature of masculinities. These analyses help to problematize gender categories by examining how meanings are assembled in local contexts. Alongside this, they provide a picture of the processes and practices of gender relations. Methodologically, such cross-cultural ana-lyses enable sociologists to respond reflexively to the conceptual frameworks that are employed. As we shall see later, this facet of cross-cultural analyses is able to destabilize the concept of masculinity itself. By taking seriously the culturally contested nature of masculinities, we begin to acknowledge that: 'it is important to capture the diversity of these signs and forms of behaviour by understanding that masculinity cannot be treated as some-thing fixed and universal' (Archetti 1999: 113).

There is a wide range of theoretical and conceptual cross-cultural ana-lyses of masculinities (Cornwall and Lindisfarne 1994). However, one of the more pervasive approaches that resonates with popularized explanations of gender has been structural functionalism. From this position, social and cultural processes do not necessarily increase difference or generate same-ness, but are overlaid onto structures that lie beneath social and cultural differences. As a result, all men are the same; there exists an ubiquitous male. This position is clearly presented in Gilmore's (1990) accounts of the variation in boys' rites of passage. Through an exploration of a number of highly geographically differentiated cultures, Gilmore suggests that all masculinities share similar fundamental structures. He maintains that mas-culinity is indispensable to societies because it acts as a means of integra-tion. The dynamic for articulation of different masculinities is based upon a psychological interrelation between mother, father and child. As a result, for him, the familial relation is a global process:

> This recurrent notion that manhood is problematic, a critical thresh-old that boys must pass through testing, is found at all levels of

socio-cultural development regardless of what other alternative roles are recognized. It is found among the simplest hunters and fisherman, among peasants and sophisticated urbanized people, it is found in all continents and environments. It is found among both warrior people and those who have never killed in anger.

(Gilmore 1990: 11)

Gilmore, using a post-Freudian analysis, suggests that the key underlying tension for boys is the detachment of a primal psychic unity with the mother. This means that when boys are born, a fusing of their identity with their mother's takes place; boy and mother exist in a unity. As boys grow up they develop a sense of public individuality that will be culturally marked as male or female. Boys are therefore caught within a contradiction of simultaneously distancing and desiring their mother. For Gilmore, cultures set up public rites of passage to resolve this contradiction. Citing Gennep (1960), he argues that rites of passage involve the public disconnection of the boy from his mother. The primal fantasy of union with the mother is a threat to their public masculine individuality. Masculinity is pitched against childhood and the rites of passage are the social mechanisms in place to 'make men' by serving to hold off the impulses to reunite with the mother. As a result, social and cultural conditions are important devices in making men, as different cultures draw upon differentiated social and symbolic practices to demonstrate masculinity.

The following three case studies critically interrogate, within a global context, the notion of the *ubiquitous male*. One of the confusing aspects of Gilmore's approach is that there is a tendency to substitute cultural difference for biological difference, without examining the political, economic and social dimensions of the particular local context. Alongside this critique, we also concentrate on the interrelationships between gendered and national identities.

Global relations and gendered nations

One way of critically exploring the 'ubiquitous male' is to focus on how masculinities are mediated through different national contexts and how their specific social and cultural interrelationships reshape the meanings of manhood. Mostov (2000) outlines how in the former Yugoslavia, gendered bodies become symbolic markers of national fertility and territory. In times of war, men and masculinity operate symbolically and materially as protectors and aggressors (Sharp 1996). In this way rather than suggest a unitary national/global maleness, it is possible to identify historically specific versions of maleness. A gendering of nations approach stresses that masculinities are formed by nationally specific images, tasks, rituals and value systems. In this way, masculinity is not a simple self-construct but is generated through an imagined community, a sense of national/ethnic belonging and racialized difference (Anderson 1983; Hall 1991).

Masai warriors, modernity and the remaking of traditional masculinities

The case of Masai warriors in the southeast African countries of Tanzania and Kenya highlights the limitations of examining masculinity as a simple global psychosocial phenomenon. Although the Masai tribe have tradition-ally lived a semi-nomadic existence with their economy built upon pastor-alism (animal herding), they have built up a fearsome reputation as brave warriors. Within the tribe, various forms of segregation exist, including the sexual division of labour and differentiated birthrights. However, one of the strongest forms of segregation between the men in the tribe is based upon age. Age is not in this culture juxtaposed within a simple child/adult binary, but consists of a five various lifecycles, each containing contested versions of manhood. These generational periods appear to operate through oppositions with young men representing values of communal sharing, wildness, and a carefree sex for pleasure ethic. In contrast, older men are understood as being individualistic, domesticated authority figures and involved in sexual relations primarily for procreation.

According to Hodson (1999) these age-differentiated definitions of man-hood became refracted through state definitions of citizenship. At different historical junctures the state became key to the arrangements of masculine meanings that were attached to male bodies. In essence, the state normal-ized and situated masculine attributes within a series of global based values. Therefore in order to understand masculinities, we need to examine the nation in terms of the processes of: colonialism, economic and social develop-ment, missionization and nation building (C. Hall 1992). For example in the 1920s, a key dynamic of British colonial rule was an attempt to develop and 'civilize' the nation. Modernist themes such as progress, order and rationality characterized state legislation. The Masai, with their indigenous traditions, represented the past and symbolized what had to be changed about the nation. Thus British colonialists attempted to increase economic productivity by encouraging farming methods. The older generation became important instruments of the state, as they attempted to use their influence to control and 'civilize' the younger men. Alongside the ring-fencing of Masai lands, Hodson suggests that the cultivation of modern masculinities involved the containment of an exoticized and eroticized 'young black wildness'.

Using the older generation to consolidate colonial rule positioned the young Masai warriors and their pastoralism as antithetical to modern nation building. As a result, the colonialists suggested that the Masai needed greater training in farming and animal husbandry. According to Hodson, the notion of complying or working with the colonialist was articulated through the category of 'Ormeek'. The 'Ormeek' was a masculinity that was colonially friendly and was typified in the dress style of shirt and trousers. It is a category that has carried through into postcolonialism (a period where subjectivity is marked by a previous imperial ruler) and has expanded to include education and training. Occupying an earlier position of devalued masculinity, Ormeek has been reconfigured to be a masculinity of high value, as education and training in the late twentieth century became a central strategy in increasing economic development in the Masai villages, with a synthesis between traditional and modern masculinities emerging.

> For Massai, the imposition of the modern/traditional dichotomy has been a profoundly gendered process in its constitution, representation and effects: the oppositional categories of modernity simultaneously valorize and stigmatise certain gender configurations, certain masculinities and femininities. Masai masculinities have become a key site for the experience and negotiation of modernity.
>
> (Hodson 1999: 144)

One interesting aspect of Hodson's work is demonstrating the nationalization of Masai culture. In place of the 1920s insistence on men of modernity, Kenya and Tanzania are now reconstructing African identities through the use of the cultural imagery of the Masai as a tourist trade attraction. With the systematic attempt at modernization, through the commercialization and commodification of Masai culture, the modern face of the nation projects what was once deemed 'uncivilized' and 'backward' as emblematic of the modern nation. The nation is now celebrating and cultivating a warrior masculinity, in spite of concerted attempts to 'civilize' it.

Ethnicity, nation and religion: Israeli masculinities

Exploring the social structure of the Masai warriors illustrates the implausibility of the ubiquitous male by highlighting how meanings of manhood are highly contingent and do not automatically stem from psychosocial processes. Within this local context, such meanings of manhood are not simply reattached to new phenomena but are reconstructed and reconstituted through definitions of nationhood. Understanding nationhood through the frame of masculinities can make explicit competing definitions of manhood. A key aspect of Gilmore's work is that differentiated geographical locations, with their diverse access to resources, produce different kinds of manhood. However, diasporas (dispersed populations) demonstrate that a notion of nation can exist without geographical boundaries (Anthias and Yuval Davies 1992; Mac an Ghaill 1999). The interrelationship between masculinity and nationhood is also illustrated by analyses of Israeli society.

The historical formation of the Israeli nation was closely connected to the Zionist movement. Significantly, early in the twentieth century a key feature of the Zionist movement was the promotion of an ideal of Jewish muscular masculinity. A central feature of the new Jewish man was shaped by a complex relationship to the Jewish diaspora. The diaspora from a Zionist position was represented as weak and effeminate. In contrast, the Zionist movement's 'ideal man' was embodied in the 'sabra' – Israeli born youth. With the Israeli settlement in Palestine, the Zionist promotion of muscular masculinity has become a dominant feature of Israeli society and has been closely aligned with militarism. From a Zionist perspective, a readiness to fight for their honour is an organizing principle of what it means to be a Jewish man.

Klein (1999) argues that with the transformation of the Jewish diaspora, there has been a reconfiguration of Jewish identity. Rather than religion being the key definer of Jewish masculinity, the new organizing feature is a military orthodoxy. For example, Kaplan (2000) transposes the bar mitzvah, a Jewish ceremony of coming of age for 13 year old boys, that involves exhibiting competence in reading from the Torah, to conscription into military service at the age of 18. He argues that the bar mitzvah, with its associations with the diaspora and its emphasis on reading, is emblematic of passive individuals and a weak nation. Conscription to the tough masculinity of the Israeli defence force has now become the new rite of passage. However Kaplan (2000) has noted that although militarized masculinities have become a dominant feature of Israeli society, the masculinities within the military are not cohesive and in many ways reflect the diversity of the Israeli nation. For example, the Parachute unit adheres to traditional Zionist ideals of the Sabra, whereas the Gi'ivati unit tends to focus on religious orthodoxy and be inclusive of new immigrants. As a result, rather than consolidate the Israeli nation into a cohesive masculinity, conscription to the defence force segregates and cultivates cultural differentiation.

For Klein (1999), this new rite of passage that is in place stresses hardness, strength, physical ability, endurance, self-control, professionalism, sociability, aggressiveness and heterosexuality. These qualities have been consolidated by Israel's national security policy, which includes three years' compulsory conscription for men (18 months for women) with reserve service lasting until their 50s. If masculinities within Israeli society are being reshaped through the cultural centrality of the military rather than religion, then threats to Israeli masculinity take the form of a militarized 'otherness'. The result of this 'otherness', according to Kaplan, is the positioning of Arab nations as devoid of any cultural characteristics and their refiguring as the 'enemy'. The absence of cultural content in the enemy allows the Israeli defence forces to reconstruct conflict. For instance, the Intifada uprising of the Palestinians within Israel reconstructed 10 year old children as men and enemies of the state. The brutalization of the Palestinians by the Israeli state is based upon a strict militarized otherness, rather than any claims to religious or cultural identifications. The interrogation and torture of Palestinians by Israeli soldiers have produced accounts that illustrate how the Israeli state regards Arabs as non-human (Peteet 2000).

Mexican masculinities

The final case study that serves to contest the existence of the 'ubiquitous male' is provided by Gutmann (1996) in his excellent account of working-class men in the suburbs of Mexico City. His sensitivity to the range and variability of being a man allows him to deconstruct assumptions that have been applied to Mexican men's lifestyles. Gutmann's account allows us to contest the cross-cultural validity of the concept, 'masculinity'. Within a western sensibility, masculinity (or masculinities) makes sense. It belongs to a range of academic and popular discourses that have identified specific social behaviours and categorized them as 'masculine'. We have a tendency to extrapolate descriptive and analytical categories to other cultures, thus practising a conceptual imperialism. The sensibilities that may be (more or less) adequate to make sense of western meanings and behaviours may not have analytical or conceptual currency in other societies. This not only opens up how we might begin to make sense of masculinities cross-culturally, or if we can actually talk about masculinity as a cross-cultural phenomenon, but also provides clarity about the explication of men's experiences and understandings in western contexts.

Within North America, Mexican men tend to be represented as adulterous, promiscuous, irresponsible to children and physically abusive in marriage. The particular concern for Gutmann (1996) was to explore this suggested hard, uncaring masculinity in the working-class suburb of Colonia San Domingo. An area built upon volcanic rock, it was made available in the early 1970s by the government and resulted in four to five thousand families claiming plots of land overnight. Through the use of ethnography, Gutmann's study interrogates what men *say* and *do* to become men. Of key interest is how he helps us to make sense of masculinity as non-translatable into Mexican language. For instance, *macho, machismo*, and *mandilon*, are expressions used by Mexican men and women to describe and explain different kinds of men. Machismo in particular has a particular cultural significance with wife beaters. However, during his fieldwork, Gutmann noticed that such terms were used interchangeably to mean a man that physically abuses his wife, a connotation of being unmanly, to a meaning that suggests authentic manliness. According to Gutmann this shifting meaning appears as historically located. Many of the respondents in his fieldwork talked about machismo as having a different meaning in the past that was courageous and principled, whereas a modern understanding is of someone who is cowardly and unworthy. In fact, he documents how in some contexts to be a machismo is to demonstrate femininity.

A further complexity surrounds a *mandilon*, which is a term used to describe a man who is dominated by a woman. Although Gutmann was provided with a number of examples of these kind of men, the men themselves did not identify with such a term, reconstructing it in terms of fairness and sharing.

Fatherhood in particular became a salient feature of his study as he tried to capture understandings of Mexican masculinity.[1] According to Gutmann a dominant image of Mexican men is that they have little contact with children, that they are carefree and that taking responsibility for children would be a display of femininity. During his fieldwork, he could find little evidence to support this claim, as many of the men and women high-lighted the fact that working-class men took an active involvement in child-care. Although women took a greater degree of household responsibility, this did not preclude an affectionate, tender and caring relationship between men and their children. A further aspect of the discrepancy between cultural assumptions and social behaviour was illustrated by the celebration of boys' assumed higher cultural capital. Again such an assumption did not make sense to the people in this matrifocal context, with many young men arguing that they treated their male and female children the same. What became salient was the notion that what fatherhood means was strongly organized around class, region and ethnicity.

Gutmann's study offers a number of important conceptual facets. The notion of a machismo or macho man – pre-1940s – was not part of popular Mexican vocabulary. Although macho was used, he argues that it was a much more obscure term. Rather, he maintains that masculinity was captured by the term *muy hombre*, which was used to celebrate both men and women's practices. For example, in the Mexican Revolution both men *and* women's courage and sacrifice were valued. However, during the reconstruction of Mexico in the 1940s, national identities became associated with Mexican men. Such an identity was captured and constituted by cinema and later by radio and television. Cinema projected a notion of the Mexican man as advocating individuality and sacrifice to the nation, establishing a cultural nationalism.

Importantly, this is a proletarian militant, as an emblem of the nation. However, this effectively consolidated a national identity that became focused around men. To be Mexican therefore became equated with a certain kind of man. Another important aspect of the establishment of this identity has been Mexico's geographic proximity to the United States.

Mexico and the United States have a strong economic and cultural inter-relationship, with around 15 per cent of Mexico's labour force working in the United States. A key element of this interrelation is the import/export of music, fashion and consumerism. At the level of subjectivity, Gutmann (1996) suggests that what it means to be a Mexican man has also been exported back to Mexico. For example, Mexicans are now able to watch television shows broadcast from the United States that discuss what it is like to be a Mexican. Machismo in the United States has a derogatory meaning that is associated with Latin Americans in general. In this way, the values and meanings that are being constructed around Mexican masculinity have been fused with nationalist understandings that in the present era are being reworked from outside the national borders.

In summary, these cross-cultural studies demonstrate that masculinity and femininity are not reducible to two discrete biological categories. As pointed out in the Introduction of this volume, there appear to be more differences among men as a social group than there are between men and women. A further limitation is that structural functionalist notions of gender roles produce false dichotomies. As the studies above indicate, within various cultural contexts a number of competing masculinities are visible that are arranged within historically contingent value systems. Operating within cross-cultural systems, it is possible to suggest that men have a number of different referents with which to display diverse masculine styles. From this more conventional analysis of world-wide masculinities, we now turn to an understanding of men and masculinity that goes beyond a modernist understanding of the nation.

Beyond the gendered nation: disembodied hegemonic masculinities

In this section we also connect masculinity with global processes and explore masculinities as constitutive features of globalized politics, labour markets and culture. We suggest that while the above section highlights the cultural differentiation of masculine meanings, they continue to identify masculinity with male bodies. In contrast, the possibilities of examining gender transnationally is that it enables us to rethink the naturalized gender order. Tensions emerge as the boundaries that mark off similarity and difference between men and women and among each social group become confused.

Globalization has become a significant conceptual tool with which critically to explore the transnational travelling of economies, politics, commodities and technologies (Harvey 1989). It is only recently that these global processes have been understood as constituting masculinities (Lancaster 1992; Ling 1999; Mac an Ghaill 1999; Connell 2000). However within the notion of transnational genders a productive paradox emerges. As Connell (2000: 40) suggests:

> This is one of the most difficult points in current gender analysis because the conception is counterintuitive. We are so accustomed to thinking of gender as the attribute of an individual, even as a particularly intimate matter, that it requires a considerable wrench to think of gender on the vast scale of global society.

Responses to globalization may vary (Appaduri 1991; Mac an Ghaill 1999). On one hand, Connell (2000) suggests globalization is not simply a recent phenomenon, arguing that we are able historically to identify a number of globalizations. As a social phenomenon, the current global gender order has been shaped by imperialism and has resulted in a broadly patriarchal society. For example, masculinities of conquest and settlement, masculinities of empire and masculinities of neo-liberalism and postcolonialism have emerged at various historical junctures to reinforce a patriarchal organiza-tion of society. At each historical moment, gender regimes have been re-constituted as male dominance. For example, in the drive for empire building, the conquest and settlement of various peoples has included as a central mechanism the reproduction of the customs and traditions of the imperial country. From Connell's perspective, imperialism disrupted traditional gender mores and has rearticulated them into new forms of patriarchy.

From a different position, Hooper (2000) argues that gender relations play an integral part in the impact of new technologies, global finances, new social divisions of labour and emerging forms of regionalism. She argues that current global relations are reconstructing gender relations but not necessarily in patriarchal ways. Modern forms of social organization that depend on a male breadwinner model are being fractured, as work becomes disconnected from a localized economy and welfare arrangements no longer support male workers, alongside changes in family formations. The hegemonic masculinity of early modernity, marked by a traditional patriarchal order, has according to Hooper been 'softened'. She identifies a number of interrelating elements involved in this transformation, includ-ing the decline of military conscription in various countries; men taking on feminine positions as they increasingly occupy the space of consumer rather than producer; and a feminization of the workforce (as discussed in Chapter 1). These processes are having an integral effect on the composition of emerging global masculinities that may not simply be equated with tradi-tional forms of oppression.

It has been argued that globalization has become a watchword for a number of different political, economic and cultural changes (Marchand and Runyan 2000). This section will concentrate on three interrelated and mutually informing categories, the political, the economic and the cultural, to illustrate how we might begin to think about masculinities as disembodied entities.

A global community of men: the Gulf War

As Parpart (1998: 204) has suggested: 'The international arena is also a place where competing hegemonic interpretations of male power and man-liness struggle for predominance'. In the early 1990s, the fall of the Berlin Wall, the shifting political dynamic in the Soviet Union and the Gulf War symbolized a new era in international relations. With Kuwait exceeding

OPEC's oil quotas and the subsequent invasion by Iraq of Kuwait in 1990, new political allegiances and coalitions were mobilized that involved 39 countries, including Afghanistan, Egypt, France, Saudi Arabia, Syria, the United Kingdom, and the United States. During the war a number of discourses were used morally to position the coalition and Iraq, in which 'masculinity' became a salient feature. Niva (1998) argues that the Gulf War is a good example of the demonstration of masculinity on the political stage. She maintains that the Gulf War became an opportunity to reconstruct national identities into a broader community of nations or a new world order. George Bush, president of the United States at the time, argued:

> It is a big idea: a new world order, where diverse nations are drawn together in common cause to achieve the universal aspirations of mankind, peace, and security, freedom and the rule of law . . . only the United States has both the moral standing and the means to back it up.
>
> (Niva 1998: 112)

Interestingly, this new world order became supported and legitimized by the projection of a particular militaristic masculinity. This was about establishing a world order, not about fighting and sacrifice for a particular nation state; it was a war for the global community. The Iraqi antipathy shown towards the West and United States became reconstructed by the West as an issue for international law and order (Mosse 1985).

Niva argues that repositioning the military coalition in this campaign was underpinned by the United States remaking its national identity. In short, the reconstruction of the United States military had a homogenizing effect on other nations. The moral purpose of the Gulf War integrated the particularities of the United States national (military) consciousness into a collectively shared masculinism. From a cultural studies perspective, Jeffords (1994) asserts that the United States national identity crisis came to be read as a crisis of manhood. She suggests that the portrayal of America through popular cultural forms represented the nation as a soft body. This soft, *feminized* body came to signify the failure of foreign policy, being held responsible for a number of military and civilian embarrassments that included the United States' defeat in Vietnam, the failure of US policy in Nicaragua, the Iran Contra Affair and the inability to capture and try Osama Bin Laden. Alongside the restructuring of gender relations institutionally, economically and domestically, Niva suggests that the Gulf War became an important showcase for American manhood and the consolidation of national subjectivity.

Jansen and Sabo (1994: 1) argue that: 'sport/war tropes are crucial rhetorical resources for mobilising the patriarchal values that construct, mediate, maintain, and, when necessary, reform or repair hegemonic forms of masculinity and femininity'. Their analysis of the Gulf War demonstrates the use of sport/war metaphors to represent different aspects of the conflict but also to consolidate the coalition's male solidarity. They argue that the language of sport represents the language of hegemonic masculinity which is constituted by 'aggression, competition, dominance, territoriality and instrumental violence'. Jansen and Sabo draw upon a range of examples where American football language became interchangeable for military operations. As the bombers returned from dropping bombs on Baghdad, they described the foray as a 'big football game'. They also cite how General Norman Schwartzkopf talked of the ground war intervention as 'Hail Mary play in football', along with numerous references to 'game plans', 'tactics' and 'war games'. As the use of such metaphors celebrated men and masculinities, they convey heroism, competitiveness and emotional hardness that in turn celebrates specific versions of men, serving to displace women and other men. The new world order coalition became reconstituted as a male team.

Another interesting aspect of this war was that it became a global media spectacle. The spectacle itself also became part of soldiering because technological development was enabling war to be fought at a 'safe' geographical distance. With a traditional cultural confluence of tough masculinity and the military, such distance was juxtaposing a hard embattled masculinity with men who were technically minded. In effect, the air attack and the ground attacks attempted to take the body out of the action. It was no longer important for the troops to be fighting machines, the emphasis was on men who operated fighting machines. In effect there was no immediate need for a tough body; the body became an appendage to the machine. As Niva (1998: 119) suggests: 'Infantry men took a backseat in war coverage to computer programmers, missile technologists, battle tank commanders, high tech pilots and those appropriately equipped and educated for the new world order'. What is interesting is that the fighting took a technological turn as laser-guided missiles resembled the explosions characteristic of home computer games. Such technological innovation enhanced a broader theme of the conflict that was based upon avoiding casualties. This conflict was represented as a soldier-friendly warfare, where those in command demonstrated a regime of caring for troops.

Importantly, this 'caring approach' resonates with the moral purpose of a world order. This tough but concerned approach towards troops in the Persian Gulf was juxtaposed with the demonization of the Iraqi leader. Interestingly, it was the Iraqi leader who was demonized rather than the Iraqi nation itself. In fact, the nation was described as a victim, with the United Nations setting up 'smart sanctions' to provide humanitarian aid while at the same time blockading the purchase of military equipment. Saddam Hussain was described as a dictator, a hyper-masculine aggressor. His aggression was fused with a religious extremism and an effeminate Arabic culture that was juxtaposed to the liberal democratic, compassionate, respectful nature of western citizenship. These values became the justification for the military action against the Iraqi army. Thus, the Gulf War became a contestation of global meanings of manhood. Following the destruction of the World Trade Center on 11 September 2001, this now reads as a dress rehearsal for the 'war against terrorism', involving what the American military refers to as a 'clash of civilizations'.

Global capitalism

One of the more pervasive accounts of globalization is that economic markets operate as a key dynamic in transnational processes. Embedded within a national political economy are global trends that are incorporating and thus reshaping local processes. Work by Fukuyama (1989) for instance equates modernity with a rationalist historicism, where all nation states are at some point absorbing western political economies. Although this modernist perspective understands history as an 'endpoint' analysis, it does allow us to think about social and economic organization as 'regimes'. However, it is important to stress that social and economic organizational regimes are gendered not simply in terms of the effects on bodies but as realized through the normative meanings and understandings that allow us to make sense of bodies.

A commonly cited theme of globalization is that it characterizes a shift from Fordism to post-Fordism. It is possible to understand this change in mode of industrial production as constituting a particular gender regime, that is certain versions of masculinity (and femininity). Fordism is a mass production system that focuses on nationally located companies, occupationally and hierarchically separated, whose market is undifferentiated. According to Young (2000), Fordism represented a particular gender regime of the white, western, male, industrialized worker. Fordism had transformed the gender regimes of agrarian industrialism, collapsing a private patriarchal productivity into a publicly gendered industrial organization. The homemaker/breadwinner dichotomy was supported politically and legitimized through welfare arrangements. Importantly, the gender regime of Fordism was characterized as a division of labour.

In contrast, the emergence of post-Fordist industrial organization, led by Japanese firms outsourcing work to non-OECD countries, can be understood as a travelling global production process. Post-Fordism, with its emphasis on increasing productivity, is often characterized as a merging of thinking and doing, that has a focus on multiskilling and the collapse of occupational hierarchies. Although there is evidence of this happening (see below), it appears that post-Fordism is often confused with multinational companies relocating Fordist working regimes into areas that have lower production costs, such as free trade zones or tax free regions, supplemented by government grants and subsidies. Inevitably, the increasing participation of women in waged work, albeit in poorly paid and insecure material conditions is reshaping gender regimes. However, research needs to be carried out that evaluates the characteristics of a regendering of poorly paid, insecure work, both of men and women (Williams and Mac an Ghaill 1998). As a result, travelling post-Fordist organizations can be seen to be significant in reconstructing gender regimes.

Hamada (1996) provides a useful account of the impact of post-Fordism and the potential for the cultural contestation of masculinity. His study focused on the middle management of a Japanese multinational company that had invested in the US. Part of that investment involved the transfer of Japanese culture to the American site. One element of the new culture was that managers did not have offices, thus enabling them to work in open spaces with secretarial staff. Another element was that managers did not have their own personal secretarial staff. Managers were also encouraged to have direct contact with the plant workers, thus seeking to undermine social hierarchies. As a result, some key resources and social relations that symbolized Fordist middle management masculinities were eroded. At the worker level of engineers, Japanese workers were much more tactile, expressing appreciation and courtesy through touching bodies. This 'touching' became reconstructed as homoeroticism by indigenous workers.

Hamada's work helps us to focus on the way that the implementation of Japanese-based production methods are simultaneously renationalizing masculinities. Ling (1999) notes that broader implications for travelling production methods coincide with cultivating the naturalization of 'manly states and manly firms'. She argues that Eastern Asia has been a region that has produced a great deal of confusion and controversy regarding globalization. Much of the controversy surrounds the clash between ancient mores, traditions and religion working against increasing consumerism and capitalist rationalization. In order to make sense of this process, Ling uses Nandy's (1991) concept of hyper-masculinity, which is defined as an intensified rejection of all aspects that are deemed feminine. In the context of globalization, consumerism and capitalist rationalism engender forms of economic and social organization that grade and prioritize one set of features while devaluing others. The terms through which these values are articulated are feminized and masculinized: weak, underdeveloped and poor as opposed to rich, strong and developed. Thus local markets are deemed 'feminized' and unproductive, whereas modernity becomes masculinized and viewed as productive. Hyper-masculinity according to Ling becomes the standard for successful globalization, while the feminine is assigned to those who are local, traditional and underdeveloped. Yet there is a sense that the West's hyper-masculinity may be internally challenged by racialized versions of Asian masculinity.

Globalized desire

Ling's analysis is also useful because it identifies global masculinities not simply as structures of economic production but as economic production articulated through cultural representations. One example of this has been the travelling economic policy that has surrounded the sex trade. Since the 1920s, western media have exported images of Asian women back to Asian societies. Ling identifies how historically, Japanese and Asian notions of beauty and desire were connected to chalked faces, blackened teeth and very long hair. She suggests that these images have been rewritten and exported as versions of western desire. For her, Asian femininity has been reconstructed as curvaceous, fun loving, free spirited and desirable. Thus, sexualized service workers are produced as westernized objects of desire. At the same time, the desire for western masculinity has also become part of Chinese culture. Ling maintains that the businessman's suit has replaced the Maoist suit of an earlier period. Media images convey masculinity as progress, action and achievement.

A similar process has taken place in terms of the globalization of beauty contests. Cohen's (1996) work in the British Virgin Islands highlights the differences between globalized versions of femininities and local island virtues. He documents two competitions, one that was directed to an international audience and the other held for the local community. The two competitions highlighted different versions of attractiveness, with the local competition celebrating attitudes rather than bodies. In the international competition, men adopted a 'MTV' style of dress that focused on individuality and creativity. Cohen's work illustrates how local objects of desire have been substituted for Americanized versions of attractiveness.

In the above studies, sexualized desire itself appears unproblematic and unchanging. However, Lancaster's (1992) work on the interrelationship between masculinities and sexualities explores how desire is constituted. Unlike western heterosexuality, which tends to be constituted through a dis-identification with same-sex acts and where engaging in homosexual acts produces a homosexual subjectivity, in Nicaragua the situation is different. Key themes that constitute Nicaraguan working-class masculinity are that of domination/submission and aggressiveness/passivity. Lancaster argues that although this gendered dichotomy is extremely rigid and fixed, access to manhood is relatively easy and that fixed meanings of gender undergo relatively little change. An interesting aspect of Lancaster's study is that such gender identifications are carried over into the sphere of sexual relations.

Part of being *machismo* in Nicaragua is to display an active sexuality. However, according to Lancaster, it is not unusual for men, who proclaim themselves *machismo*, to engage in sexual relations with other men. This relationship in itself does not contest their claims to manhood. These claims are contested only if the man becomes a submissive partner and appears to take up a passive role in a relationship. As a result, same-sex relationships take on a range of passive–shame and active–honour associations. Consequently, although a man has sex with another man it does not necessarily impact upon their gender. Same-sex behaviour conveys sexual stigma in

Nicaragua but it is only projected onto the person who is anally penetrated, that is the passive partner, labelled as a *cochon*. As Lancaster (1992: 248) points out: 'In Nicaragua, insecurity about one's masculinity or sexuality could be dispelled by mounting – thus sexually subordinating a cochon'.

It could be argued that a typical process of globalization is taking place with a western sexual subjectivity (anchored within homosexual/hetero-sexual categories) impacting upon the traditional, native and popular sexual subjectivities. It would be easy, Lancaster suggests, to equate the *cochon* with the Anglo-American homosexual. However, 'Nicaragua's *Cochones* are ontologically different from Anglo-American homosexuals . . . It is not that homophobia is more intense in a culture of machismo, but that it is a different sort of thing altogether' (Lancaster 1992: 269).

The impact of a global sexual subjectivity is illustrated by the increas-ing prevalence of models of sexual healthcare in Nicaragua that are being imported from western countries. These models tend to hold onto a cultur-ally specific interrelationship of sexuality and masculinity. For example, the fight against HIV/AIDS is designed and understood through a categorical sensibility of a heterosexual/homosexual binary. A similar process was taking place during Nicaragua's revolution as visiting supporters attempted to set up gay and lesbian self-help groups. In promoting lesbian and gay identities, Lancaster argues they were also articulating a sexual colonialism by marginalizing local sexual subjectivities.

There is an increasing number of commentaries on these aspects of globalization. In this section we have used the themes of politics, economy and desire as devices to make sense of globalized masculinities. In short, we are suggesting global processes are gendered and that we find it useful to understand global processes beyond corporeality (Featherstone *et al.* 1991). The theoretically challenging aspect of this latter understanding of global-ization is that naturalized gender, racial/ethnic and sexual categories become detached from the epistemological anchor of the body. This means that essentialized oppositions such as male and female, black and white or heterosexual and homosexual collapse.

Conclusion

We have suggested that examining men within an international context provides an important conceptual space to interrogate existing analyses of identity and subjectivity. We have concentrated on two distinct approaches. The first suggests examining masculinities cross-culturally with the inten-tion of tracing the themes of gender and nation. This was carried out through a critical examination of a structural functionalist perspective, which is a pervasive perspective in the literature on international masculinities. The second section provided an approach that is informed by more recent understandings of globalization, poststructuralism and postcolonialism (Brah *et al.* 1999; Mac an Ghaill 1999). International relations, economic development and reconstituted forms of desire have in turn provided alternative ways of thinking about the international context of men and masculinities. At the centre of this approach is the notion of masculinities as disembodied, that forms of masculinization are not necessarily dependent on male bodies and may at numerous times include female bodies. In turn, this serves to highlight the highly contradictory constitution of the notion of masculinity.

Questions for your reflection

1 Do ways of being men differ from culture to culture?

2 Can we think about nations in gendered ways?

3 What are the cultural variations involved in becoming a man?

4 Do nations import and export masculinities?

5 Do masculinities need male bodies?

Suggested further reading

Connell, R. W. (2000) *The Men and the Boys*. London: Polity.
Ghoussoub, M. and Sinclair-Webb, E. (2000) *Imagined Masculinities: Male Identity and Culture in the Modern Middle East*. London: Saqi Books.
Hooper, C. (2000) *Manly States: Masculinities, International Relations, and Gender Politics*. New York: Columbia University Press.
Zalewski, M. and Parpart, J. (1989) *The Man Question and International Politics*. Oxford: Westview Press.

Note

1 This discussion makes an interesting contrast to the one on fathering in Chapter 2.

CHAPTER 5

COMING OUT AS A MAN: METHODOLOGIES OF MASCULINITIES

Key concepts

Positivist paradigm; empiricist approaches; standpoint epistemology; categorical sensibility; poststructuralist methodology; realism; crisis of representation; multiple subjectivities; technologies of truth production; transference; research as praxis.

Introduction

This chapter examines sociological research frameworks that have explored the issue of men and masculinities. We begin with a cautionary note. After much theoretically-led critical thinking on men and masculinity, there continues to be a remarkable absence concerning the epistemological and methodological implications of carrying out research in this field of inquiry (Digby 1998). There appears to be little work that transports the theoretical developments of studies on men and masculinities into developing representations of the research process. In an early contribution to feminist methodological and epistemological debates, Morgan (1981: 108) concluded that: 'this chapter is impressionistic and polemical in tone, designed more to hint at work to be done than to present achievements accomplished. Clearly, there is still a lot of further investigation and reanalysis required'. In short, we still have little sense of what it means to do masculinity research. This chapter contributes to a further investigation and reanalysis.

Since the early 1970s sociological research has been subject to increasing philosophical tensions and breaks that have resulted in current approaches to research on men and masculinity being contextualized by growing uncertainty over understandings of truth, validity and reliability. Guba's (1990) three part model of fundamental research questions enables us to frame this uncertainty and interrogate each layer of the research process by examining *how* knowledge is produced. First is the ontological question: what is there that can be known – what is knowable? It deals with the assumptions one is willing to make about the nature of reality. Second is the epistemological question: what is knowledge and what is the relationship of the knower to the known? The assumption that one makes about how knowledge is produced depends on how one conceives reality (ontology). Third is the methodological question: how do we find things out? How this is answered depends on what decisions have been made about the above ontological and epistemological questions. Sociological studies on men and masculinity address these questions in a variety of ways, producing differentiated masculinity research frameworks. We now examine such frameworks by exploring empiricist, standpoint, and poststructuralist approaches.

Gendered methodologies

The sociohistorical approach that we are advocating in this book enables us to locate contemporary methodological questions within the histories and geographies of sex/gender exclusion. In other words, earlier texts have underplayed the collective subject position of men. This hegemonic logic renders 'men and masculinity' absent to the 'gender majority', who assume that gender is something to do with women. Here we might usefully adapt Dyer's (1993) critique of whiteness as the invisible but normative presence in studies of race and ethnicity. Until recently, masculinity as the signifier of dominance had become the unexamined norm. In the realm of categories, 'woman' is always marked as a gender and is always particularizing; whereas men/masculinity is almost anything, not an identity, not a particularizing quality, because it is everything. Therefore, men/masculinity is no gender because it is all genders. Surprisingly, as argued above, this continues to be a relatively underexplored area as gender issues appear almost outside the fieldwork setting. Rather, we need to emphasize the importance of understanding the research context of men and masculinities as a *gendered field* (Bell *et al.* 1993). By examining the research context in this way, we insert a theoretical and conceptual analysis of the research process itself.

Empiricist approaches to masculinity

Empiricist sociologists offer a productive starting point for our exploration of researching men and masculinities. They view the social world as an arrangement of social facts. The collection of these social facts, via objective methods, is seen to generate valid, reliable and 'testable' theories. Empiricist approaches tend to operate in a positivistic manner so that a set of independent objective social laws and formulas can be identified. Research in this tradition generally takes a quantitative form, associated with the collection of *numerical data*, as opposed to qualitative approaches, focusing on the collection of *meanings*. Of key importance for empiricist approaches is the suggested neutral content of research methods, as partiality in the process of data collection is seen as producing distorted results. Those researching men and masculinity within this tradition have learnt much from feminists, who argue that traditional forms of impartiality generate distorted data because of their inherent sexist assumptions. It is an issue to which we now turn.

Empiricist approaches to social life have been a dominant feature in American and European social sciences. However, during the 1960s and 1970s, the growing influence of hermeneutic sociological perspectives, such as phenomenology and symbolic interactionism, were increasingly sceptical of scientific analyses of society. At the same time, second-wave feminism began challenging the normative and regulative biases of androcentrism/ phallocentricism (centred on men) of traditional research methods (see Ramazanoglu 1989). In placing on the research map the significance of gender as an explanatory category of social phenomena, feminism began to reframe old methodological issues and also raise new questions about the absence of women and the visibility of men as legitimate makers of knowledge. In short, feminist empiricist approaches problematize traditional sociological research for carrying out bad science, which they argue, rather than producing objective facts, results in distorted images of the social world (Millman and Kanter 1987). Of particular significance for feminist empiricists is that scientific values of objectivity, validity and reliability are not stringent *enough*; 'sexist and androcentric biases are eliminable by stricter adherence to the existing methodological norms of scientific inquiry' (Harding 1987b: 182).

While acknowledging feminists' shared assumptions with traditional empiricist tendencies, Harding (1987b: 183–4) identifies three potential ways that researchers on gender, working within this frame, can undercut the assumptions of the (male) empiricist. She argues that the context of discovery is as important as the context of justification, that the scientific method is not effective at eliminating endemic social biases such as androcentrism, and for social scientists to follow existing research norms more rigorously. In other words, it has produced a useful method, as indicated in Eichler's (1988) work:

1 To avoid sexism in titles: titles should be explicit (for example, *The Affluent Worker Study* should be retitled *The Male Affluent Worker Study*).
2 Sexism in language has to be eliminated: language should be used that makes it clear whether men or women or both are being addressed or referred to.
3 Sexist concepts need to be eliminated (for example, defining class by reference to the occupation of the head of household).
4 Sexism in research designs has to be overcome so that men and women are both included in the research where this is relevant.
5 Sexism in methods has to be eliminated.
6 Sexism in data interpretation has to be eliminated – the interpretation of the data from the perspective just of men or just of women.
7 Sexism in policy evaluation has to be eliminated, so that policies that serve the needs of both men and women are advocated.

An illustration of the impact of impartiality on social research is outlined by Lee's (1997) examination of sexual harassment. One-taken-for-granted aspect of social research is the ethics of confidentiality. The right of research subjects to confidentiality, with its attendant requirements of privacy and discretion, appears as an automatic feature of contemporary sociological studies. For Lee, ethically sound research procedures create a gender problematic in fieldwork situations. In her work, masculinity and femininity are conceptualized as opposites; being 'male' and being 'dangerous' are closely connected. As a female researcher, the ethical code of confidentiality neglects women's potential vulnerability when conducting research with men in private situations. As a result, Lee argues that holding on to the principle of confidentiality can actually construe to men that female interviewers are inviting sexual relations (see also Abbott 1983). Lee does suggest, however, that mutually supportive and reciprocal relationships between male respondents and a female researcher can be achieved once sexist gendered expectations have been neutralized.

This issue has been explored in more philosophical depth by Morgan (1981). Within the context of arguing for gender to be a central category in sociological scholarship, he emphasized that methodological questions concerning the gendered nature of fieldwork could not simply be reduced to issues of social exclusion as an effect of difference. Rather, these differences located within specific fieldwork spaces constituted a source of knowledge. Hence, what is involved here is not simply a technicist response of attempting to limit the way in which the gender of the researcher impacts on the research process but reflexively to explore how the researcher's gender identity is intimately connected to ways of knowing. In the light of emerging feminist methodological critiques, he re-examined his own research, including studies on Anglican bishops, factory life and the Bloomsbury set (Morgan 1969a; 1969b). This addressed the issue of whether the dominant rationality in sociological inquiry constitutes a *male rationality*. He raised an interesting distinction between formal, scientific rationality and the substantive culture of sociological (or academic) rationality, constituted by the symbols, rituals and regular routinized practices that indicate ways of *doing rationality*. The former involves a cluster of concepts found in methodological textbooks, such as reliability, validity, falsifiability, verifiability, internal consistency, bias and objectivity, all central to the claims and counterclaims by which the discipline's social inquiry is evaluated. Morgan argued that, in principle, the claims of formal academic rationality are non-gender specific, with the possible exception of the use of personal experience in sociological studies. However, it is at the level of culture that the above typification of sociological evaluation becomes complexly interlinked with the dominant male culture of the university environment. Morgan explicates how academic machismo shapes the social practices that underpin the processes of selecting research areas and negotiating specific modes of methodological investigation.

In a similar vein, Goodwin (1999) acknowledges that empiricism has been used as a form of machismo through its continued neglect of looking at males as men. Through the collection of numerical data on the men in the workforce, he invites the reader to ask questions about the changing nature of masculinity. He suggests that large-scale empiricist research can clarify the broader social processes influencing men and masculinity. Goodwin is one of the few researchers whose work has absorbed methodological issues that surround the study of this subject. The aim of generating empirically-based research on men and work initially began with a self-administered questionnaire distributed to British companies. The return rate of the questionnaire was extremely low, prompting Goodwin to adopt a research position indebted to a qualitative feminist approach. Through personal relationships and contacts, men were encouraged to attend an unstructured interview. For Goodwin, this again proved inadequate, as few men were willing to participate. Finally, Goodwin took up a feminist politics in relation to large-scale empiricist approaches to men and work. In this way, research data that had been previously collected could be explored through the lens of masculinity. As a result, he adopted a *quantitative case study approach* that used longitudinal birth cohort studies.

Goodwin uses statistical datasets to test out various hypotheses, thereby establishing the absence of an empiricist understanding of British-based sociological research on masculinity. He extrapolates the 'actuality' of men's experiences from the data sets of the National Child Development Study.[1] For instance, in exploring men's sex-role ideology in the home, attitude statements coded through traditional and non-traditional views become the evidence through which Goodwin makes his claims. Although other researchers on gender might contest the uniqueness of his quantitative approach, it does offer important methodological suggestions, including: research should make men's experience more visible; it should reflect critically on the impact of feminism and the concept of patriarchy; it needs to explore men's experience empirically as well as theoretically; and that men must not be treated as a homogeneous category. Making men a visible gender category enables the capturing of trends, locations, and positions on a larger scale. However, one of the limitations of large-scale empirical studies on men and masculinity is that a categorical sensibility imposes itself. In other words, in order to manage and comprehend large-scale information, masculinity needs to be decontextualized by removing it from the minutiae of everyday experience. An example of this can be found in Hofstede's (1998) cross-cultural mapping of masculinity in different national cultures. This study operationalizes a fixed universalistic measure of masculinity which is seen as a combination of descriptors such as toughness or aggression. Masculinity in this way can operate objectively, existing as an ideal type or as a benchmark for 'proper' masculine behaviour.

From the perspective of getting men as a *gender* onto the research map, feminist empiricism provides a very useful resource, though at the same time implying that (pro-feminist) men (as with women feminists) have no distinctive contribution to make. What is clearer from a contemporary perspective is that the inclusion of the social category *gender* and the accompanying social group *women* is a serious disruption to existing conventional categories of western thought. In short, what began as critical questioning of scientific practices developed into destabilizing science's methodological and epistemological foundations.

Critical theory, men's experience and standpoint epistemology

Most researchers on gender agree with the ethos of non-sexist research produced by the above perspective, yet many see it as providing necessary but insufficient conditions to explore a gendered experience of the social world. Some researchers therefore adopt a more radical stance, challenging those positivistic assumptions, such as methodological individualism and a

narrow conception of rationality, that make empiricists implicitly masculinist. Such a stance is seen to support or naturalize a social distinction
between men and women while establishing the superiority of certain types
of behaviour over others. This standpoint epistemology has its roots in the
Hegelian argument about the slave–master relationship and its subsequent
development into a Marxist-based proletarian standpoint (Harstock 1983).
It shares with empiricism a realist philosophical position that believes in
the existence of an underlying material reality that structures the social
world, with which social experts should engage. However, it also takes up
a novel intervention into justificatory claims to knowledge in mainstream
science. While accepting the idea of science, standpoint epistemology
argues that it is not the disengaged scientist but rather the politically-
engaged researcher who provides objectivity within the research process.

The starting point for standpoint epistemology is experience. Because
this position takes power as a central organizing principle of social relations, it is able to reveal the underlying interests that shape social life. It
locates experiences within a wider social order and accompanying public
world of relations of ruling from which certain groups are excluded (Smith
1987). There is a tradition within a wide range of academic disciplines of
identifying a specific social group, named as *existential outsiders*, the *theological
remnant* or *anthropological strangers*, who are positioned as having special
insight into what is 'really' going on in society. Feminist standpoint epistemology shares such a stance, claiming that women as strangers are in a unique
social position to reproduce less distorting knowledge as social researchers.
In her book *Whose Science? Whose Knowledge? Thinking from Women's Lives*,
Harding (1991: 124) explains:

> The stranger brings to her research just the combination of nearness
> and remoteness, concern and difference, that are central to maximizing
> objectivity. Moreover the 'natives' tend to tell a stranger some kinds of
> things they would never tell each other; further, the stranger can see
> patterns of belief and behaviour that are hard for those immersed in
> the culture to detect.

This structurally-located double consciousness with which female social
researchers operate provides them with a wider angle of view in which they
see things from the position of the dominant social group (men) as well as
that of the oppressed (women) (Smith 1987: 99).

For some feminists, men's social location within wider patriarchal relations, together with the cultural institutionalization of the male gaze makes
them unable to contribute to feminist research that focuses on women's
experiences and exhorts researchers to adopt the same critical plane as
the subjects of social inquiry (Cook and Fonow 1986; Kremer 1990). In
contrast, early research manuals, informed by realist empiricism, attempted
to produce a 'hygienic' research context. This involved identifying and

eliminating particular variables that served to distort research findings, as well as devising strategies to neutralize and eradicate social categories such as gender, race and class. More specifically, research frameworks were designed to resolve the researcher's anxiety that respondents would read off particular meanings from the social categories that confronted them. Second-wave feminism productively responded to traditional research method formats. Early work by Oakley (1981) and Finch (1984) and later work by Ramazanoglu (1992) highlighted how their research methods were antithetical to the traditional collection of data. By treating research participants as though they were scientific variables, quantitative research techniques were seen as limiting access to participants' meanings, understandings and interpretations. At the same time, such research situations were deemed unethical as they appeared to re-produce and insert the patriarchal power relations found in wider society. From this perspective, if sociological researchers were not engaging research participants in reciprocal relationships and allowing their voices to be heard, research methods were masculinist. As such, power relations within the fieldwork situation had to be broken down, so that research participants should be equally involved in the formation of research questions, the research schedule, data analysis, coding and dissemination of results.

Against a background where few men have taken up feminist methodology in the study of men and masculinity, feminist standpoint epistemology has probably been the most influential stance in this field (Connell 1990; Christian 1994; Pease 2000). For May (1998: 335), a progressive male standpoint provides 'an egalitarian theoretical and practical position from which men can critically assess male experience and traditional male roles'. Men who take up such a standpoint, working within an anti-oppressive political frame can produce social knowledge that challenges gender inequality. May develops a model of progressive male standpoint with four dimensions:

> First, there is the striving for knowledge or understanding based on experience, especially personal experience of traditional male roles and activities. Second, there is a critical reflection on that experience in the light of possible harms to women, as well as men, of assuming traditional male roles and engaging in traditional male activities. Third, there is the moral motivation to change at least some aspects of traditional male roles and activities. And finally, there are practical problems for changes in traditional male roles that are regarded as believable by other men.

A critical aspect of standpoint epistemology then, is to validate the authenticity of research subjects' oppressive experience. But what are the implications of this for men's experience? If men occupy a patriarchal privileged position, two questions emerge: can the exploration of men's experience be a productive research agenda and can men do gender research on other men?

Some researchers suggest that the history of men's dominant modes of social inquiry and the typical constitution of men's standpoints means that men doing gender research with men cannot simply replicate feminist knowledge-making (Flood 2000: 17). However, Hearn (1993a) argues that exploring men's experience is vitally important, given that men have different experience of practices to which being male gives access. However, men's positioning as members of an oppressing class poses important questions to the political viability of men researching other men; for example, male to male relations may generate anti–feminist knowledge. Hearn evaluates ways in which male researchers can overcome these potential limitations. For example, research on men might be conducted in 'the context of world patriarchy'. There might also be ways of exploring men's subjectivities through in-depth interviews, such as those carried out in psychoanalysis. A third way might be to examine males in less powerful situations who might also be subject to the oppressive nature of patriarchal power. Finally, Hearn suggests that methodologies examining men and masculinity could be useful, if they employ both qualitative and quantitative techniques that include triangulation.

The issue of men, masculinity and methodology is particularly important in Hearn's exploration of men's violence. With open-ended interviews and biographical data, the contradictory implications of men researching men through feminist methodology come into sharper focus. In one sense, the interview situation simply replicates the power relations of traditional interview formats that removes power and objectifies its subjects. At the same time, male researchers are in the process of doing what we have noted earlier as 'women's work'. Although Hearn recognizes the importance of differences between men – male social researchers and the male researched – both have access to the experience of being men, a shared knowledge that is often worked through traditional male relationships deriving from fraternity (see also McKegany and Bloor 1991). Yet while this can be seen as simply reinforcing a 'natural' oppressive order of gender relations, the research situation may, in itself, be considered as a political instrument since it can encourage men to acknowledge and identify the oppressive nature of their practices. In the context of researching violence against women, this is a highly salient point.

The difficulties of simply applying a feminist framework to men's experience reveals broader tensions in sociology. The discipline evolved as a science of society and carries the modernist hopes of a risk-free society, with sociological methodologies tending to develop around the needs and politics of vulnerable groups. Researching men from a feminist standpoint epistemology generates new complexities in the pursuit of researching the powerful (Mills 1956). In the context of developing sexuality policies, Redman (1994) considers the possibilities of 'empowering men to dis-empower themselves'. Hence, social research situations can be politically strategic. Such strategies are not simply aimed at particular research subjects but also male researchers themselves. For example, those working within a pro-feminist framework name themselves as white heterosexual middle-class men. In so doing, they point out the need for their work to focus on the deconstruction of the privileged social categories and subject positions that they occupy.

Other researchers on masculinity report a more complex picture of the research arena. For example, Schacht's (1997) work explores the pervasive misogyny and homophobia of a group of American rugby players. His study generated a conflict between his political beliefs and analytical approach. The pervasive misogyny and homophobia of this group of young men stood in opposition to Schact's radical feminism. As a consequence, he interpreted this opposition as mediated through various masculinities, positioning his own as compliant to the dominant masculinity of sport, toughness and hardness. His study identifies differences that exist between men and maintains that the notion of commonality as a strategy for research methods may have a limited purchase.

In contrast to the overt political approaches above, Drummond's (1994) pro-feminist methodology on the sociocultural construction of sport adopts a less interventionist style in researching men and masculinity. It focuses on how masculine identities and the structure of sport can be captured through phenomenological interviewing – interviews that are designed to generate the experience of the phenomenon. He records: 'I attempted to minimise any power or status inequities so they might see me as a friend and be willing to share their thoughts and feelings in a non-threatening environment' (1994: 101). The aim of the research was to make men feel comfortable in order to relate to men in an egalitarian, reciprocal manner.

This conceptual and empirical concern with placing patriarchy at the centre of pro-feminist men's inquiry is often set up in opposition to the Men's Studies methodological assumptions, which the former claim have anti-feminist tendencies.[2] Key questions for pro-feminist men are whether men can change and what it means methodologically to answer this question in a valid way. Research on fathers, explored in Chapter 2, indicated that this is a highly contested question producing contradictory responses. As discussed earlier in the book, a key difficulty here is the undertheorization of social change. From a methodological perspective, a major issue is the dependence of pro-feminist men on earlier feminist frameworks, with their limited conception of patriarchy and an accompanying simple male–female oppositional structure.

Shifting beyond pro-feminist men's standpoint

Many men currently involved in researching men and masculinity appear to have adopted an overly defensive methodological stance. One major aspect of this response is the question of how they position themselves in relation to feminist methodology. There seems often to be a preoccupation with the desire to be designated a *male feminist*, rather than the feminist methodological concern with producing less partial representations of the social world and women and men's cultural habitation of it. Feminist methodologies have made explicit the social processes involved in the production of research. Of central importance here is the assertion that research involves a process and that: 'consciousness is *always* the medium through which research occurs' (original emphasis; Stanley and Wise 1990: 34). However, a main concern of this chapter is that research into men and masculinities has given little space to the research process. We argue that the unseen gendered relationships in studies of men and masculinities actually mediate what we come to understand as masculinities. In short, the research site is constitutive of the object of inquiry, that of the gendering of men and masculinities. As Frank (1993: 336–7) suggests, awareness of how gender is socially constructed within patriarchal relations does not appear to be a sufficient condition to ensure analysis of the historicity and social construction of theories and methods themselves that produce knowledge. He continues:

> The power of these historical and social products (the theoretical stance and methodological procedures) produced within the patriarchal gaze used to gain an understanding of people's lives and the resulting consequences, are taken for granted, and thus temporalized and depoliticized. Insofar as these disciplinary practices produce women, and some men, as subordinate, their methods of observation and inquiry and the resulting production of theory do little to reorganize the objectified 'ways of knowing'.

A deep sense of methodological pessimism infuses pro-feminist men's fieldwork. A major flaw is that their critical focus in exploring male interviewer/interviewee interaction and the resulting assumed limited self-disclosure, ascribes a simplistic format to what is a complex dynamic arena, for example, that of the interview situation. Their work on men serves to reinscribe static notions of gender identity that assume that male modes of interaction are the effect of masculinity per se and its attendant dominant power in a patriarchal society. In so doing, they return us to an identity politics position (see Chapter 6) marked by homogeneity, tight boundaries and cultural fixity. This means that gender categories do not inflect with a diverse range of social categories, such as sexuality, class, ethnicity, disability and generation, that shapes men's and women's social behaviour and modes of relating.

Addressing this issue, contemporary social and cultural theoretical frameworks have problematized the implicit assumptions of feminist standpoint epistemology for its universalizing tendencies around a unitary understanding of women (Nicholson 1990; Sedgwick 1990; Butler 1993). Most significantly, the paradox of attempts to construct a uniform model of patriarchy is that they seem to lose the ability to explain the dynamics of change and conflict within specific fieldwork locations. In so doing, they fail to analyse the processes which lead to the social relations of gender being imbued with patriarchal domination in particular societies, institutions and social practices.

One of the effects of holding onto a reductionist male–female dualism is that it produces a one-dimensional view of men, with a range of negative characteristics (patriarchal practices) ascribed to them. Working within this conceptual frame, men doing research on men are projected as simply producing another male space in which these negative characteristics are reinscribed. The latter includes attributes identified as defining men in the social organization of their lives: their emotional illiteracy, their macho male bonding, male-on-male competitiveness and their tendency to collude in sexism and homophobia. The research site is reduced to a space where male research participants enact a defensive self-representation to the male interviewer. Hence, the major methodological concern of pro-feminist men appears to be a self-conscious attempt to challenge the limitations of this collective performance. There is little sense here of feminist researchers providing a representational space for the subjects of their research (Skeggs 1997).

The shift to anti-oppressive research frameworks invites the operation of particular scripts for the researcher and the research participants. Adopting empowering research methods may simply be a more ethically sensitive way of extracting information from the researched. Work on the genealogy of identities (Walkerdine 1984; Rutherford 1990; Probyn 1993) offers useful frameworks to evaluate critically how fieldwork relations are constructed and provides valuable resources for a more rigorous reflexive production of sociological knowledge. Nevertheless, anti-oppressive methodologies have helped push the limits of sociological analysis by inviting alternative readings of the research process. The increased recognition of the research process as generated by gendered epistemological and theoretical positions has produced increased visibility of reflexivity around research designs, data collection, coding and analysis.

Emerging paradigms *for* masculinity research

During the last decade, we have been involved in a number of ethnographic research projects with young heterosexual and gay males in the process of becoming adult men, within particular institutional settings of the home, the school, the workplace and popular culture. In so doing, we have developed our own epistemological and methodological understandings which do not resonate with pro-feminist men's accounts. As described by the latter, we have explored how male theorists of young men have systematically failed to acknowledge the implicit male knowledges, understandings and desires that we share with male research participants' biographies. We have evaluated how male studies on masculinity, with their specific emphases and absences, may be read as a form of male bonding in terms of the research processes, the selected representations of masculinities and femininities and the production of specific gendered/sexual subjects. However, pro-feminist men's methodology fails to capture the complexity of the multidimensional arena of men doing research with men.

Although there has been a growing exploration of the implications of poststructuralism/postmodernism for men and masculinity, at the time of writing, there has been little application of those theoretical and conceptual insights to the research process (see Saco 1992; MacInnes 1998; Petersen 1998; Pease 2000). Sociologists' general lack of transparency of their research methodology exacerbates this invisibility. A main concern in our own work has been to capture 'what is going on'. We have found some of the strategies outlined below to be informative analytical devices, with theory used as a tool to 'make sense' of social relations. This section establishes the case that poststructuralist research paradigms may be useful *for* researching men and masculinities. At the present time, this is important because there is much uncertainty amongst sociological researchers about the relationship between contemporary cultural theoretical frameworks such as postmodernism and poststructuralism and their relationship to methodology.[3] Such debates open up a range of possibilities or 'ways of looking' at men and masculinity. In short, it may be argued that the current explosion of *new* knowledges are accompanied by *old* methodological techniques. In order to explore this, we focus upon the crisis of representation, multiple subjectivities and methods of research as technologies of truth production.

Crisis of representation

In a review of methodological positions, Lowe (2000) argues that postmodernism problematizes the authorial positions of both the researcher and the researched. Anthropological ethnographic studies are a productive area for debate about representation. With its traditional empiricist claims to authenticity, ethnography has attracted much criticism. Within a positivistic stance that focuses on systematic observation and experiment, ethnographers often claim to let those being researched 'speak for themselves'. Thus, it is claimed that this 'objectively' collected data produces a 'natural' *in situ* account of the research arena. One example is Gilmore's (1990) collection of data on masculinity in different cultures where he argues that masculinity can speak for itself, with the researcher's role being simply a collector of gendered phenomena (see Chapter 4, this volume). More specifically, such accounts tend to correspond with broader methodological research procedures that position the author as a 'roving microphone' generating faithful and varied research accounts. It is argued that ethnographic methodologies act as strategies to filter out 'false' information, enabling the objective reporting of 'what is *really* going on'.

However, this approach to research has undergone what Marcus and Fischer (1986: 8) term a 'crisis of representation', where authorial status is deemed problematic. This resonates with Derrida's (1978) focus on the indeterminacy of the author in the articulation of ideas. He questions the notion of the text as simply conveying the author's perspective. Derrida contends that meanings within texts are subject to multiple interpretations. Therefore the author's representations are active attempts to stabilize (justify and legitimate) interpretations of fieldwork incidents. Research accounts become the *forcible* presentation of a semantic unity between researcher and the researched. Hence, a postmodern approach to researching men and masculinity questions the author's authority and the meanings that he or she attempts to stabilize. As Alvesson and Skoldberg suggest (2000: 192):

> The author is made visible and the reader is compelled to become involved. Appropriate parts of the researcher's subjectivity should emerge from the page. Avoiding jargon, rhetorical tricks, ritualistic references and other authority-promoting devices can also help to produce a more open text.

Postmodernism does not simply ask questions about the legitimacy of sociological research accounts but also sociology's claims to academic legitimacy through the operation of meta-narratives. Lyotard (1994: 8) claims that rather than establish and legitimate a methodology of truth, researchers should adopt postmodernism in order to recognize difference and 'reinforce our ability to tolerate the incommensurable'. The crisis of representation is based upon the author not having direct access to 'facts' which problematizes the connection between experience and its textual representation (Denzin 1994). Research on men and masculinity therefore requires the researcher to apply a certain amount of reflexivity to the authority *bases* of his or her research accounts in order to interrogate critically epistemological claims to gendered knowledge.

Importantly, reflexive awareness of how epistemologies may simply *produce versions of reality* rather than being a mirror or device to *access reality* is a key departure from empiricist and standpoint epistemologies. Poststructuralist methodology deploys a reflexivity that allows the researcher to examine the researcher/researched relationship as a localized, dialogical production; understanding *research as praxis* is of key concern (Lather 1991). At the same time, problematizing representations of the research process is also a recognition of reader epistemologies, that is, how readers access texts. With its disciplinary traditions in literary theory, poststructuralism emphasizes the complexity of writing up research. In what can be seen as an overly anxious attempt to demonstrate the contrived nature of sociological research, poststructuralists seek out new ways with which to convey processes of data collection. For example, in writing up research data, King (1999) outlines two metaphors that characterize postmodern research: pastiche and montage. *Pastiche* is a representation that follows no structured norms (Jameson 1985), where a series of influences without logic can be collated. *Montage* characterizes research accounts where the text is multilayered and the making of meaning connects with readers' subjectivities rather than an author's intentions. Of major importance for those working in the field of masculinity is that, the author's (arranger's) subjectivity is not cleansed by objective research procedures or critical standpoints but rather is made actively explicit. As Denzin (1994: 296–7) points out:

> Critical post-structuralism reads the discussions of logical, construct, internal, ethnographic, and external validity, text based data, triangulation, trustworthiness, credibility, grounding, naturalistic indicators, fit, coherence, comprehensiveness, plausibility, truth, relevance as attempts to re-authorise a text's authority in the post-positivistic moment. Such moves cling to the conception of the 'world-out-there' that is truthfully and accurately captured by researchers' methods.

Closely linked to the poststructuralist critique of researchers' claims to authority is the issue of multiple interpretations. Hutchinson and Wilson (1994: 302) argue that poststructuralism: 'refuses appeals to epistemological absolutes and embraces the wisdom of a multiplicity of positions acknowledging the contradictions implicit in them and accommodating ambiguity.' For Lemert (1990), traditional sociological frameworks adopt models as mirrors of reality. However, given that poststructuralism aims to disperse a natural view of reality, the use of models are merely a representation of a representation. As a result, the application of pregiven theories or received understandings of social encounters between and within genders and sexualities are dismissed. It is to the issue of interpretations to which we now turn.

Multiple subjectivities

An immediate concern for poststructuralists is that social relations often operate through a series of historically-situated discourses. These contain categorically organized narratives that use techniques such as binarism, othering, repositioning and inverting. As a result, Davies and Harre (1990: 46) suggest that: 'An individual emerges through the process of social interaction, not as a relatively fixed end product but as one who is constituted and reconstituted through the various discursive practices in which they participate.' As an individual in different discourses, he or she is located in a number of subject positions that results in the constitution of multiple subjectivities. The task of the poststructuralist researcher on masculinity is to develop sensitivity to an individual's differentiated subject positions. For example, the administrative ordering of individuals as teachers and students in educational institutions is often taken as unproblematic by researchers. In contrast, researchers that draw upon poststructuralism suggest that institutional categories are historically produced. For example, for a researcher on gender, categories of teacher/student may exclude other relations of power that may be transferred through gender relations. Alongside this, the poststructuralist researcher on masculinity would also be reflexive about how identities around ethnicity, sexuality or generation work through masculinity practices. An acknowledgement of the multiple discursive positions that research subjects occupy simultaneously demands a re-evaluation of the research context.

This re-evaluation may entail a methodological insistence to incorporate, or to make visible, unheard voices. Such an approach is also taken up by feminist and anti-racist theorists on identity formation. In contrast, the poststructuralist seeks out subtle differences and convergences between and within identities. Such a perspective encourages an analytical dissonance. For instance, problematizing the appropriateness of masculinity to 'male' experience makes it possible to disconnect masculinity from the body. However, 'male' often appears as the only (culturally) legitimate body that can carry masculinity. An important exception is found in Halberstram's (1998) work on female masculinity which destabilizes gender categories, allowing masculinity to be a subjectivity through which females can make their identities. She does this without reverting to a psychological methodology that depends upon attributes or personality traits. A key element of this categorical destabilizing in research on men and masculinity involves simultaneously collapsing the homogeneity of social majorities and minorities and (con)fusing distinct and incompatible categories.

Given the social and cultural changes outlined in other chapters of this book, we have highlighted how categories of identity have limited purchase, where meanings cannot be simply 'read off' from (male/female) bodies. At the same time, sociological methods conceptualized at an older historical juncture continue to be the key devices to capture contemporary social processes and cultural practices. A central question around research methods emerges. If the bodily signifiers that carry the relationship between men and masculinity no longer correspond, can research methods that integrally contain this correspondence continue to be useful? Equally problematic is that if we hold onto an understanding of multiple and shifting masculine subjectivities, how can, for example, a one hour structured interview capture and contain these multiple subjectivities?

Research methods: technologies of truth production

Although sociological methodologies have undergone considerable revision over the last century, little attention has been paid to the techniques of data collection. For example, sociological researchers on men and masculinity continue to use research techniques as methods of truth production. We discussed above how realist standpoint epistemology methods are given special status by pro-feminist men as politicized practice. In an article that exemplifies one style of postmodern writing, Tyler (1991: 85) argues: 'Method, the technology of truth, the rational means that make truth, relativizes truth not to time, place or purpose, but to its instrumentality. Method is the ritual that brings forth the truth.' With poststructuralism making visible the semantic technologies that systematically produce truth claims, research methods also need examination. A poststructural approach to methods on masculinity emphasizes that interviews are constituted through local contexts, multiple identities and cultural scripts. These affect the emergence of truth about gender categories.

Studies of men and masculinity that lay claim to poststructuralist insights often do so through the unreflexive use of conventional sociological methods. For example, although some studies of masculinity contest the notion of role and propose a theory of performativity, their poststructuralist assertions are often generated through quasi-positivist or critical realist methods. By reflexively turning theory in on its methods, poststructuralist research techniques are ascribed increased epistemological distinction. In this way, research contexts are a locally produced accomplishment or arrangements of meanings. For example, whether interviews are structured, unstructured, semi-focused or non-focused, they act as technologies to produce information that is bound by localized sensibilities and practices. In short, the micropolitics of the interview do not distort the collection of real facts as there are no existentially real objects. The idea that the interview situation is more than a simple technical procedure is discussed in Spradely's (1979) work, where the interview becomes a social context in itself. Ethnomethodologists also adopt the idea that interviews can only be understood as local contexts of meaning making. For the poststructuralist, the contextual features of the interview are so indeterminate, that the researcher on masculinity could do the same interview with the same man (or woman), ask the same questions but get different answers.

Hollway and Jefferson (2000) provide another example of an emerging paradigm that may be productive in researching men and masculinity. They explore the use of transference and counter-transference to capture the dynamic nature of the interview. In their psychoanalytical theoretical position, the researcher and the researched are 'anxious, defended subjects, whose mental boundaries are porous where unconscious material is concerned' (2000: 45). Internal fantasies that enter unconsciously into the interview serve to mediate how the interview emerges. In this sense, the researcher and the researched take up ways of being that are historically informed by significant relationships developed prior to the interview. As a result, a process of transference and counter-transference of subjective positions takes place. Hollway and Jefferson neatly outline how in interviews (grand)mother and daughter positions were taken up and lived out while carrying out interviews. In our own work on masculinity, we have been aware of how those interviewed often invoke social scripts through which they make sense of the interview and their ways of being during the interview. For example, categories of father, teacher, boyfriend, doctor, brother have all been used by research participants (male and female) as vehicles to make sense of the research relationship.

Scheurich's (1995) poststructuralist approach conceptualizes the interview as a place where the conscious and the unconscious desires of the researcher and the researched come into play. One effect is that the language emerging from the research context shifts from person to person and is culturally and temporally located. In the traditional interview, as indicated above, the researcher fixes meanings and attempts to enforce categories through reflexively sifting out ambiguity. Scheurich (1995: 245) argues that interview interactions do not have some essential, teleological tendency towards an ideal of 'joint construction of meaning'; 'human interactions and meaning are neither unitary nor teleological. Instead, interactions and meanings are a shifting carnival of ambiguous complexity, a moving feast of difference interrupting differences'. Scheurich goes on to argue that meanings may be agreed, rejected, confused or misunderstood and that social relations are fleetingly accomplished. Implicit in the approach for sociologists of masculinity is a more fluid, relational approach to power relations.

It is not that the power differentials articulated by the researcher and the researched do not enter the interview context, rather it is that their forms may be unpredictable. The slave–master relationship invoked by critical theorists does not provide a space for power relations to be reversed without rejecting that relationship. From a poststructuralist position, power is distributed through a number of discourses that do not fall within hierarchical binaries. Alvesson and Skoldberg (2000: 187) demonstrate the exclusive nature of identity categories in an interview situation.

> By interviewing someone *qua* woman, or asking someone to describe their relationship with their 'boss', we construct or fix a certain identity (such as 'woman' or 'subordinate,' and accordingly also an identity of dependence, independence or rejection in relation to the Other (man or manager). Identities or categories are themselves problematic: they fix and exclude.

The interview might therefore be a space where more varied rational or emotional literacies may articulate themselves. With the emphasis on the plurality of voices, during the interview, individuals are not locked within researcher/researched roles but operate through different discourses and occupy various subjective positions. Anthropological studies highlight the difficulty of simply holding onto the researcher/researched relationship. Warren's (1988) work provides us with examples of how research roles operate simultaneously through other cultural scripts. For example, being 'fictive kin' or taking the role of family members is a common feature of women's anthropological fieldwork. Another form that women can operate in gendered situations is that of taking up the position of honorary male. Warren argues that such culturally ascribed positions are imperative to gaining access to research informants. In short, we suggest that research situations resonate and circulate through existing gendered social processes and cultural practices that are taken up *at the same time* as the researcher/researched relationship.

Late modernity, fieldwork and normalizing masculinity

It is not simply academic representations of the research context that condition the generation of research data but the interpretation and reflection of those involved. We suggested that a key element of bringing masculinity into the fieldwork setting includes negotiating an appropriate masculinity of the researcher. The confusion that surrounds qualitative research often elides with a troubling relationship of males researching men, masculinity and sexuality. In our own work we have experienced personal attacks and been subject to countless rumours regarding our gender and sexual identities. At the level of common sense, being male carries with it a number of connotations that activates a gendered and sexual normalizing. At particular times, we have been warned that the study of gender and sexuality can be potentially career-threatening. We suggest that such responses to our work need to be contextualized within the social and cultural milieu in which the work is being carried out.

An example of how the cultural context can shape masculinity is clearly evident in the English context. At the end of the 1990s, a media-inspired frenzy erupted around the issue of the sexual abuse of children, often termed 'stranger danger'. The target of this media concern centred on older men (strangers) who planned the abduction and subsequent abuse of young people. Given the climate of sexualized panic, social research could also be read through a sexualized discourse of 'dangerous men'. Male social researchers do not stand outside these concerns, rather their research is contextualized by it. For example, the negotiation of access into schools to carry out research on young boys' sexual identities always appears as a contentious part of gaining access. A resulting researcher's defensive position, alongside that of institutional anxiety, may serve to regulate the display of a normalized heterosexual masculinity. At the same time, the institutional request for a police check on the researcher now appears as a standard feature of school research.

Another area where the cultural context of dangerous men infuses school relations in research contexts is the interrelationship between the researcher and students. On introducing a recent research project that took up the theme of exploring children's social development, one of the boys in the class asked: 'Sir, are you a paedophile?' Although other members of the class laughed and the teacher present smiled reassuringly, the position of an older male watching younger boys was pertinently contextualized. Further on in the study, when the students left their friends to accompany the researcher to a classroom to be interviewed, the friends would shout out: 'Are you off with the "paedophile"?' or 'Watch he doesn't try to touch you up'. Alongside the ambivalent nature of qualitative research with its seemingly laissez-faire approach, involving such social practices as hanging about, sitting around, and chatting, the male researcher takes on particular cultural significance. For the students, the dominant cultural positioning of children and men gave them a certain amount of institutional literacy in making sense of the research process.

To some respondents, the male qualitative researcher may appear to act in an effeminate manner. Qualitative research practices that involve listening, sensitivity to detail, appreciation and generosity with time and an interested approach, can signal a softer/effeminate masculinity. As masculinity in western contexts operates as a cultural resource of sexuality, the expression of a soft/effeminate masculinity may be reconstructed as a deficit heterosexuality. The subject itself, men and masculinity, can provide gendered dissonance. Mort's (1996) historical mapping of cultures of masculinity and consumption in England demonstrates an example of this gendered /sexual dissonance. Carrying out interviews with young men and women, he recalls one of the interviews with a black actor model, whom Mort describes as 'confident and mildly flirtatious'. He suggests that the interview contained ambiguity and innuendo:

> 'I'd do anything for money, strip naked as long as there's cash involved. Anything, I have done.' Excited by a fruitful research lead I tried to push him further, in order to render his tantalising remarks more discursively clear. His response became hostile. Abruptly, he terminated the interview with an aggressive rejoinder. David's parting remark deftly overturned the balance of power. He exploded: 'Do you think I'm queer or something?'
>
> (Mort 1996: 198)

Conclusion

Sociology is an old discipline and carries with it the signatures of an early modern enlightenment approach. Part of its predictive capacity relies upon humanist readings of categories of identity that contain behavioural patterns and identifiable meaning systems. These have been central to sociology's continued existence and importance in contemporary social and cultural systems. Attempts are now being made to destabilize realist approaches. As a result, the historically generated (dominant) laws of social research are subject to intellectual interrogation. This raises the question: how can traditional sociology's epistemological and methodological formats continue to make sense against poststructuralist claims about the multiplicity of selves, notions of decentred forms of power and the intersections of highly relational social categories? In our response, we have found that theoretical and conceptual developments tend to remain underconnected to methodological reflexivity. For example, while there is much talk of poststructuralist accounts of masculinity, these have not yet produced a consistent methodology. In fact, sustained methodological discussions of masculinity have yet to take place.

As outlined in the introduction, we locate ourselves within conceptual frameworks that provide analyses of masculinities that can offer a direct understanding of the research process. Using these frameworks as methodological resources enables us to bring the process of research back into theoretical analysis, thus highlighting the centrality of the mutually reinforcing nature of social research (Smith 1987; Lather 1991). More specifically, in studying men as a gendered category, we consider the methodological implications of a key argument in this book, namely holding onto the productive tension between materialist, poststructuralist and psychoanalytic explanations of men and masculinities. In the research process, materialist accounts have helped us recognize the importance of social relations, practices and organization. Poststructuralist accounts have helped us recognize how contextual aspects of masculinities can influence the specificities of relational aspects of masculinities. In turn, this helps us begin to think through what we understand and acknowledge as masculinity. For instance, there is a need to recognize that in certain instances masculinity is spoken through sexuality, ethnicity, class, etc. Alongside this, psychoanalytic studies of masculinities provides us with ways in which we can begin to understand the constitution of masculinities, especially around the processes of expression and articulation.

We end with a number of caveats. In response to the invisibility of men as a gendered category in the research process, we are not suggesting that we should develop a 'masculinity methodology'. Rather, we adopt an exploratory position that focuses on the ways that theoretical developments in the study of masculinity can be used to inform understandings of the research process. In effect, this chapter attempts critically to explore *what it means* and *the ways that we come to understand* (our justificatory claims) when we engage in sociological research on men and masculinities. Second, as Harding (1987a) in her classic text *Feminism and Methodology* maintains, it is useful to make a distinction between method (techniques for gathering evidence), methodology (a theory and analysis of how research should proceed), and epistemology (an adequate theory of knowledge or justificatory strategy). Third, criticisms of early materialist feminist methodologies, both internal and external, often assume that it constituted a unitary intel- lectual phenomenon. In reality, as with the range of theoretical accounts of second-wave feminism, traditionally constructed within the tripartite typology of liberal, socialist/Marxist and radical positions, we also find a range of epistemological stances, represented as: empiricism, standpoint and poststructuralism (Ramazanoglu 1989; Humm 1992). Fourth, these epist- emological differences among feminists should not distract from their shared beliefs that, taken collectively, constitute a major challenge to western orthodox science, thus providing alternative accounts of how we know the social world alongside a theory of what 'exists' and the specificities of being (ontology) (Roberts 1981; Lather 1991).

Questions for your reflection

1 What main contributions have feminist empiricism and standpoint epistemology made to researching men and masculinity?

2 Can men do research on men?

3 What are the main implications of allowing masculinity to be a subjectivity through which females can make their identity?

4 What are the main aspects of a poststructuralist approach to method- ology and methods in exploring gender relations?

Suggested further reading

Alcoff, L. and Potter, E. (1993) *Feminist Epistemologies*. London: Routledge.
Alvesson, M. and Skoldberg, K. (2000) *Reflexive Methodology: New Vistas for Qualitative Research*. London: Sage.
Bell, D., Caplan, P. and Karim, W. J. (1993) *Gendered Fields: Women, Men and Ethnography*. London: Routledge.
Haddad, T. (ed.) (1993) *Men and Masculinities: A Critical Anthology*. Toronto: Canadian Scholars' Press.
Harding, S. (1991) *Whose Science? Whose Knowledge? Thinking from Women's Lives*. Buckingham: Open University Press.
Nicholson, L. J. (ed.) (1990) *Feminism/Postmodernism*. London: Routledge.
Pease, B. (2000) *Recreating Men: Postmodern Masculinity Politics*. London: Sage.

Notes

1 The National Child Development Study (NCDS) is a continuing, multidisciplinary representative longitudinal study which takes as its subjects all those living in Great Britain. It has followed various generations since the 1950s.

2 See Chapter 6 for further discussion.
3 A diversity of terms are used to pin down new epistemological approaches to sociological research. In discussion of other perspectives, we use postmodernism and poststructuralism as they do. When conveying our own epistemological position we use poststructuralism for reasons outlined in the Introduction.

MASCULINITY POLITICS IN LATE MODERNITY

Key concepts

*Masculinity politics; postidentity politics; masculinity therapy; mythopoetic men,
modernization of masculinity; the politics of cultural difference; sexual minorities;
dissident masculinities; coming out.*

Introduction: 'unchanging men' or 'men in crisis'

Throughout the book we present major theoretical frameworks, exploring the continuities and discontinuities in the interplay of local and global changes, with shifting ideologies, discourses and representations of men and masculinity. This provides a clearer picture of the main sociological ways of understanding the complex relationship between notions of sex, gender and sexuality (see Rubin 1993). In this chapter, we locate within the changing conditions of the sex/gender order, three forms of masculinity politics, marked by the impact of feminism, namely, male liberationists, men against sexism and the New Men's Movement. In turn, this enables us to examine the question of the future of masculinity politics in the long history of sexual politics (Clatterbaugh 1990; Pease 2000). We explore gay men's collective mobilization, including the early modern gay movement and queer activism, as one of the most dynamic elements of recent sexual politics in destabilizing sociological and common-sense meanings of men and masculinity within the broader structure of gender relations (Bristow and Wilson 1993; Kirsch 2000).

Talk of the recent emergence of masculinity politics is surprising. Politics might be seen as the defining cultural space that delineates the public (masculine) from the private (feminine), thus serving to legitimate this space as an exclusive male preserve. As with so much social theory concerning contemporary gender relations, we are presented with a paradox. Men are highly visible in mainstream politics. However, they are conventionally represented and represent themselves not as men per se, as an embodied male sex or as a gendered social group, but rather as generically representative of humanity. Hence, *men* tend to be *visible*, while *masculinity* remains socially *invisible* (but normatively present). In 'normal times', masculinity politics within the public arenas of the governing state, economic management and institutional regulation is served by and in turn produces dominant forms of heterosexual masculinity. This is to understand politics in general terms as the power that men exercise that has a long history from Plato's Polis to the contemporary governance of nation states (Phillips 1998; Lovenduski 1999). Connell (1995: 205) offers a more specific definition of masculinity politics as 'mobilizations and struggles where the meaning of masculine power is at issue, and with it, men's position in gender relations. In such politics masculinity is made a principal theme, not taken for granted as background'. It is in this critical sense that it has recently emerged.

Reading the sociological literature on gender and sexuality reveals highly divergent positions that have been adopted historically, since the inception of second-wave feminism in western societies. However, even within such a context of shifting explanations the representation of masculinity politics appears as an intensely contested terrain. A major question raised by feminists – have men changed? – is contradictorily answered in terms of yes, no and not really sure. In turn, men's groups' projection of a *crisis masculinity* across western contemporary societies is marked by bitter debates about the assumed changing social location of men and accompanying threatened male subjectivities. Alongside media-led high profile images of a collapsing modern manhood, there appears to be general political pessimism among an earlier generation of feminists and gay activists about contemporary sexual politics. They see this as being marked by a 'backlash politics', attempting to recuperate a regressive heterosexual masculinity. A political understanding of this field of inquiry is not simply an empirical question. As we argue throughout this book, specific conceptual and methodological limitations emanate from the undertheorization of social and cultural change. In short, there is little political consensus about what constitutes change in a patriarchal society. Hence, there is a difficulty in recognizing or measuring it.

Over the last 20 years, the New Right agenda across Europe and America has been dominant, occupying the high moral ground with its projected atavistic representations of a consumer-based acquisitive individualism, the heterosexist patriarchal family, the strong state and the patriotic nation. For example, within a British context, this response was part of a wider project to construct an alternative to the post-war social democratic settlement, with its underlying values of egalitarianism and collectivism. Metcalf (1985: 11) provides the political and ideological background to the 1980s' shift from the 'soft' welfare state to the 'harder' new realism of market economics. He writes:

> In the popularization of a monetarist economic policy on both sides of the Atlantic, care has been taken to present these strategies as being proper to the competitive instincts of red-blooded American and British males. The call goes out to kill off lame ducks, to forswear compassion. It is asserted that in the market-place only the fittest should survive, and that a hard, lean industrial sector is necessary. Appeals to machismo and to disdain soft emotions are quite naked, as politicians of the radical right pour scorn on the need for the less fortunate, on the whole idea of the welfare state.

We are currently in a period of the descendancy of the more extreme version of market economics that was graphically signalled in Britain by the collapse of the Conservative government in 1997. However, the New Labour government is continuing the old Conservative tunes, with its emphasis on the inevitable political–economic logic of late capitalism, as the grand metaphor of the global market continues to shape our lives. This has been reinforced with the return of the Republican Party in the United States and the increased parliamentary success of extreme right-wing political parties in Fortress Europe (Mac an Ghaill 1999). Significantly, at the time of writing, an alternative progressive and coherent framework to the politically conservative social democratic project in Britain has not been developed. Within this context it appears difficult, conceptually and politically, to evaluate the achievements and limitations of feminist, gay/lesbian and pro-feminist activism.

The politics of masculinity: a limited cultural project

Morgan (1992: 24) discussing the problems of studying men, referred to the wide range of writing styles and accompanying different focuses, including personal, autobiographical, theoretical and analytical. He writes that:

> Some have celebrated men and masculinity, some others have denounced their own gender; many, if not most of all, have seen a need for some kind of change, personal and/or political. Men have demanded (as have some women) that men should 'get in touch with their feelings', or that they should confront the violence that they perpetrated or of which they are capable, that they should take a critical look at all their practices in the home, in interpersonal relationships, in public life and at work. Yet, perhaps, we still have a long way to go.

Connell (1987: xi) reminds us that 'theories don't grow on trees, theorizing is itself a social practice with a politics'. The studies to which Morgan refers were greatly indebted to the politics of feminist and gay liberation movements. Throughout early chapters we made reference to the different theoretical and methodological positions taken up by feminist scholars. These different positions produce different political perspectives with reference to an understanding of how men *can* and *should* respond to feminist explanations of gender relations. Adopting the rather simplified typology of liberal, Marxist/socialist and radical positions, we can map out a crude potted history of feminist responses, which are explored below. However, this fails to capture the complexity of what is at stake in this arena regarding the ambivalences and contradictions of feminist responses to men's involvement in sexual politics. As Segal (1990: 205) notes, the increased awareness of masculinity as plural, heterogeneous and contradictory is accompanied by the continuing 'problem of men'. She writes: 'We may come to understand sexual difference in terms of a shifting reality – a multiplicity of meanings rather than simple opposition – but the cultural, social and political domination of men over women persists'.

For a 1970s generation of progressive young men, the women's liberation movement was highly formative in their sexual and emotional coming-of-age. At one level, when contemporary male theorists, writing about masculinity, speak of their indebtedness to feminism, they often appear less concerned with the detailed specificity of particular positions; rather they are invoking the cultural significance of feminism as a political movement to understand contemporary men and masculinities (see also Kimmel 1987c). However, conventional male academic representations of masculinity politics map out men's involvement in sexual politics as reflecting early political feminist debates, with different men's groups aligning themselves with or against specific feminist positions. For example, Clatterbaugh (1990), writing of the American situation, identifies six main contemporary political perspectives: conservative, pro-feminist, men's rights, spiritual, socialist and group-specific. The danger here is to think of these groups as developing mutually exclusive practices. It is important to emphasize as Hearn (1993b) suggests, that individual men take up different, including contradictory responses, and that the politics of any particular position adopted by men's groups have developed a number of strands. His argument helps to explain what often appears as a confused history of heterosexual men's involvement in sexual politics alongside confusing shifts in popular understandings of the men's movement across western societies (Reynaud 1983; Bertoia and Drakich 1995).

In *Men and Masculinities* we argue that conceptualizing masculinity needs to be located within the wider gender order and dominant political regimes of representation, just as masculinity politics needs to be located within the bigger picture of sexual politics. Masculinity politics is conventionally represented within the academy and in sociological textbooks as an aspect of men's studies, with the gendered/sexual majority as its object of inquiry, placed alongside that of women's studies and gay and lesbian studies. However, compared to the cultural dynamism and political appeal of the latter two new social movements, the conceptualization and living out of masculinity politics appears to be remarkably narrow, defensive and reactive to a self-projected crisis of western masculinity in late modernity.

Male liberationists: a reformist agenda

This suggested crisis needs to be placed within a broader political framework in which to understand the structure and meaning of men's sexual politics. From their conception in the early 1970s, the constitution of men's groups was marked by a number of limitations. In terms of internal relations, there was a real tension about their purpose, with different emphases on men's liberation and anti-sexism, that produced a long-standing fundamental suspicion about each other's intentions and practices (Seidler 1991; Pease 2000). Male liberationists, working within a sex-role approach, mobilized liberal feminist discourses of equal rights and fairness to argue that both women and men suffered from the sexism generated from negative gender stereotypical socialization (Farrell 1974; Nichols 1975). They spoke of the burden and emotional damage of being men, thus focusing upon the negative attributes of the male role as *oppressed* rather than that of *oppressor*. As Pease (2000: 124) points out:

They saw consciousness-raising groups as vehicles by which men could get in touch with their feelings, free themselves from sex-role stereotyping, learn to be more caring for other men and struggle together against the imposition of the socially oppressive male role.

A particular strength of this approach is to challenge biologically-based determinist explanations of women's oppression. It suggests that if young boys are socialized into acting out society's expectations of the male role – 'a chip off the old block' – dominant masculine characteristics, such as aggression, competitiveness and fear of intimacy, can be relearned. Hence, from this reformist agenda, women and men can (and should) form political alliances that address their shared needs, enabling them to eradicate the sexism inherent in traditional sex roles. There is evidence of the political success of this approach in local and national European spaces including: implementing equal opportunities initiatives within institutions, developing anti-sexist educational material, co-parenting, and developing anti-discrimination laws at a local state level (European Commission Network on Childcare 1993).

'Men Against Sexism': a radical agenda

'Men Against Sexism' groups have produced rich accounts of their political activities (Snodgrass 1977; Tolson 1977; Metcalf and Humphries 1985; Jardine and Smith 1992). Seidler's (1992) British collection of writings, written from 1978 to 1984, that were published in *Achilles Heel*, the journal of men's sexual politics, makes clear the innovativeness of this position (see also *Changing Men* from the United States and *XY* from Australia). The index to the collection indicates the critical self-exploration and reflexivity of a group of men, who made their sex and sexuality the key object of political inquiry. Aligning themselves with socialist and radical feminist positions, Men Against Sexism named themselves as complicit with patriarchal power relations and the accompanying institutional oppression of women. Remembering their sexual and domestic biographies, they focused upon diverse sexist practices around issues of the self, sexuality, violence and pornography. The techniques and processes of the women's liberation movement were adopted and practised, as they collectively imagined non-oppressive, life-affirming ways of being men in their relationships with women, gay men and other heterosexual men.

Men Against Sexism creatively developed a political strategic approach that opposed a tendency by some men of a radical rejection of their masculinity, which was seen as essentially tied up with a relationship of power. This is illustrated in Stoltenberg's *Refusing to be a Man* (1989). At the same time, they focused on the political limitations of the men's liberationist approach, which emphasizes a voluntarism. This underplays the social structures and cultural ideologies within which individual men and women are embedded. The political terrain on which they worked was circumscribed by the question of how to respond positively to feminism. They sought to challenge the radical feminist argument that privileged social groups do not give up power without great resistance, maintaining in a highly optimistic way that men can and need to change because it is in their individual and collective interest. However, no positive vision emerged from among themselves about what kind of modern movement they constituted in relation to the feminist and gay liberation movements. Connell (1987: 276) articulates the problems involved for the gender majority, suggesting that it is difficult to construct a social movement of heterosexual men that is based upon the attempt to dismantle their hegemonic interest. Rutherford (1992) makes the case for those active within Men Against Sexism groups experiencing a sense of cultural and gendered dislocation. As we argue throughout this book, there was and continues to be a real sense of gendered and sexual (and indeed ethnic/national) dislocation among groups of contemporary men. However, for a group of white middle-class, heterosexual men, who could make no appeals to a shared political oppression, a collective identity from which to speak seemed indelibly marked by internal disputes, recriminations and ambivalences. This is a shared political and moral problem for social majorities, for whom the motivation to change is more likely to develop 'from an ethical rather than experiential position' (Kimmel and Messner 1989; Morgan 1992: 39).

Although feminism was a key formative influence on the origins and development of contemporary men's groups, it was and remains a highly ambivalent relationship. Recently Squires (1999) has spoken of the continuing reluctance within much feminism to engage fully with men's writing on masculinity. For her, these texts provide important insights and are profoundly productive in developing a full understanding of gender theory. In fact, there has been a long history to this reluctance, particularly from feminists working in the academy, who have argued against the development of men's studies with its suggestion that it is complementary to women studies (Brod 1987; Canaan and Griffin 1990; Luxton 1993). Male liberationists and pro-feminist men are often perceived by feminists as promoting a modernization rather than an eradication of patriarchy, in which they gain the advantages of such a move without giving up the fundamental privileges of a dominant social group. However, given that politics is about forming successful strategic alliances, such feminist responses added to the weakness of progressive heterosexual men's sexual politics, that was marked by their own suspicion of 'traditional male forms of organising and politicking to be able to create a coherent movement' (Baker 1994: 12). Anti-sexist heterosexual men failed to gain legitimacy, either philosophically or practically, for their political project either among themselves or from other progressive social movements, while at the same time been highly visible and vulnerable to ridicule from other men. Some feminists saw them as continuing to enact *too much masculinity*, while other hetero-sexual men saw anti-sexist men as enacting *too little masculinity*. Most importantly, progressive men's groups continued conceptually to conflate notions of men and masculinities, that are conventionally elided in the social science literature. Hence, in living out the contradictions of em-bodied heterosexual masculinities, it was not clear if the object of their political organizing was to change themselves, as a gendered social major-ity, or to change the wider structures, ideologies and discourses that shaped the sex/gender order and the accompanying dominant political regime.

Interestingly, as discussed in Chapter 2 in contrast to feminists work-ing within academia, those working with men in specific institutional sites are more optimistic about building alliances across gender divisions, such as feminists commenting upon the increased involvement of nurtur-ing men in paternal relationships. At the same time, male academics who were involved in anti-sexist men's groups have written extensively about the demise of their formal meetings and networks. However, what is underexplored is the wide range of men who were not members of organ-ized men's groups in the 1980s but were actively involved in anti-sexist practices in trade unions, the media, community and youth groups and university campuses (Hearn 1987). Dunphy (2000: 141–2) writing from an identity politics position (see below) makes the important political point that the

> progressive men's movement does have an effect, for example in the influence its politics have on male counsellors working with young male offenders or drug abusers – especially those convicted of violent crimes against women and children – and by working also to change attitudes within the police force.

While progressive heterosexual men's groups responded to feminism, they failed to engage with the gay liberation movement (see below). Dunphy (2000: 64–5) has described the difficulty that social theorists have in answer-ing questions concerning the meaning of heterosexuality. More specific-ally, with reference to male writers on masculinity, he notes that they claim *masculinity* rather than *sexuality* as their sexual identity. Dunphy continues:

> They write of 'male sexuality', 'masculinity sexuality', the 'sexuality of men', effectively conflating their gender and sexual identities. Yet it is often the case that they are universalising from their own experience as men whose sexual desires, feelings, needs and fears are directed towards women. Their heterosexuality remains unnamed, and subsumed within their masculinity. By equating masculinity with their sexuality, they ignore gay and bisexual men who are often confined to the limbo of non-men.

As argued in Chapter 2, with reference to familial masculinities, gay men's activism around the issue of redefining social ways of being men, as part of the latter's longer history of having to invent a self, a social identity and a wider community, might be adopted as alternative cultural resources by heterosexual men. In so doing, they might begin to operate beyond the institutional ideologies and discourses of gender regulation and self-surveillance that maintains the fixed boundaries of modern manhood. This is particularly salient at a time when it is claimed that heterosexual men are in crisis. For example, Faludi (1999) in her study found a generation of American men whom she sympathetically portrays as unable, personally and collectively, to find a progressive resolution to the effects of contemporary social transformations that they interpret as challenging their sense of manhood. She suggests that they are asking the wrong questions and that instead of relentlessly seeking the meaning of masculinity, they should concentrate on what it means to be human.

What becomes clear from such texts is that the heterosexual male crisis is premised on a cultural shift from a social identity that is assumed to be fixed, coherent and stable, being displaced by the experience of doubt and uncertainty (Mercer 1990: 43). This is experienced at individual, social and psychic levels, that is circumscribed by the local–global nexus of cultural transformations, which the new men's movement has addressed. In so doing, they adopt a conservative political position in their attempt to recuperate an assumed lost masculinity.

The New Men's Movement

At one level, male liberationists and anti-sexist men tend to define political positions and more specifically their political alliance to feminism against each other, producing debates that have little resonance outside their own membership. At another level, these progressive groups define themselves against men who take up a conservative position in relation to feminism. Again, this results in debates with limited political effects. Conservatively orientated men's groups are often represented by the former as a homogenous movement. In fact, we can identify a number of strands, involving variants of pro-male, anti-feminism and anti-women stances, which illustrate both the changing historical development and cultural specificity of conservative men's sexual politics within different nation-states (Reynaud 1983; Bertoia and Drakich 1995). For example, a number of articles in *The Guardian* newspaper, including Baker (1994) and Millar (1997) have usefully mapped out the development of the UK men's movement during the 1990s, with its challenging the legitimacy of the Equal Opportunities Commission, its arguments for repealing equal rights legislation and direct attacks on rape crisis centres.

Alongside, and sometimes overlapping with this embryonic movement, a range of grassroots action groups have emerged in Britain around men's issues. There is a tendency in the academic literature to overpoliticize these groups, often drawing upon American experiences that are not appropriate to understanding the cultural specificities of the British gender social order. This is most clearly illustrated in relation to the activities of the Child Support Agency, which acted as a major catalyst for mobilizing men. In an analysis of the politics surrounding the agency, Westwood (1996) makes clear the way in which ethnicity and class are articulated via masculinity, providing a key moment in the generation of a collective subject in opposition to the British state. Many of these fathers were not politically active around masculinity issues but rather were mobilized into protest against what they interpreted as a specific injustice with major difficulties for their current domestic arrangements.

Writing from a different location, Connell (1995) names the gun lobby as a specific form of masculinity politics that he sees as central to defending hegemonic masculinity in the United States. He also identifies the changing politics surrounding masculinity therapy since the 1970s, which he sees as presently the most talked about in the United States. He traces its shift from the early 1970s association with counter-cultural therapy and its pro-liberal feminist stance of breaking out of the traditional male role, to a 1980s emphasis on a separation from the feminine in search of the deep masculine.

Bly's (1990) *Iron John* is one of the most celebrated books about men, among academics, professionals and journalists. Invoking 'mythopoetic' concepts, he argues for the restoration of a lost, traditional masculinity – for the urgent need to encounter the 'hairy man'. From a British perspective, there is much scepticism about 'meeting the god – woman in the garden', 'bringing interior warriors back to life' and 'the wild man in ancient religion, literature and folk life' – which are chapter headings in Bly's book. However, there is much resonance with emotional self-exploration, male bonding and recovering damaged relationships with fathers.

Placed within a structure of a traditional masculinity, this enables individual men to be actively involved in affective relations, underpinned by the security of images that do not threaten their participation in the traditionally feminine world of emotional work. In short, gendered and sexual power relations are reinforced rather than subverted – you can discover your authentic masculinity becoming a 'hard warrior' rather than a 'soft wimp'. Schwalbe's (1996: 119) three year ethnographic study is one of the most insightful commentaries on this new men's movement. Most interestingly he reports how these men's rituals, as part of a wider search for positive affirmation and validation of their sense of being men, including being emotional and sensitive, enable them 'to reinterpret their feminine traits as "deep masculine"'.

Bly claims a pro-male rather than an anti-feminist stance. However, feminism is cited as one of the key sources of the feminization of contemporary men. Hence, he maintains there is a need for men to renegotiate their relationship to feminism. Schwalbe (1996: 245) in a critical appreciation of the mythopoetic men whom he researched, challenged them:

> to think more critically about the dangers of archetypalizing social roles, embracing essentialism, celebrating masculinity, using stories that are full of sexist imagery, engaging in activities that encourage andro-centrism, and insulating feelings from analysis.

He concludes that a major limitation of this movement is its failure to engage with questions of 'structural inequalities and injustices that are the root causes of trouble in men's and women's lives' (1996: 245). Others working within masculinity therapy have developed a more stringent anti-feminist stance in reworking this relationship. In contrast, the British thera-pist, Rowan (1987), who like Bly is working within a Jungian tradition, describes the productive engagement of men with strong women produced in feminism, arguing for the need to get in touch with a female goddess tradition (see also Rowan 1997).

The men's rights lobby is probably the form of masculinity politics that currently has widest resonance across different societies, including Britain, Australia and the US. It has been central to a cultural shift in which the idea of the men's movement, which from the early 1970s was associated with a progressive identification with feminist politics is now popularly understood as an organized defence of men as the victims of gender arrange-ments. In contrast, failing to develop a language to explain the changing meanings of what it is to be a heterosexual man, progressive men's groups have made little impact on challenging a popular media image of men being forced to make adjustments to structural changes in the workplace and family life under increasing pressure from feminist and gay activists. Key texts on men's rights include Lyndon (1992), Thomas (1993) and Farrell (1994). Farrell moved from an earlier pro-feminist position, as a member of the influential National Organization of Women (NOW) in the US, to an attempt to provide a theoretically coherent framework for a men's rights politics. In an interview with him, Grant (1994: 2) records the contemporary appeal of the projected men's movement and the pertinent questions that Farrell raises.

> Why did men live one year less than women in 1920 but seven years less than women in 1990? ... Why is breast cancer such a glib issue and prostate cancer no issue at all? Why are men more likely to commit suicide? ... When we talk about male power, aren't we actually talking about the power of white, heterosexual, middle-class men? Why do we never talk about the powerlessness of black men growing up in the ghetto and the strategies of violence forced on them by their culture? Why are men so alien to so many women when we grow up in

families with fathers? Is it because the definition of success as a father has been that he will never be there, always out at work supporting his children?

The above pro-male position might implicitly indicate the need for a class and race analysis to make sense of these complex sets of contemporary material changes in late modernity. However for Farrell these complex questions are answered in terms of a simple explanation that men are now the gender victims as a result of feminism having gone too far, with men having increased responsibilities but few rights around issues of marriage, divorce, child custody and access to children. Modern legislation is seen to be overprotective of women's interests, resulting in discrimination against men at a time when they are under increasing threat within a rapidly changing society. For example, the feminization of institutional life is experienced within the context of the decline of traditional male work, and its accompanying implications for the male 'bread winner' role, alongside the increase of women in the feminine-friendly service sector (see Chapter 1).

For all the differences between different strands of men's groups, a number of underlying themes can be identified. First, arguments for a more inclusive approach to gender relations – that is, to include men as central participants – can be read as politically important in highlighting the interdependence of men and women, masculinities and femininities. This might suggest the need to modernize our understanding of relations between men and women. For example, Connell (1995: 211) is undoubtedly right that:

> although such texts like Bly's are nostalgic and the mythopoetic imagery can be strikingly reactionary, the tendency of therapeutic practice is towards accommodation between men and women, adjustment at the level of personal relations. The larger consequence of the popular forms of masculinity therapy is an adaptation of patriarchal structures through the modernization of masculinity.

Second, the historical development of men's groups has marked a theoretical shift of interest from men's patriarchal presence in the public world and an accompanying politics of social justice for women and men to that of a preoccupation with men's emotionally damaged inner world. For conservatives, this is translated into challenging their projected disempowerment. For progressive men's groups, this has resulted in a movement into therapy.

The future of masculinity politics: searching for a postidentity politics position

Within western societies, at the start of the 2000s, masculinity and sexuality have come to speak of a wider sense of social dislocation in globally-based, postcolonial, deindustrializing societies. Early pro-feminist men's groups, in responding to the much vaunted masculinity crisis, have been criticized in the sociological literature for their profile as white, middle-class males, thus excluding working-class, gay and black men. These exclusions are read through an identity politics position that serves to challenge the under-representation of minority groups.

Throughout this book we examined the limitations of this position, building on what we identified and developed as innovative frameworks for making sense of men's sexual politics, namely the dynamics of: sexuality, age/generation, social class and ethnicity. Holding on to the tension between identity politics (feminism/gay liberation) and the politics of cultural difference (postmodernism/poststructuralist/queer theory) positions, we explored this both in terms of the absence of social minorities and the constitution of the multidimensional heterosexual male subjectivity.

Men and Masculinities critically explores materialist accounts of a feminist problematic. We are particularly concerned with the limitations of an anti-oppressive position as a conceptual framework and its failure to capture the dynamics of local, that is, nationally-based, institutional spaces that are experiencing and producing major social, economic and cultural change. In this way, we locate an anti-oppressive analytical position, promoted by earlier versions of socialism, feminism, anti-racism, and gay and lesbian rights, as theoretically incomplete. In testing the limits of the new social movements, we are suggesting that a postidentity politics position provides a wider vocabulary to capture the complexity of our gendered/ sexual lives. At the same time, there continues to be a need to identify structural relations of social power and the resulting patterns of collective social justice.

Gay men's sexual politics: forging dissident masculinities

A major aim of *Men and Masculinities* is to denaturalize sex, gender and desire, emphasizing the active cultural production of masculinities within the wider context of the social organization of the sex/gender order. We suggest that one productive arena in which to accomplish this is to explore those who have not taken up the cultural injunction to become heterosexual men, that includes a wide range of sexual minorities: gay men, bisexuals, transsexuals and transgendered groups. Gay men's collective organization is one of the most dynamic elements of recent sexual politics in destabilizing sociological and common-sense meanings of men and masculinity within the broader structure of gender relations (Bristow and Wilson 1993; Kirsch 2000).[1] At the same time, we emphasize the analytical purchase of gay narratives and concepts in helping to reshape mainstream sociology – leading to the extension and development of our theoretical understanding of the processes and patterns or conflicts that produce the gender order within specific historical and geographical spaces. As Pronger (1990: 2), writing of the political paradox of contemporary meanings of gay masculinity, argues:

> In our culture male homosexuality is a violation of masculinity, a denigration of the mythic power of men, an ironic subversion that significant numbers of men pursue with great enthusiasm. Because it gnaws at masculinity it weakens the gender order. But because masculinity is at the heart of homerotic desire, homosexuality is essentially a paradox in the myth of gender.

This collective organization of contestation and resistance, played out in reformist and radical/utopian forms, has involved a repertoire of political strategies and organizational forms for mobilization, including HIV/AIDS activism, parliamentary lobbying, formation of support networks/telephone helplines, counselling services, partnership rights/same-sex marriages, gay fathering, fostering and adoption, and the playfulness of gay camp style and gay male drag (Rubin 1993; Forrest 1994).[2] In turn, the changing forms of social ways of being men lived out by gays resonate with the wider picture of changing institutions, fluid and changeable relationships, a shifting emotional landscape and the complex transformations of intimate life in a global age of uncertainty (Giddens 1992; Rubin 1993; Sedgwick 1994; Weeks 1995; Jamieson 1998).

June 1969 marked the birth of gay liberation as a modern social movement, with the Stonewall riots in New York City, when gay men fought back against police harassment in a gay bar (D'Emilio 1983). The Gay Liberation Front formed a month later and was launched in Britain in 1970 (Edwards 1994). The legacy of this influential cultural moment in the political history of gays is still resonant in what might be referred to as the Americanization of British gay sexual politics. Edgar (1981: 218) describes the background to this global influence that was grounded in and mediated through racial politics:

> Without Black Brotherhood, there would have been no sisterhood: without Black Power and Black Pride there would have been no Gay Power and Gay Pride. The movement against the abuses of the powers of the state . . . derived much of its strength and purpose from the exposure of the FBI's surveillance and harassment of the Black Panthers and the Black Muslims . . . only the Environment Movement did not have the Black Movement as a central organisational fact or as a defining metaphor and inspiration.

Within the context of Britain, among new social movements, particularly in public-sector institutional sites such as social services and education, second-wave feminism might claim this pivotal cultural position

(Rowbotham 1997). This early period has become associated with the notion of *coming out* – a real sense of rebirth – an invention of a collective subject hidden from history, marking a decisive break with the major historical regulatory forces that have operated to pathologize homosexuality and homosexuals, that of criminalization and medicalization (Weeks 1977).

Dunphy (2000: 57) explains the significance of the concept:

> This in its most politicised form involved three over-lapping procedures: coming out to oneself by accepting one's homosexuality as an identity to be proud of; entering into a community by forming not just relationships but social and political alliances with others of a similar sexual orientation in safe places, and creating such safe places if they didn't exist; and coming out to the wider heterosexual society of family, friends and workplace.

In short, 'coming out', by forging a new social self and seeking community identity recognition and validation can be read as a highly productive sociological idea, focusing upon a traditional concern of the discipline, that of rethinking the conceptualization of the individual – society couplet, within conditions of late modernity. The early autobiographical sexual stories of inventing dissident masculinities – written in the 1970s and early 1980s, which provide fascinating insights into gay men's disinvestment in traditional modes of (heterosexual) masculinity are marked by a highly reflexive self. As Weeks (1990: 134) maintains:

> lesbians and gays have a sense of their own creativity because they are, day by day, involved in self-making, constructing their own meanings, networks, rituals, traditions, calling on inherited traces of the past, but responding all the time to the challenges and possibilities of the present.

Emerging decentred male gay subjectivities provide concrete evidence that masculinity is not something one is born with or an inherent possession, but rather an active process of achievement, performance and enactment (Weeks 1977; Plummer 1981). Furthermore, the development of a wide range of gay male styles makes clear the meaning of the living out of fractured masculinities – involving a diverse range of men's investments, anxieties, fantasy identifications and contradictory emotions – in modes of masculinity that they were actively manufacturing within safe social spaces. These texts, which were informed by the radical intention of liberating all genders, illustrate the internal cultural technologies involved in sex/gender identity work, reordering meanings, rescripting roles and reinventing values, that has emerged into the development of a new moral economy and sexual citizenship (Evans 1993; Weeks 1995).

Currently, the historical dual influence of black politics and feminism on British gay men's collective organization is often erased, particularly with the ascendancy of globally-based consumer capitalism (Mort 1996). This is captured in the phrase 'the pink pound' and its attendant hedonistic gay lifestyle, as part of the promotion of the commercial gay scene. Here, the emphasis is on youthfulness, designer clothes and toned bodies, invoking the cult of the individual, with (homo)sex as the ultimate commodity. This 'depoliticized' community self-image has been picked up and circulated by the media, who make claims for the modernization of the representation of gay lifestyle, within a range of genres – soap operas, game shows and reality television. For Simpson (in Branigan 2001: 7) this represents a cultural shift from 'gay is good' to 'gay is goods'. A main limiting element of such a shift is that while *old negative stereotypes* of the homosexual ghetto are exchanged for *new positive stereotypes* of the gay village, dominant sexual and gendered binaries are reproduced and reinscribed. During the last decade across the western world, these concerns have been intensely debated within gay and lesbian communities, which have witnessed the emergence of queer politics, which as a deconstructive project seeks to destabilize socially given identities, categories and subjectivities. At the heart of this destabilization, the established gay and lesbian movement is being provoked into exchanging the (partial) security of their social *identity* for a range of political identifications/alliances that are in the process of being assembled (Mercer 1991).

Simpson (1996) writing from a British context, describes the queering of politics as a move beyond the limitations of an identity politics position of gay rights groups such as Stonewall. The latter formed in 1989 on a reformist political agenda and concentrates on lobbying parliament for the social inclusion of sexual minorities. For queer activists in Britain such as OutRage! and the Manchester-based HomoCult, the major focus of agitation is the media rather than parliamentary lobbying. With relatively few activists, they have been remarkably successful in attracting attention for such activities as kiss-ins, mass queer weddings and the forcible 'outing' of allegedly gay public figures whom they claim support homophobic practices (Dunphy 2000: 135). Queer activism has had an uneven development across Europe, with its major political influence located within the US. Two key elements in the development of queer theory/activism have been first the scholarship of literary and cultural theorists working in gay and lesbian studies. They have provided a philosophically rich range of concepts that have been explored throughout this book, including deconstructing the hetero/homo boundary, the heterosexual matrix and gender performativity (Butler 1990; Sedgwick 1990; Dollimore 1991). The second element has been emerging political responses to the AIDS crisis in the 1980s/early 1990s. For example the radical activist group Queer Nation deployed forms of political activism promoted by ACT UP (the AIDS Coalition To Unleash Power).

For queer activists, the established gay community, in campaigning for community identity recognition and validation by straight society, has adopted an assimilationist position. The perceived limitations of this political strategy are resonant of those voiced by black radicals in the 1970s concerning the state setting the agenda on which racialized ethnic minority groups were to be included within white society, on terms of liberal acceptance rather than human rights (Mac an Ghaill 1999). Furthermore, this partial social inclusion extends to individual gay men but not homosexuality, with an accompanying official prescription/proscription of specific types of gays, that is, those embodying dominant modes of male heterosexuality. A major concern for queer activists, operating from an anti-essentialist identity position, is that mainstream inclusion involves the state regulation and surveillance of a sexual minority identity that implicitly produces the homohetero boundary of a fixed subcultural type. In his latest book, *The Queen is Dead*, Simpson (with Zeeland) (2001) provides a critique of masculinity and urban gay lifestyle, illustrating the serious flaws of equating men's behaviour around the issue of same-sex desire, with specific sexual categories, whether politically regressive or progressive. Furthermore, for queer activists, the gay movement in targeting its political energies towards straight society has not addressed a wide range of internal sexual exclusions, including bisexuals, transexuals and transgendered groups, alongside social closures, around age, ethnicity and disability, arising from the narrow conception of gay identity itself. In contrast, queer politics, adopting a utopian stance, is open to all dissident eroticized minorities, while simultaneously claiming that the effect of transcending the homo/hetero divide is to challenge the sexual regulation and repression of the sexual majority – heterosexual desire.

This political position makes clear that 'queer is also a way of cutting against mandatory gender divisions' (Warner 1993: xxvii). Though, Warner adds, gender continues to be a dividing line. In other words, working against traditional sexual and gender hierarchies, in which sexuality and gender as social categories of analysis act as containers that operate normatively to fix the boundaries of how we should live our lives, queer activists emphasize the openness, fragmentation and diversity that infuses contemporary ways of being. As a postmodern politics, it celebrates the transgressive potential, both discursive and social, of the implosion of existing gender and sexuality categories, enabling us to reimagine inhabiting a range of masculinities and femininities and the full diversity of sexual desire.

Exploring a politics of masculinity, we find queer theory particularly productive in our ethnographic work on the shifting identity formations among both young men and women, which test the limits of new social movement explanations of feminism and gay liberation. For example, in Chapter 3 we used Butler's claim that gender is routinely spoken through a 'heterosexosexual matrix', in which heterosexuality is presupposed in the expression of 'real' forms of masculinity and femininity. However, in suggesting that masculinities are 'spoken through a heterosexual matrix', it is not argued that laddishness, for example, is inevitably coded as heterosexual.

Nor is it suggested that everyone who inhabits hegemonic forms of masculinity experiences themselves as heterosexual and that everyone who inhabits subordinated forms of masculinity experiences themselves as homosexual. As the gay men's 'clone' style of the 1970s and 1980s demonstrated, highly physical and macho forms of masculinity can be successfully rearticulated so that they signify homosexuality. Equally, as we have found with a younger generation of English males, groups of friends organized themselves around a version of high camp that flaunted characteristics identified as quintessentially 'feminine' and 'poofy' by the forms of masculinity hegemonic in school life (Redman and Mac an Ghaill 1996; Redman 2001). Despite this, not all such groups identified as gay.

The existence of gay machismo and heterosexual camp should alert us to the fact that the subject positions made available by discourses of masculinity do not determine subjectivity. Within particular constraints, they can be read against the grain. In the examples given, both hegemonic and subordinate forms of masculinity are deployed as cultural resources and their meanings are rearticulated: gay is macho; 'poofy' is superior, more refined. However, while the subject positions of hegemonic masculinities can be clearly subverted or lived in contradictory ways, they more commonly act as resources through which heterosexual subjectivities are produced, lived out, and policed in local circumstances; they provide the social vocabulary through which heterosexual men are both 'spoken' and come to 'speak themselves' as heterosexual.

There are a range of criticisms of queer theory/politics, including that it is a development of a social constructionist tradition rather than a radical break with established social theory; in privileging significatory systems, discourse and discursive power, it colludes with postmodernism in underplaying the importance of the socioeconomic structural differences; that its concern with abstract theorizing and accompanying disinterest in the 'ordinary' is elitist; and most significantly that it downplays gender in its discussion of heteronormativity (McIntosh 1993; Morton 1995; Dunphy 2000; Kirsch 2000). Queer theory remains highly abstract, disconnected from the way people are living their lives within the institutional constraints of economics, the state and cultural traditions (McIntosh 1993; Edwards 1998; Kirsch 2000). The histories of gay and lesbian politics illustrate the need to reconnect contemporary material conditions to questions of representation, culture and the self in order to grasp what is at stake in troubling the dominant sex/gender system and the accompanying production of masculinities and femininities.

Recent British texts, such as Weeks *et al.* (2001) and Dunne (2001) have achieved this fusion. They explore a fascinatingly diverse range of sexual stories of how everyday experience is reordered with new meanings that serve to open up discussion of masculinity politics (Plummer 1995). These stories are being lived out within the specific context of two critical developments: the changing age profile of non-heterosexuals, and the gay community's creative response to the AIDS epidemic, mediated through safe-sex practices, new reproductive technological advances and repressive state legislation. The latter involved the British government's introduction of Section 28 of the Local Government Act 1988, which banned local authorities from supporting the 'promotion of homosexuality' or the validation of 'pretended family' (homosexual) relationships (Aggleton *et al.* 1999; Stacey 1991).

Against this background, HIV/AIDS activism has made an important contribution at a conceptual level in its rethinking of the nature of the state, 'maintaining a complex view of [it] as both process and institutional apparatus, with various levels and sectors of state action producing conflicting rationalities' (Connell 1990: 106). From this position, as was illustrated in the organized oppositional response to Section 28 in Britain, attempts to control and repress sexuality produced the opposite effects. In arguing that the state is a complex nexus of institutional arrangements involving ideological, juridical and repressive mechanisms, masculinity can be understood as occupying varying degrees of centrality in different state institutions and at different historical moments.

This examination of the interrelationship between the state and masculinity suggests the need politically to hold on to the complex interaction between state ideologies, institutionally-based cultural representations and gender and sexual subject positions. This is particularly salient at a time of pessimism around the question of political interventions, when contemporary homogenizing technologies of state power associated with processes of western globalization, modernization and collective consumption are represented as overly determining 'local' national responses. HIV/AIDS activism serves to challenge the tendency in much globalization theory to underplay the role of the state in reproducing gender and sexual ideologies and boundaries and more specifically nationally-based politics of masculinity (Brah *et al.* 1999).

Conclusion

Presently this is a difficult period for anti-sexist/pro-femininist and gay/ lesbian politics with the shift from 'movement' politics to 'lifestyle' politics. For example, the 1990s in Britain has witnessed the privatization of morality with which the public, collectivist stance of new social movements is not in tune. At the same time, there is currently a general alienation from parliamentary politics. As Brunt (1989: 150) argued:

> The way to characterise the present situation of Britain entering the 1990s is in terms of a gaping disparity: a tiny minority of various strands of the British Left and progressive movement busy rethinking and reviewing its politics while the vast majority of the British people

continue to anathematise the very idea of being involved in politics of any sort.

At the beginning of the 2000s these trends have intensified, with the implosion of the Conservative Party, accompanied by the ascendancy of an overly-managed New Labour government. The latter is detached from its traditional constituencies, such as the trade union movement, while showing little critical interest in masculinity politics.

Young (1993: 123–4), writing within an American context, has provided a productive way forward that moves beyond the limits of an identity politics problematic, while suggesting the complex interrelation between social positioning and subjective identity formation. In her paper that explores how political actors conceive group difference and how they might best conceive it, she writes that:

> Historically, in group based oppression and conflict difference is conceived as otherness and exclusion, especially, but not only by hegemonic groups. This conception of otherness relies on a logic of identity that essentialises and substantialises group natures. Attempts to overcome the exclusion which such a conception generates usually move in one of two directions: assimilation or separation. Each of these political strategies itself exhibits a logic of identity; but this makes each strategy contradict the social realities of group interfusion. A third ideal of a single polity with differentiated groups recognising one another's specificity and experience requires a conception of difference expressing a relational rather than substantial logic. Groups should be understood not as entirely other, but as overlapping, as constituted in relation to one another and thus shifting their attributes and needs in accordance with what relations are salient. In my view this relational conception of difference as contextual helps make more apparent the necessity and possibility of political togetherness in difference.

A key issue for theorists is whether we can identify differentiated forms of social power without relinquishing forms of structured oppression. In other words holding onto the tension between a politics of redistribution and a politics of difference. The development of policies aimed at reducing inequality requires a more sophisticated conceptual framework accompanied by a more empirically grounded critique, which we illustrate throughout the book through use of ethnographic studies. Producing more coherent analyses within the sociology of gender and sexuality demands an understanding of the tension between identity politics and the new postidentity politics position. We agree with Gamson (1995: 400) when he argues that: 'The problem, of course, is that both the boundary strippers and the boundary defenders are right'. He suggests that a distinction between the two approaches can be understood as one of identity building and identity blurring.

Questions for your reflection

1 Is there a crisis in masculinity?

2 Do you agree that the politics of masculinity is a limited cultural project?

3 Why does the men's movement have such popular appeal in the media?

4 What can gay and queer politics offer masculinity politics?

Suggested further reading

Bly, R. (1990) *Iron John: A Book about Men*. Reading, MA: Addison-Wesley.

Dunphy, R. (2000) *Sexual Politics: An Introduction*. Edinburgh: Edinburgh University Press.

Edwards, T. (1994) *Erotics and Politics: Gay Male Sexuality, Masculinity and Feminism*. London: Routledge.

Segal, L. (1990) *Slow Change: Changing Masculinities, Changing Men*. London: Virago.

Squires, J. (1999) *Gender in Political Theory*. Cambridge: Polity Press.

Weeks, J., Heaphy, B. and Donovan, C. (2001) *Same Sex Intimacies: Families of Choice and Other Life Experiments*. London: Routledge.

Notes

1 Historically, the relationship of gay men to gender relations is highly contested, including criticism that they were simply seeking equality with straight men. See Edwards (1994) and Mary McIntosh's (1993) discussion of whether queer theory can transcend the binary divisions between women and men in the gay movement.

2 See Edwards (1994: 16–30) for a classification of the history of modern homosexuality in western society.

CONCLUSION

Introduction

One function of a conclusion is to bring together various strands of a book's argument and offer some form of resolution. Indeed, we highlight key themes to emerge in *Men and Masculinities*. At the same time, our resolution might be deemed incomplete. In the Introduction, we spoke of the book's rationale as providing a synthesis of main approaches and key concepts. However, this synthesis does not correspond to traditional philosophical conventions. For example, we have not adopted a Hegelian approach, where through a triadic progression, ideas are proposed, negated and then transcended. Neither have we adopted a Kantian approach, of combining isolated themes into a recognized whole. We write from a specific location, that of late modernity, in which we are experiencing a fundamental cultural shift, marked by discontinuity, fragmentation and uncertainty. Within this wider context, questions of men, masculinity and gender relations are central to explanations of the configurations of contemporary social and cultural change. However, there is a sense that no one theory can give the whole picture of an ever-increasingly complex global arena in which shifting gender meanings are experienced and negotiated in complex ways. Hence rather than try to tie up the understandings and definitions of masculinity, we suggest that masculinity needs to remain conceptually open and disputed. It should not preclude differences but should actively acknowledge incongruity as an important process of developing the field of inquiry. As a result, our own readings of the various arenas featured in the book are reflexively sensitive to shifts in the theoretical and conceptual frames used to explain men and masculinities.

Emerging themes: the importance of the social

A fundamental aspect of developing frameworks that name men's experiences and describe their practices is to stress the importance of the *social*. Our first aim was to explore the main sociological approaches to men and masculinities within the broader context of gender relations. What emerged from this process is the highlighting of the social nature of masculinity. Yet media representations of current social problems focus on men and masculinity, such as absent fathers, paedophilia or football hooliganism, through a (dominant) framework of common-sense psychology. Sociologies of men and masculinity have much work to do in problematizing these re-presentations. As pointed out in the Introduction, the difficulty of discussing gender is that we tend to know in a common-sense way (implicitly), the meanings and significance of masculinity. By exploring various approaches to masculinity, specific tools, such as theories of sex-role, discourse analysis, multiple identities and hegemonic masculinities, enable us to understand masculinities as socially constituted and challenge the pervasive psychologicalism in contemporary societies. In this way, sociology may be used as a tool not only to problematize what we know but also as a means of exploring what we have yet to name.

Guided by our second aim, we considered approaches that emphasize the social organization of masculinity and its active cultural production within institutional sites. Institutions such as the state, the family, the workplace and schools are understood as 'masculinity (and femininity)-making devices'. This means that masculinities are institutionally produced with their formations influenced both at local and national levels. At the same time, within these institutional sites, we suggested that masculinities do not exist as exclusive categories but are constituted in complex interrelationships with other social and cultural relations. As a result, corresponding questions of power emerge. Do the contextual specificities that form and inform the constitution of masculinities designate and result in contextually specific power relations? Or does the national context simply act as a filter for the mediation of underlying structures of power?

Feminist thinking has been a major influence on understanding masculinity as a social phenomenon. It has been central to putting masculinity on the gender map, with patriarchal frameworks producing highly insightful analyses of how men's practices are organized (Cockburn 1983; Hearn 1987; Segal 1990; Connell 1995; Kimmel 1996). A key aspect of these frameworks is that they are premised upon the dual oppositions of male and female. As Collinson and Hearn (1996: 63) point out: 'Indeed we find it helpful to see 'men' as a gender that exists or is presumed to exist in most direct relation to the generalised male sex, that being the sex which is not female, or not the sex related to the gender of women'. From this perspective, experiences and practices are epistemologically connected to an identifiable source: the materiality of the body. As Brittan's (1989) work usefully acknowledges, men's practices have been subject to much revision. However while representations of what constitutes the *masculine* have changed historically, he maintains that there has been little change in the power dynamics that are conveyed by those representations. For example, although men's fashions have changed over the last century, the symbolic meanings that are articulated by men's clothing have not. In short, as the male body remains undisturbed, the power relations that flow from it remain untroubled. In making sense of cultural arenas and social relations, male bodies have to be politically accommodated *prior* to any analytical investigations.

Throughout the book materialist approaches have been problematized by emerging approaches that disconnect masculinity from male bodies. Moving beyond engendered bodies is an uncertain project. Uncertainties arise because if the signs of masculinity are free floating, then access to power that these signs carry also become available. As a result, power relations between sexes become unpredictable. We would also want to give visibility to the argument that masculinity is materially unconnected to biology and exists as part of a political relation/understanding of gender;

that any link to biology is created discursively, through language and material practices. In this way we would suggest that 'maleness' – the condition that enables masculinity – is problematically linked to biology and that maleness is a social representation of biology. It is a concept, Butler (1993: 10) suggests, that demands the question: 'Through what regulatory norms is sex materialised?' Analyses of masculinity have too often asserted the social construction of gender, while forcefully and unproblematically authorizing an acknowledgement of differences in sex. It is an acknowledgement that developing a sophisticated and more adequate usage of masculinity needs greater engagement.

The theoretical and conceptual tensions outlined above exist as key dynamics for the exploration of understanding gender in contemporary societies. Our third aim explored the suggested crisis of masculinity. We located this in relation to wider social and cultural transformations in late modernity, drawing upon an historical approach that makes links with earlier periods of structural change. It is popularly believed that men are currently experiencing an intensified sense of disillusionment with what it means to be a man. The question for sociologists is: what does this mean? In contrast to a conservative political explanation that men are now the 'new gender victims', most sociologists of masculinity suggest that men are experiencing the downside of their privileged gender position, what Connell (1995) refers to as the patriarchal dividend. For example, in the sociology of education there is much concern about the suggested disengagement of boys from academic work (Mac an Ghaill 1994a; Haywood and Mac an Ghaill 1995). This is occurring at a time when female students are seen to be achieving higher levels of success. What is important about these different explanations is that they suggest different answers to the question of what is to be done. If boys are the new victims of the gender system, then it may follow that extra material resources should be allocated to them in order that they achieve equity with female students. On the other hand, if their levels of underachievement are connected to the downside of their dominant gender position, then curriculum interventions might be more productively directed to engage with deconstructing contemporary forms of masculinity (Davies 1993).

Our fourth aim allowed us to trace the shift from earlier monocausal models of power to more inclusive forms of power, thus exploring the interplay between different social divisions. This enabled us to understand masculinity as being central to more traditional sociological concerns with conceptions of power and stratification, alongside more recent questions of the body, desire and subjective identity formation. Thus we argue that men and boys experience the patriarchal privilege in different ways. For example, gender relations as a social structure impacting on men and women are cross-cut by other social relations. *Men and Masculinities* draws upon theoretical work that focuses upon current interconnections between gender, sexuality, class, race, ethnicity, nation, age relations and the more subtle inflections of these positions in people's lives (Mercer and Julien 1988; Cohen 1989; Harvey 1989; Giddens 1991; Anthias and Yuval Davis 1992; Bauman 1992; Brah 1992). Empirical findings and theoretical arguments from a range of sociological texts propose a more comprehensive understanding of the social, cultural and psychic investments that males make and remake in institutionally located masculinities and accompanying power relations. Such accounts suggest the need for a multilevel analysis that incorporates explanations at the level of state discourses, institutions, social groups and individuals.

Through our final aim, we explored emerging forms of contemporary masculinities crossculturally, highlighting multiple, collective and multi-layered social practices at local and global levels (Connell 2000). At various points in *Men and Masculinities* we review research on masculinity that has been conducted outside British, American and Australian social contexts. An emphasis is placed on how academic concepts developed and used in the latter national contexts have limited purchase in different social and cultural arenas. One aspect of this is to examine how masculinity has a strategic place in the social and economic infrastructure of developing countries. For example, we explored how other cultures may produce different kinds of genders that are not confined to a rigid fe/male binary. These studies also highlight the symbolic differences in becoming a man. At the same time, the discussion of local cultural formations is contextualized by an exploration of how men and masculinity are implicated in the ascendance of globalization. This complex involvement includes the continuing impact of western capital on men working within a dependency economy, alongside international corporate media representations projecting highly seductive ethnic/cultural masculinities.

Rethinking sex, gender and sexuality

Sociological studies of men and masculinities have emerged through an often disparate and sometimes self-contained development. *Men and Masculinities* suggests that intellectual inquiries can be useful in enhancing existing research in the field, while also establishing social relations and cultural arenas, where a gendered perspective of men may be of strategic need. In this book, arenas such as Work (Chapter 1), Education (Chapter 3) and Politics (Chapter 6) draw upon established sociologies of masculinity that contain sophisticated critical analyses. For example, in the chapter on politics a range of perspectives are available that enable us to make sense of the political nature of men's social practices. At the same time, in areas such as fathering (Chapter 2), globalization (Chapter 4) and researching masculinity (Chapter 5), we argued for the development of sociological analysis which uses masculinities as devices to explore men's lives. At the same time, discussions in these chapters have highlighted a literacy that is developing through which we can speak with greater fluency of the complex relationship between notions of sex, gender and sexuality and the broader social processes surrounding the gendering of men. The key concepts outlined at the beginning of each chapter illustrate how such a literacy is taking shape. Yet creating alternative theoretical and conceptual tools to capture men's experiences and practices are fraught with ambivalence and uncertainty. Studies of masculinities have the potential to collude in the current backlash against feminism by implicitly suggesting that men are now the 'real victims'. Skelton asks: 'What are girls going to get out of the work and effort currently being invested in the focus on boys/masculinities?' (1998: 218). In response, it is intended that *Men and Masculinities* builds on feminist, gay/lesbian and queer scholarship and activism, contributing to the political deconstruction and reconstruction of masculinities (and femininities).

KEY CONCEPTS

Boyness A way of being that is socially ascribed to pre-adolescent males.

Categorical sensibility An understanding of the world that is based on social categories. For example, a categorical sensibility may organize the world through notions such as gender, disability, sexuality or race/ethnicity.

Coming out Private and public performance of sexual identity. It is usually associated with gay/lesbian identities, yet can also be productively used to explore the processes of becoming heterosexual.

Compensatory masculinities Originally understood as masculinities in class relations of production. With capitalism distorting true relations of being, masculinities are developed that compensate for alienating work. The concept can also be used to describe male responses to other existing power relations such as sexuality or disability.

Complex identity formation A recognition of the importance of a range of knowledges that explain how identities are formed. It attempts to move away from simple theories of socialization and singular all-encompassing accounts, such as sex role theory.

Compulsory heterosexuality When heterosexuality is automatic, presumed, or attributed. It often concerns the process of normalizing, where sexual alternatives are excluded and abjected.

Crisis of representation Refers to the philosophical crisis that surrounds the status of 'representation'. For example, it captures the tension between understanding representations as mirror – like reflections of reality and representations as meaning – making devices that constitute reality.

Cross-cultural analysis Research that seeks to identify the origins of cultural ideas, social structures, or ecological arrangements by comparing different societies.

Cultural turn A suggested shift away from the study of structure alongside an increased critical interest in language and how it used to produce meaning in social life. It is within this context of current theoretical advances, particularly in postmodernism and poststructuralism, that, for example, queer theorists have argued for the need to return culture to the centre of the debate on how we are to understand contemporary changing meanings of cultural forms of sexuality and gender.

Culture Has a variety of definitions. It can be used to identify the norms, values and beliefs shared by a given group. It is often used in a variety of contexts, for example: institutional culture, peer culture, subculture, and popular culture. The concept of culture has become a central theme in a wide range of current debates about social change within social and human sciences.

Diaspora Refers to the dispersion of populations across nations. Originally used to refer to a movement of Jewish people. More recently, the term provides ways of exploring the relationship of diverse migrations across fields of social relations, subjectivity and identity.

Dis-embodied masculinity Ways of being masculine that are not sex specific but can be inhabited regardless of social ascriptions of sex, race/ethnicity, sexuality, class or age.

Discourse Refers to specialized and common sense regulated systems of meaning through which we make we make sense of the world. They are constructed in and through particular practices, which make available social identities or subject positions, and which simultaneously entail relations of power. For example, we identify ourselves as female or male, or as gay/lesbian or heterosexual, and could not do so if categorising discourses of gender and sexuality did not exist. In this limited sense, we can be said to be 'produced' by discourses and discursive practices.

Discourse analysis This term has a variety of definitions. One useful way of understanding this method is that it views social relations as texts. As a result, the same principles or rules of language may be applied to social relations. For example, social relations can be considered as authored by a set of narratives.

Dissident masculinities Ways of being male that trouble dominant images of masculinity as projected by, for example the state or the media.

Empiricist approaches Drawing upon positivist philosophies, this perspective emphasizes the collection of facts and observations. Currently this is the major British methodological approach.

Family wage Income from one wage earner used to support a family.

Feckless fathers A term used by the political right to identify men who it is claimed take no social or economic responsibility for their children.

Female homemaker A popular assumption that managing the domestic sphere is a specific female attribute.

Femininity Gendered ways of being and becoming a woman in a given culture.

Feminization A term used to indicate the changing nature of social institutions that is used in a variety of ways. Most commonly it refers to the increasing numbers of women in the workforce. Other definitions focus on the changing culture of work that operates through socially ascribed feminine attributes. For example, the suggested shift from a (masculine) industrial sector to a (feminine) service sector.

Fordism An assembly line system of mass production and standardized goods.

Gay fathers Fathers who identify as gay/the promotion of a lifestyle that is conducive to successful parenting.

Gender identity This concept is used to mark the difference between sex and gender. It highlights the distinction between the *biological determinism* of men and women and the *social construction* of male and female identities. More recently, feminists have problematized this distinction and explored how biological knowledge is itself socially and historically constituted.

Gender regime The institutionally dominant/ascendant arrangement of gender relations.

Gendered nation Refers to ascriptions of gendered characteristics to a national community.

Global masculinities Transnational ways of being and becoming men. In other words, masculinities that are not nationally or locally located.

Globalization The development of extensive worldwide patterns of cultural, social and economic relationships across nations.

Hegemonic masculinity An ascendant masculinity in a particular time and place.

Hegemony Commonly used to describe the domination of one class, nation, or group of people over others. This Gramscian concept emphasizes that domination has to be 'won' and sustained. It includes a notion of complicity carried by those being dominated.

Heterosexual matrix A structure of meaning where heterosexuality is assumed to be a constitutive element of authentic forms of masculinity and femininity.

Heterosexual state The deployment of sexual regulation through government institutions advocating heterosexual lifestyles by promoting particular social and economic policies.

Homophobia The fear of homosexuality in oneself or others.

Hyper-masculinity Extreme performances of (ascribed) masculine norms and values. Often articulated through styles of dress, speech and/or social behaviours.

Macho or *machismo* Usually refers to the exaggerated public display of masculine behavior. The content of the display and enactment can vary within and between cultures.

Male breadwinner A common assumption of the wage earner as a specific male attribute. It tends to be connected with the traditional masculinity of the family patriarch, for whom work is a key element of identity formation.

Masculine schizophrenia A term used to convey oppositional value systems within the masculine psyche.

Masculinism Pertains to the perspectives, practices and institutions which are masculine in orientation. It is sometimes used to compare the continuity of the underlying processes of manhood to the historical variability expressed in 'male' styles.

Masculinities Acknowledges the wide social and cultural variations in being and becoming male.

Masculinity Ways of being and becoming a man in a given culture.

Masculinity politics A set of strategies designed to manage the everyday experience and practice of masculinities. Current mobilizations and struggles around the meaning of masculine power, which foregrounds men's position in gender relations (Connell 1995).

Materialism Refers to a broad philosophical perspective held by those who insist on the primacy of 'matter' as a source of meaning and experience. This means that social relations are based upon a 'fixed' source. For example, early feminist studies located the source of women's oppression in the male body.

Melancholy A grieving for something lost that was never attained in the first place.

Methodology The process involved in the generation of knowledge. Methodology refers to a theory and analysis of how research should proceed, while method refers to techniques for gathering evidence and epistemology refers to an adequate theory of knowledge or justificatory strategy (see Harding 1987a).

Misogyny A term used to refer to the hatred of women.

Masculinity therapy An approach that claims that social change is damaging to men's identity. Key themes include emotional self-exploration, male bonding and recovering damaged relationships with fathers. While some have written of the productive engagement of men with strong women produced in feminism, the dominant position within masculinity therapy often appears to be anti-feminist.

Modernization of masculinity An attempt by masculinity therapy politics to insert traditional meanings of manhood (usually patriarchally orientated) into the modern ways of living.

Multiple masculinities A term used to convey the diversity of ways of enacting masculinity, individually and/or collectively.

Multiple subjectivities Refers to the institutionally defined possibilities of experience. It also captures how experience is multilayered and contradictory.

Mythopoetic men A masculinity therapy movement which asserts that in order for men to gain spiritual stability, they need to get in touch with their true masculine selves. For some groups, myths play an important part as they reveal the true nature of masculinity.

New fathers Refers to an emerging representation of fatherhood as a display of caring, empathy and emotional commitment.

Paternal masculinities Refers to ways of being and becoming men through fatherhood. Also, they may refer to contemporary ascriptions of fathering.

Paternal rights Civil rights assigned by the state to a child's (biological) father.

Patriarchy Commonly understood as a social organization that structures the dominance of men over women.

Patriarchal state Government institutions that sustain and produce a structured inequality between men and women.

Politics of cultural difference An acknowledgement of the complex and contradictory processes involved in the negotiation and reinvention of being, becoming and belonging.

Positivism The study of society based upon the philosophies of the natural sciences. Methods associated with positivism often include scientific observations and experiments.

Postcolonialism A period where subjectivities are generated by and marked by a previous imperial ruler.

Post-Fordism Complex production systems that emphasize flexibility of working relationships (non–hierarchical) in order to meet the specialized demands of a competitive global economy.

Post-identity politics A term used to describe people who do not use social categories to convey commonality and difference, as demonstrated in queer politics.

Poststructuralism As a result, meanings can not be 'read off' in a simplistic manner from an identifiable source. In terms of exploring men and masculinities, this means that the living of sexual/gender categories and divisions is more contradictory, fragmented, shifting and ambivalent than the dominant public definitions of these categories suggest.

Poststructuralist methodology An approach that involves key features of poststructuralist theory in the production of knowledge. For example, poststructuralists tend to view interviews as truth creating mechanisms rather than techniques to access the 'real world'.

Private/public masculinities A term used to capture ways of being and becoming men in private and public spaces. Often refers to a number of social dichotomies such as: domesticity/work, inside/outside, family/state.

Product fetishism A concept used to describe how a cultural identity can be constructed and sustained through identifications with products. Late capitalism offers a diverse range of consumer goods through which differentiated lifestyles are expressed.

Protest masculinity A way of being a man that observes in an exaggerated manner, socially ascribed conventional male behavior.

Queer theory Seeks to destabilize socially given identities, categories and sub-jectivities. At the heart of this destablization, the established gay and lesbian movement is being provoked into exchanging the (partial) security of their social *identity* for a range of political identifications/alliances that are in the process of being assembled (see Mercer 1991).

Sexual minorities Refers to sexualities that are assumed not be to be shared by the sexual majority of a given time or place.

Realist perspective A realist philosophical position that believes in the existence of an underlying material reality that structures the social world.

Relativism Disputes the existence of absolute truth, suggesting that norms, values and beliefs are relative to time and place.

Remasculinization A process whereby existing social and cultural values are superceded by an alternative set of beliefs and values associated with other/particular masculine attributes.

Research as praxis Usually refers to a methodological approach that actively seeks to transform social relations in the process of carrying out research, rather than merely as the result of research outcomes.

Rites of passage Formal and informal cultural initiation ceremonies. Often used to describe the challenges that boy/girls and young men/women have to face and successfully negotiate in order to attain the status of manhood/womanhood.

Second-wave feminism A social movement that has equality of the sexes as a central concern. With its origins in the sixteenth century, second wave feminism developed in the 1960's as an international movement.

Sex role The sex specific behaviour that a person is expected to learn as a member of a particular society.

Sex-role segregation Segregation based upon socially ascribed gender qualities.

Standpoint epistemology A methodological approach that argues that truth can be found in the accounts of people in specific social and cultural situations. The researched are positioned as having special insight into what is 'really going on' in society (Smith 1987).

State Government institutions ruling over a given territory, whose authority is backed by law, enabling the legitimate use of force.

Structural functionalism The study of social and cultural phenomena that emphasizes interrelated functions of society. Structural functionalism is particularly concerned with how institutional norms, values and beliefs determine social behaviours.

Theoretical synthesis The bringing together of different theories. Often used to acknowledge the productiveness of diverse explanatory frameworks.

Technologies of the self A Foucauldian concept used to identify the subjective aspects or processes of identity formation.

Transference Involves the projecting of understandings and feelings generated from relationships in one context onto relationships in another. For example, the researcher or/and the researched may transfer the ways of relating in a family context onto a research relationship.

Transnational genders Genders (masculinities and femininities) that are not specifically connected to localized regions, cultures or practices.

Ubiquitous male A term that presupposes a commonality of masculinity. The ubiquitous male refers to a set of masculine traits that appear to be 'everywhere'.

Working-class resistance A collective response to the capitalist organization of wage labour.

REFERENCES

Abbott, S. (1983) 'In the end you will carry me in your car': Sexual politics in the field. *Women's Studies*, 10: 161–78.

Acker, J. (1992) Gendering organizational theory, in A. Mills and P. Tancred (eds) *Gendering Organizational Analysis*. Newbury Park, CA: Sage.

Addelston, J. and Stirratt, M. J. (1996) The last bastion of masculinity: Gender politics at the Citadel, in M. Kimmel and M. A. Messner (eds) *Men's Lives*. New York: Allyn & Bacon.

Adkins, L. (1998) Feminist theory and economic change, in S. Jackson and J. Jones (eds) *Contemporary Feminist Theories*. Edinburgh: Edinburgh University Press.

Aggleton, P. (1987) *Rebels Without a Cause? Middle Class Youth and the Transition from School to Work*. Lewes: Falmer.

Aggleton, P., Hurry, J. and Warwick, I. (1999) *Young People and Mental Health*. New York: John Wiley.

Ali, T. (1996) *We Are Family: Testimonies of Lesbian and Gay Parents*. London: Cassell.

Alvesson, M. and Billing, Y. D. (1997) *Understanding Gender and Organizations*. London: Sage.

Alvesson, M. and Skoldberg, K. (2000) *Reflexive Methodology: New Vistas for Qualitative Research*. London: Sage.

Anderson, B. (1983) *Imagined Communities: Reflections on the Origin and Spread of Nationalism*. London: Verso.

Anthias, F. and Yuval-Davis, N. (1992) *Racialised Boundaries: Race, Nation, Gender, Colour and Class and the Anti-Racist Struggle*. London: Routledge.

Appaduri, A. (1991) Global ethnoscapes: Notes and queries for a trans-national anthropology, in R. G. Fox (ed.) *Recapturing Anthropology: Working in the Present*. Santa Fe, NM: School of American Research.

Archetti, E. P. (1999) *Masculinities: Football, Polo and the Tango in Argentina*. Oxford: Berg.

Arnot, M. (1984) How shall we educate our sons? in R. Deem (ed.) *Co-education Reconsidered*. Milton Keynes: Open University Press.

Askew, S. and Ross, C. (1988) *Boys Don't Cry: Boys and Sexism in Education*. Milton Keynes: Open University Press.

Baker, P. (1994) Who's afraid of the big bad woman? *The Guardian*, 24 January.

Ballard, J. A. (1992) Sexuality and the state in time of epidemic, in R. W. Connell and G. W. Dowsett (eds) *Rethinking Sex: Social Theory and Sexuality Research*. Melbourne: Melbourne University Press.

Bauman, Z. (1992) *Intimations of Postmodernity*. London: Routledge.

Beechey, V. (1987) *Unequal Work*. London: Verso.

Bell, D., Caplan, P. and Karim, W. J. (eds) (1993) *Gendered Fields: Women, Men and Ethnography*. London: Routledge.

Bem, S. L. (1974) The measurement of psychological androgeny. *Journal of Consulting and Clinical Psychology*, 42: 155–62.

Bertoia, C. E. and Drakich, J. (1995) The fathers' rights movement: contradictions in rhetoric and practice, in W. Marsiglio (ed.) *Fatherhood: Contemporary Theory, Research and Social Practice*. London: Sage.

Beynon, J. (1989) A school for men: An ethnographic case study of routine violence in schooling, in S. Walker and L. Barton (eds) *Politics and the Processes of Schooling*. Milton Keynes: Open University Press.

Bingham, C. (2001) *Schools of Recognition: Identity Politics and Classroom Practices*. Boulder, CO: Rowman & Littlefield.

Biron, R. E. (2000) *Murder and Masculinity: Violent Fictions of Twentieth Century Latin America*. Nashville, TN: Vanderbilt University Press.

Bjornberg, U. (ed.) (1992) *European Parents in the 1990s: Contradictions and Comparisons*. New Brunswick, NJ: Transcation Publication.

Bly, R. (1990) *Iron John: A Book about Men*. Reading, MA: Addison-Wesley.

Bly, R. (1993) *A Book About Men*. Shaftesbury: Element.

Bowles, S. and Gintis, H. (1976) *Schooling in Capitalist America. Educational Reform and the Contradictions of Economic Life*. London: Routledge and Kegan Paul.

Bradley, H. (1996) *Fractured Identities: Changing Patterns of Inequality*. Cambridge: Polity Press.

Bradley, H. (1999) *Gender and Power in the Workplace: Analyzing the Impact of Industrial Change*. Basingstoke: Macmillan.

Brah, A. (1992) Difference, diversity and differentiation, in J. Donald and A. Rattansi (eds) *'Race', Culture and Difference*. Buckingham: The Open University/Sage.

Brah, A., Hickman, M. and Mac an Ghaill, M. (eds) (1999) *Global Futures: Migration, Environment and Globalization*. London: Macmillan.

Branigan, T. (2001) Pink pound rated an adman's chimera, *The Guardian*, 13 August.

Breugal, I. (2000) No more jobs for the boys? Gender and class in the restructuring of the British economy, in M. Cully, S. Woodhead, A. O'Reilly and G. Dix (eds) *Britain at Work*. London: Routledge.

Bristow, J. and Wilson, A. R. (eds) (1993) *Activating Theory: Lesbian, Gay and Bisexual Politics*. London: Lawrence and Wishart.

Brittan, A. (1989) *Masculinity and Power*. New York: Blackwell.

Brod, H. (ed.) (1987) *The Making of Masculinities: The New Men's Studies*. London: Allen & Unwin.

Brunt, R. (1989) The politics of identity, in S. Hall and M. Jacques (eds) *New Times: The Changing Face of Politics in the 1990s*. London: Lawrence and Wishart.

Burgess, A. (1997) *Fatherhood Reclaimed.* London: Vermilion.

Burgess, A. and Ruxton, S. (1996) *Men and Children: Proposals for Public Policy.* London: Institute for Public Policy Research.

Burman, E. (1995) What is it? Masculinity and femininity in cultural representations of childhood, in S. Wilkinson and C. Kitzinger (eds) *Feminism and Discourse: Psychological Perspectives.* London: Sage.

Butler, J. (1990) *Gender Trouble: Feminism and the Subversion of Identity.* London: Routledge.

Butler, J. (1993) *Bodies that Matter, On the Discursive Limits of 'Sex'.* London: Routledge.

Butler, J. (1997) *Excitable Speech: A Politics of the Performative.* New York: Routledge.

Campbell, B. (1993) *Goliath: Britain's Dangerous Places.* London: Methuen.

Canaan, J. and Griffin, C. (1990) The new men's studies: Part of the problem or part of the solution? in J. Hearn and D. Morgan (eds) *Men, Masculinities and Social Theory.* London: Unwin Hyman.

Carlsen, S. (1993) New Scandinavian experiences, in *Fathers in Families Tomorrow.* Report from the Conference held in Copenhagen, 17–18 June, Copenhagen: Ministry of Social Affairs.

Castells, M. (1997) *The Information Age: Economy, Society and Culture. Vol. II: The Power of Identity.* London: Routledge.

Central Statistical Office (CSO) (2001) *Social Trends.* London: The Stationery Office.

Chapman, R. and Rutherford, J. (eds) (1988) *Male Order: Unwrapping Masculinity.* London: Lawrence and Wishart.

Cheal, D. (1991) *Family and State Theory.* Hemel Hemstead: Harvester Wheatsheaf.

Christian, H. (1994) *The Making of Anti-sexist Men.* London: Routledge.

Clatterbaugh, K. (1990) *Contemporary Perspectives on Masculinity.* Oxford: Westview Press.

Cockburn, C. (1983) *Brothers: Male Dominance and Technological Change.* London: Pluto.

Cockburn, C. (1985) *Machinery of Dominance: Women, Men and Technical Know-how.* London: Pluto.

Cohen, C. B. (1996) Contestants in a contested domain: Staging identities in British Virgin Islands, in C. Cohen, R. Wilk and B. Stoeltje (eds) *Beauty Queens on the Global Stage: Gender, Contests and Power.* New York: Routledge.

Cohen, P. (1989) *Really Useful Knowledge: Photography and Cultural Studies in the Transition from School.* London: Trentham.

Collier, R. (1995) *Masculinity, Law and the Family.* London: Routledge.

Collier, R. (1998) *Masculinities, Crime and Criminology: Men, Heterosexuality and the Criminal(ised) Other.* London: Sage.

Collinson, D. L. (1992) *Managing the Shopfloor: Subjectivity, Masculinity, and Workplace Culture.* New York: W. de Gruyter.

Collinson, D. L. and Hearn, J. (eds) (1996) *Men as Managers, Managers as Men: Critical Perspectives on Men, Masculinities and Managements.* London: Sage.

Connell, R. W. (1987) *Gender And Power: Society, the Person and Sexual Politics.* Cambridge: Polity Press.

Connell, R. W. (1989) Cool guys, swots and wimps: the inter-play of masculinity and education. *Oxford Review of Education,* 15(3): 291–303.

Connell, R. W. (1990) The state, gender and sexual politics. *Theory and Society,* 19(5): 507–44.

Connell, R. W. (1995) *Masculinities.* Cambridge: Polity Press.

Connell, R. W. (2000) *The Men and the Boys.* London: Polity.

Connolly, P. (1998) *Racism, Gender Identities, and Young Children: Social Relations in a Multi-ethnic, Inner-city Primary School*. New York: Routledge.

Cook, J. A. and Fonow, M. M. (1986) Knowledge and women's interests: Issues of epistemology and methodology in feminist sociological research. *Sociological Inquiry*, 56: 2–29.

Cornwall, A. and Lindisfarne, N. (1994) Dislocating masculinity: Gender, power and anthropology, in A. Cornwall and N. Lindisfarne, *Dislocating Masculinity: Gender, Power and Anthropology*. London: Routledge.

Davies, B. (1993) *Shards of Glass: Children, Reading and Writing beyond Gendered Identities*. Sydney: Allen & Unwin.

Davies, B. and Harre, R. (1990) Positioning: The discursive production of selves. *Journal for the Theory of Social Behaviour*, 20(1): 43–64.

Davies, B. and Hunt, R. (1994) Classroom competencies and marginal positionings. *British Journal of Sociology*, 15(3): 389–408.

Delphy, C. (1984) *Close to Home: A Materialist Analysis of Women's Oppression*. London: Hutchinson in association with Explorations in Feminist Collective.

D'Emilio, J. (1983) *Sexual Politics, Sexual Communities: The Making of a Homosexual Minority in the United States 1940–1970*. Chicago, IL: University of Chicago Press.

Dennis, N., Henriques, F. and Slaughter, C. (1969) *Coal is Our Life*. London: Tavistock.

Denzin, N. K. (1994) Evaluating qualitative research in the post-structural moment: the lessons James Joyce teaches us. *International Qualitative Studies in Education*, 7: 64–88.

Department for Social Security (DSS) (1991) Child Support Act. London: Sweet & Maxwell.

Derrida, J. (1978) *Writing and Difference*. Chicago, IL: University of Chicago Press.

Dicken, P. (1998) *Global Shift: Transforming the World Economy*. London: Paul Chapman.

Digby, J. (1998) *Men Doing Feminism*. London: Routledge.

Dobash, R. E., Dobash, R. and Harry Frank Guggenheim Foundation (1998) *Rethinking Violence Against Women*. Thousand Oaks, CA: Sage Publications.

Dollimore, J. (1991) *Sexual Dissidence: Augustine to Wilde, Freud to Foucault*. Oxford: Clarendon Press.

Douglas, A. (1977) *The Feminization of American Culture*. New York: Alfred A. Knopf.

Drummond, M. (1994) Masculinity from a feminist perspective: Or how feminism helped construct the new man. *Issues in Educational Research*, 4(2): 95–102.

Du Gay, P. (1996) *Consumption and Identity at Work*. London: Sage.

Dunne, G. A. (1999) A passion for 'sameness'? Sexuality and gender accountability, in E. B. Silva and C. Smart (eds) *The 'New' Family?* London: Sage.

Dunne, G. A. (2001) *The Lady Vanishes? Reflections on the Experiences of Married and Divorced Gay Fathers*. http: www.scoresonline.org.uk/6/3/dunne.html (accessed 27 January 2002).

Dunphy, R. (2000) *Sexual Politics: An Introduction*. Edinburgh: Edinburgh University Press.

Dyer, R. (1993) *The Matter of Images: Essays on Representation*. London: Routledge.

Easthope, A. (1990) *What a Man's Gotta Do: The Masculine Myth in Popular Culture*. Boston, MA: Unwin Hyman.

Edgar, D. (1981) Reagan's hidden agenda. *Race and Class*, 22(3): 207–23.

Edwards, T. (1994) *Erotics and Politics: Gay Male Sexuality, Masculinity and Feminism*. London: Routledge.

Edwards, T. (1998) Queer fears: Against the cultural turn. *Sexualities*, 1(4): 471–84.

Eichler, M. (1988) *Non-sexist Research Methods: A Practical Guide*. Boston, MA: Allen & Unwin.

Epstein, D. (ed.) (1994) *Challenging Lesbian and Gay Inequalities in Education*. Buckingham: Open University Press.

Epstein, D. and Johnson, R. (1998) *Schooling Sexualities*. Buckingham: Open University Press.

Ervo, S. and Johansson, T. (eds) (1999) *Bending Bodies: Moulding Masculinities*, Vol. 2. Aldershot: Ashgate.

European Commission Network on Childcare (1993) *Men as Carers: Report of an International Seminar in Ravenna*. Brussels: European Commission Network on Childcare.

Evans, D. (1993) *Sexual Citizenship: The Material Construction of Sexualities*. London: Routledge.

Faludi, S. (1999) *Stiffed: The Betrayal of the Modern Man*. London: Chatto Windus.

Fanon, F. (1970) *Black Skins, White Masks*. London: Paladin.

Farrell, W. (1974) *The Liberated Man*. New York: Random House.

Farrell, W. (1994) *The Myth of Male Power: Why are Men the Disposable Sex?* New York: Fourth Estate.

Featherstone, M., Hepworth, M. and Turner, B. (eds) (1991) *The Body: Social Processes and Cultural Theory*. London: Sage.

Finch, J. (1984) 'It's great to have someone to talk to': The ethics and politics of interviewing women, in C. Bell and H. Roberts (eds) *Social Researching: Politics, Problems, Practice*. London: Routledge and Kegan Paul.

Flood, M. (2000) Lust, trust and latex: Why young heterosexual men don't use condoms. Unpublished PhD thesis, Australian National University.

Forrest, D. (1994) 'We're here, we're queer, and we're not going shopping': Changing gay male identities in contemporary Britain, in A. Cornwall and N. Lindisfarne (eds) *Dislocating Masculinity: Comparative Ethnographies*. London: Routledge.

Foster, V., Kimmel, M. and Skelton, C. (2001) 'What about the boys?': An overview of the debates, in W. Martino and B. Meyenn (eds) *What about the Boys? Issues of Masculinity in Schools*. Buckingham: Open University Press.

Foucault, M. (1977) *Discipline and Punish*. London: Allen Lane.

Foucault, M. (1981) *The History of Sexuality*, Vol. 1. Harmondsworth: Penguin.

Fox, K. (2000) Time to commit, *The Pink Paper*, 5 December, 31–6.

Frank, B. W. (1993) The 'new men's studies' and feminism: Promise or danger? in T. Haddad (ed.) *Men and Masculinities: A Critical Anthology*. Toronto: Canadian Scholars' Press.

Frosh, S. (1994) *Sexual Difference: Masculinity and Psychoanalysis*. London: Routledge.

Fukuyama, F. (1989) 'The end of history?' *National Interest*, 16: 3–18.

Furstenberg, F. F. (1988) Good dads – bad dads: Two faces of fatherhood, in A. J. Cherlin (ed.) *The Changing American Family and Public Policy*. Washington DC: Urban Institute.

Gamson, P. (1995) Must identity problems self destruct? A queer dilemma. *Social Problems*, 42: 390–407.

Gennep, A. V. (1960) *The Rites of Passage*. London: Routledge & Kegan Paul.

Gerwitz, S. (1997) Post-welfarism and the reconstruction of teachers' work in the UK. *Journal of Education Policy*, 12(4): 217–31.

Gheradi, S. (1995) *Gender, Symbolism and Organizational Cultures*. London: Sage.

Giddens, A. (1991) *Modernity and Self-Identity*. Cambridge: Polity Press.

Giddens, A. (1993) *The Transformation of Intimacy: Sexuality, Love and Eroticism in Modern Societies*. Cambridge: Polity Press.

Gilbert, R. and Gilbert, P. (1998) *Masculinity Goes to School*. Sydney: Allen & Unwin.

Gilmore, D. (1990) *Manhood in the Making: Cultural Concepts of Masculinity*. New Haven, CD: Yale University Press.

Golde, P. (1970) *Women in the Field: Anthropological Experiences*. Berkeley, CA: University of California Press.

Goodwin, J. (1999) *Men's Work and Male Lives: Men and Work in Britain*. Aldershot: Ashgate.

Goss, R. E. and Strongheart, A. A. S. (eds) (1997) *Our Families, Our Values: Snapshots of Queer Kinship*. New York: Haworth Press.

Gramsci, A. (1971) *Selections from the Prison Notebooks*. London: Lawrence & Wishart.

Grant, L. (1994) Soldiers in the sex war, *The Guardian*, 22 February.

Grint, K. (1998) *The Sociology of Work: An Introduction*. Cambridge: Polity Press.

Guba, E. G. (1990) Subjectivity and objectivity, in E. W. Eisner and A. Peshkin (eds) *Qualitative Inquiry in Education: The Continuing Debate*. New York: Columbia University Press/Teachers College Press.

Gutmann, M. C. (1996) *The Meanings of Macho: Being a Man in Mexico City*. Berkeley, CA: University of California Press.

Halberstam, J. (1998) *Female Masculinity*. Durham, NC: Duke University Press.

Hall, C. (1992) *White, Male and Middle-Class: Explorations in Feminism and History*. Cambridge: Polity, Press.

Hall, S. (1991) The local and the global: Globalization and ethnicity, in A. D. King (ed.) *Culture, Globalization and World System*. London: Macmillan.

Hall, S. (1992) The question of cultural identity, in S. Hall, D. Held and T. McCrew (eds) *Modernity and Its Futures*. London: Polity/The Open University.

Hamada, T. (1996) Unwrapping Euro-American masculinity in a Japanese multinational corporation, in C. Cheng (ed.) *Masculinities in Organization*. Thousand Oaks, CA: Sage Publications.

Hansard (2001) Written Answers, 5 April 2002. Part 10, column 498W. London: HMSO.

Harding, S. (1987a) Introduction: Is there a feminist method? in S. Harding (ed.) *Feminism and Methodology*: Social Science Issues. Milton Keynes: Open University Press.

Harding, S. (1987b) Conclusion: Epistemological questions, in S. Harding (ed.) *Feminism and Methodology: Social Science Issues*. Milton Keynes: Open University Press.

Harding, S. (1991) *Whose Science? Whose Knowledge? Thinking from Women's Lives*. Buckingham: Open University Press.

Harrison, M., Snider, G. and Merlo, R. (1990) *Who Pays for the Children?* Melbourne: Australian Institute of Family Studies.

Harstock, N. E. M. (1983) The feminist standpoint: Developing the ground for a specifically feminist historical materialism, in S. Harding and M. Hintikka (eds) *Discovering Reality: Feminist Perspectives on Epistemology, Metaphysics, Methodology and Philosophy of Science*. Dordrecht, Holland: Reidel Publishing Company.

Harvey, D. (1989) *The Conditions of Post-Modernity*. Oxford: Blackwell.

Hawkes, G. (1996) *The Sociology of Sex and Sociology*. Buckingham: Open University Press.

Haywood, C. P. (1993) Using sexuality: An exploration into the fixing of sexuality to make male identities in a mixed sex sixth form. Unpublished MA dissertation, University of Warwick.

Haywood, C. P. (1996) 'Out of the curriculum': Sex talking, talking sex. *Curriculum Studies*, 4(2): 226–49.

Haywood, C. P. (2003) Schooling and sexuality: The politics of desire. Unpublished PhD thesis, to be submitted University of Newcastle.

Haywood, C. and Mac an Ghaill, M. (1995) The sexual politics of the curriculum: Contesting values. *International Studies in Sociology of Education*, 5(2): 221–36.

Haywood, C. and Mac an Ghaill, M. (1997a) Materialism and deconstructivism: education and the epistemology of identity. *Cambridge Journal of Education*, 27(2): 261–72.

Haywood, C. and Mac an Ghaill, M. (1997b) A man in the making: Sexual masculinities within changing training cultures. *The Sociological Review*, 45(4): 576–90.

Haywood, C. and Mac an Ghaill, M. (1997c) Masculinity and social change: Rethinking sexual politics. *Social Alternatives*, 16(3): 11–13.

Haywood, C. and Mac an Ghaill, M. (2001) The significance of teaching English boys: Exploring social change, modern schooling and the making of masculinities, in W. Martino and B. Meyenn (eds) *What About the Boys?* Buckingham: Open University Press.

Hearn, J. (1987) *The Gender of Oppression: Men, Masculinity and the Critique of Marxism*. Brighton: Harvester Wheatsheaf.

Hearn, J. (1992) *Men in the Public Eye: The Construction and Deconstruction of Public Men and Public Patriarchies*. London: Routledge.

Hearn, J. (1993a) *Researching Men and Researching Men's Violences*. Research Paper No. 4. Research Unit on Violence, Abuse and Gender Relations: University of Bradford.

Hearn, J. (1993b) The politics of essentialism and the analysis of the men's movement. *Feminism and Psychology*, 3: 405–10.

Hearn, J. (1996) Is masculinity dead? A critique of the concept of masculinity/masculinities, in M. Mac an Ghaill (ed.) *Understanding Masculinities: Social Relations and Cultural Arenas*. Buckingham: Open University Press.

Hearn, J. and Morgan, D. (eds) (1990) *Men: Masculinities and Social Theory*. London: Hyman and Unwin.

Hearn, J. and Parkin, W. (2001) *Gender, Sexuality and Violence in Organizations*. London: Sage.

Hemphill, E. (ed.) (1991) *Brother to Brother: New Writings by Black Gay Men*. Boston, MA: Alyson.

Henriques, J., Hollway, W., Urwin, C., Venn, C. and Walkerdine, V. (eds) (1984) *Changing the Subject: Psychology, Social Regulation and Subjectivity*. London: Methuen.

Heward, C. (1988) *Making a Man of Him: Parents and their Sons' Careers at an English Public School 1929–1950*. London: Routledge.

Heward, C. (1991) Public school masculinities: An essay in gender and power, in G. Walford (ed.) *Private Schooling: Tradition, Change and Diversity*. London: Paul Chapman.

Hewlett, B. (1991) *Intimate Fathers: The Nature and Content of Aka Pygmy Paternal Infant Care*. Ann Arbor, MI: University of Michigan.

Hodson, D. L. (1999) 'Once intrepid warriors': Modernity and the production of Massai masculinities. *Ethnology*, 38(2): 121–51.

Hofstede, G. H. (1998) *Masculinity and Femininity: The Taboo Dimension of National Cultures*. Thousand Oaks, CA: Sage Publications.

Hollway, W. (1989) *Subjectivity and Method in Psychology: Gender, Meaning and Science*. London: Sage.

Hollway, W. (1996) Masters and men in the transition from factory hands to sentimental workers, in D. Collinson and J. Hearn (eds) *Men as Managers, Managers as Men: Critical Perspectives on Men, Masculinities, and Managements*. London: Sage.

Hollway, W. and Jefferson, T. (2000) *Doing Qualitative Research Differently: Free Association, Narrative and the Interview Method*. London: Sage.

Hood, J. C. (1993) *Men, Work and the Family*. Beverly Hills: Sage.

Hood-Williams, J. (1996) Good-bye to sex and gender. *Sociological Review*, 44(1): 1–16.

Hooper, C. (2000) *Manly States: Masculinities, International Relations, and Gender Politics*. New York: Columbia University Press.

Horna, J. and Lupri, E. (1987) Fathers' participation in work, family life and leisure: A Canadian experience, in C. Lewis and M. O'Brien (eds) *Reassessing Fatherhood: New Observations on Fathers and Modern Family*. London: Sage.

Humm, M. (1992) *Feminisms: A Reader*. London: Harvester Wheatsheaf.

Hutchinson, S. and Wilson, H. (1994) Research and therapeutic interviews: A poststructuralist perspective, in J. M. Morse (ed.) *Critical Issues in Qualitative Research Methods*. Newbury Park, CA: Sage Publications.

Jameson, F. (1985) Postmodernism and consumer society, in H. Foster (ed.) *Postmodern Culture*. London: Pluto Press.

Jamieson, L. (1998) *Intimacy: Personal Relationships in Modern Society*. Cambridge: Polity Press.

Jansen, S. C. and Sabo, D. (1994) The sport/war metaphor: Hegemonic masculinity, the Persian Gulf War and the New World Order. *Sociology of Sport Journal*, 11: 1–17.

Jardine, A. and Smith, P. (eds) (1992) *Men in Feminism*. New York: Methuen.

Jefferson, T. (1994) Theorising masculine subjectivity, in T. Newburn and E. Stanko (eds) *Just Boys Doing Business: Men, Masculinities and Crime*. London: Routledge.

Jeffords, S. (1994) *Hard Bodies: Hollywood Masculinity in the Reagan Era*. New Brunswick, NJ: Rutgers University Press.

Kahn, A. J. and Kamerman, S. B. (1988) *Child Support*. New York: Sage.

Kaplan, D. (2000) The military as a second bar mitzvah, in M. Ghoussoub and E. Sinclair-Webb (eds) *Imagined Masculinities*. London: Saqi Books.

Kehily, M. (2001) Boys in school: Young men, embodiment, and heterosexual masculinities. *Men and Masculinities*, 4(2): 173–85.

Kim, S. K. (1997) *Class Struggle or Family Struggle: The Lives of Women Factory Workers in Korea*. Cambridge: Cambridge University Press.

Kimmel, M. (1987a) *Changing Men: New Directions in Research on Men and Masculinity*. New York: Sage.

Kimmel, M. S. (1987b) Rethinking 'masculinity': New directions in research, in M. S. Kimmel (ed.) *Changing Men: New Directions in Research on Men and Masculinity*. London: Sage.

Kimmel, M. S. (1987c) The contemporary 'crisis' of masculinity in historical perspective, in H. Brod (ed.) *The Making of Masculinities: The New Men's Studies*. London: Allen & Unwin.

Kimmel, M. (1996) *Manhood in America: A Cultural History*. New York: The Free Press.

Kimmel, M. and Messner, M. (eds) (1989) *Men's Lives*. London: Macmillan.

Kincaid, J. R. (1992) *Child-loving: The Erotic Child and Victorian Culture.* New York: Routledge.

Kinealy, S. (1999) *A Disuniting Kingdom: England, Scotland and Wales.* Cambridge: Cambridge University Press.

King, J. R. (1999) Am not! Are too! Using queer standpoint in postmodern critical ethnography. *International Journal of Qualitative Studies in Education,* 12(5): 473–90.

Kirsch, M. H. (2000) *Queer Theory and Social Change.* London: Routledge.

Klein, M. (1964) *Love, Hate and Reparation.* New York: Norton.

Klein, U. (1999) 'Our best boys': The gendered nature of civil-military relations in Israel. *Men and Masculinities,* 2(1): 47–65.

Knights, D. (1990) Subjectivity, power and the labour process, in D. Knights and H. Willmott (eds) *Labour Process Theory.* London: Macmillan.

Kremer, B. (1990) Learning to say no: Keeping feminist research for ourselves. *Women's Studies International Forum,* 13: 463–8.

Ku, L., Sonenstein, F. L. and Pleck, J. H. (1993) Neighbourhood, family and work: Influences on the pre-marital behaviours of adolescent males. *Social Forces,* 72(2): 479–503.

Lancaster, R. N. (1992) *Life is Hard: Machismo, Danger and the Intimacy of Power in Nicaragua.* Berkeley, CA: University of California Press.

Lather, P. (1991) *Getting Smart: Feminist Research and Pedagogy with/in the Postmodern.* New York: Routledge.

Lee, D. (1997) Interviewing men: Vulnerabilities and dilemmas. *Women's Studies International Forum,* 20(4): 553–64.

Lee, D. (2000) Hegemonic masculinity and male feminization: The sexual harassment of men at work. *Journal of Gender Studies,* 9(2): 47–65.

Lemert, C. C. (1990) Post-structralism and sociology, in G. Ritzer (ed.) *Frontiers of Social Theory.* New York: Columbia University Press.

Lewis, C. (1986) *Becoming a Father.* Milton Keynes: Open University Press.

Lewis, C. and O'Brien, M. (1987) Constraints on fathers: Research, theory and clinical practice, in C. Lewis and M. O'Brien (eds) *Reassessing Fatherhood: New Observations on Fathers and the Modern Family.* London: Sage.

Ling, L. H. M. (1999) Sex machine: Global hyper-masculinity and images of the Asian woman in modernity. *Positions,* 7(2): 277–306.

Lovenduski, J. (1999) Sexing political behavior, in S. Walby (ed.) *New Agendas for Women.* New York: St. Martin's Press.

Lowe, A. (2000) *Past Postmodernism: Interviews, Accounts and the Production of Research Stories.* http://visar.csustan.edu/papers/Lowe95.pdf (accessed 5 January 2001).

Luxton, M. (1993) Dreams and dilemmas: Feminist musings on the 'man question', in T. Haddad (ed.) *Men and Masculinities: A Critical Anthology.* Toronto: Canadian Scholars' Press.

Lyndon, N. (1992) *No More Sex War: The Failures of Feminism.* London: Mandarin.

Lyotard, J. F. (1994) The postmodern condition, in S. Seidman (ed.) *The Postmodern Turn: New Perspectives on Social Theory.* New York: Cambridge University Press.

Mac an Ghaill, M. (1994a) *The Making of Men: Masculinities, Sexualities and Schooling.* Buckingham: Open University Press.

Mac an Ghaill, M. (1994b) (In)visibility: Sexuality, masculinity and race in the school context, in D. Epstein (ed.) *Challenging Gay and Lesbian Inequalities in Education.* Buckingham: Open University Press.

Mac an Ghaill, M. (1994c) The making of black English masculinities, in H. Brod and M. Kaufman (eds) *Theorizing Masculinities*. London: Sage.

Mac an Ghaill, M. (ed.) (1996a) *Understanding Masculinities*. Buckingham: Open University Press.

Mac an Ghaill, M. (1996b) Irish masculinities and sexualities, in L. Adkins and V. Merchant (eds) *Sexualizing the Social: Power and the Organization of Sexuality*. London: Macmillan.

Mac an Ghaill, M. (1999) *Contemporary Racisms and Ethnicities: Social and Cultural Transformations*. Buckingham: Open University Press.

Mac an Ghaill, M. (2000) What about the lads? – Emigrants, immigrants, ethnics and transnationals, in R. Lentin (ed.) *Emerging Irish Identities*. Dublin: Trinity College Dublin/The National Consultative Committee on Racism and Interculturalism.

MacInnes, J. (1998) *The End of Masculinity: The Confusion of Sexual Genesis and Sexual Difference in Modern Society*. Buckingham: Open University Press.

McKee, L. and O'Brien, M. (eds) (1982) *The Father Figure*. London: Tavistock.

McKegany, N. and Bloor, M. (1991) Spotting the invisible man: The influence of male gender on fieldwork relations. *British Journal of Sociology*, 42(2): 195–210.

McKeown, K., Ferguson, H. and Rooney, D. (eds) (2000) *Changing Fathers? Fatherhood and Family Life in Modern Ireland*. Cork: The Collins Press.

McKinnon, C. A. (1989) *Toward a Feminist Theory of the State*. Cambridge, MA: Harvard University Press.

McIntosh, M. (1993) Queer theory and the war of the sexes, in J. Bristow and E. Wilson (eds) *Activating Theory: Lesbian, Gay and Bisexual Politics*. London: Lawrence and Wishart.

McLean, C., Lewis, S., Copeland, J., O'Neil, B. and Lintern, S. (1997) Masculinity and the culture of engineering. *Australian Journal of Engineering Education*, 7(2): 143–56.

McRobbie, A. (1991) *Feminism and Youth Culture: From 'Jackie' to 'Just Seventeen'*. London: Macmillan.

Marchand, M. H. and Runyan, A. S. (2000) Introduction: Feminist sightings of global restructuring, in M. H. Marchand and A. S. Runyan (eds) *Gender and Global Restructuring: Sightings, Sites and Resistances*. London: Routledge.

Marcus, G. and Fischer, M. (1986) *Anthropology as Cultural Critique: An Experimental Moment in the Human Sciences*. Chicago, IL: University of Chicago Press.

Martino, W. (1999) 'Cool boys', 'party animals', 'squids' and 'poofters': Interrogating the dynamics and politics of adolescent masculinities in school. *British Journal of Sociology of Education*, 20(2): 239–63.

Marx, K. (1972) *Karl Marx: Economy, Class and Social Revolution: Selected Writings of Karl Marx*, ed. Z. A. Jordan. London: Nelson.

May, L. (1998) A progressive male standpoint, in T. Digby (ed.) *Men Doing Feminism*. London: Routledge.

Maynard, M. (1990) Trend report: The reshaping of sociology? Trends in the study of gender. *Sociology*, 24(2): 269–90.

Mayo, E. (1933) *The Human Problems of Industrial Civilization*. New York: Macmillan.

Mercer, K. (1990) Welcome to the jungle: Identity and diversity in post-modern politics, in J. Rutherford (ed.) *Identity, Community and Difference*. London: Lawrence and Wishart.

Mercer, K. (1991) Skin head sex thing: Racial differences and homoerotic imagery, in Bad Object Choices (eds) *How Do I Look? Queer Film and Video*. Seattle, WA: Bay Press.

Mercer, K. and Julien, I. (1988) Race, sexual politics and black masculinity: a dossier, in R. Chapman and J. Rutherford (eds) *Male Order: Unwrapping Masculinity*. London: Lawrence and Wishart.

Messerschmidt, J. W. (1995) Managing to kill: Masculinities and the space shuttle Challenger explosion, *Masculinities*, 3(4): 1–22.

Metcalf, A. (1985) Introduction, in A. Metcalf and M. Humphries (eds) *The Sexuality of Men*. London: Pluto Press.

Metcalf, A. and Humphries, M. (eds) (1985) *The Sexuality of Men*. London: Pluto Press.

Middleton, P. (1989) Socialism, feminism and men. *Radical Philosophy*, 53: 8–19.

Middleton, P. (1992) *The Inward Gaze: Masculinity, Subjectivity and Modern Culture*. London: Routledge.

Miedzian, M. (1991) *Boys Will Be Boys: Breaking the Link Between Masculinity and Violence*. New York: Doubleday.

Millar, J. (1994) State, family and personal responsibility: The changing balance for lone mothers in the United Kingdom. *Feminist Review*, 48: 24–40.

Millar, S. (1997) Here comes trouble, *The Guardian*, 13 February.

Millman, M. and Kanter, M. K. (1987) Introduction to another voice: Feminist perspectives on social life and social science, in S. Harding (ed.) *Feminism and Methodology: Social Science Issues*. Milton Keynes: Open University Press.

Mills, C. W. (1956) *The Power Elite*. New York: Oxford University Press.

Mirandé, A. (1997) *Hombres y Machos: Masculinity and Latino Culture*. Boulder, CO: Westview Press.

Morgan, D. (1969a) Theoretical and conceptual problems in the study of social relations at work: an analysis of the differing definitions of women's roles in a northern factory. Unpublished PhD thesis, University of Manchester.

Morgan, D. (1969b) The social educational backgrounds of Anglican bishops – continuities and changes. *British Journal of Sociology*, 20: 295–310.

Morgan, D. (1981) Men, masculinity and sociological enquiry, in H. Roberts (ed.) *Doing Feminist Research*. London: Routledge.

Morgan, D. (1992) *Discovering Men*. London: Routledge.

Mort, F. (1996) *Cultures of Consumption: Masculinities and Social Space in Late Twentieth-Century Britain*. London: Routledge.

Morton, D. (1995) Birth of the cyberqueer. *PMLA*, 110(3): 369–81.

Moss, P. (1995) *Father Figures: Fathers in the Families of the 1990s*. Edinburgh: HMSO.

Mosse, G. L. (1985) *Nationalism and Sexuality: Middle Class Morality and Sexual Norms in Modern Europe*. Madison, WI: University of Wisconsin Press.

Mostov, J. (2000) Sexing the nation: Politics of national identity in the former Yugoslavia, in T. Mayer (ed.) *Gender Ironies of Nationalism*. London: Routledge.

Mumford, K. J. (1993) 'Lost manhood found': Male sexual impotence and victorian culture in the United States. *Journal of the History of Sexuality*, 3(1): 5–14.

Murray, C. (1989) *The Emerging British Underclass*. London: Institute of Economic Affairs.

Murray, C. (1994) *Underclass: the Crisis Deepens*. London: IEA Health and Welfare Unit.

Nandy, A. (1991) *The Intimate Enemy: Loss and Recovery of Self under colonialism*. Delhi: Oxford University Press.

Nichols, J. (1975) *Men's Liberation*. New York: Penguin.

Nicholson, L. J. (ed.) (1990) *Feminism/Postmodernism*. London: Routledge.

Niva, S. (1998) Tough and tender: New World Order masculinity and the Gulf War, in M. Zalewski and J. Parpart (eds) *The Man Question and International Politics*. Oxford: Westview Press.

Oakley, A. (1974) *The Sociology of Housework*. London: Martin Robertson.

Oakley, A. (1981) Interviewing women: A contradiction in terms, in H. Roberts (ed.) *Doing Feminist Research*. London: Routledge and Kegan Paul.

Office of Population Censuses and Surveys (OPCS) (1999) *Labour Force Survey: Spring Quarters Historical Supplement*. London: HMSO.

Office of Population Censuses and Surveys (OPCS) (2001) *Labour Force Survey: Quarterly Supplement (February)*. London: HMSO.

Pahl, R. E. (1984) *Divisions of Labour*. Oxford: Blackwell.

Pajaczkowska, C. and Young, L. (1992) Racism, representation, psychoanalysis, in J. Donald and A. Rattansi (eds) *Race, Culture and Difference*. London: Sage.

Parpart, J. (1998) Conclusions: New thoughts and directions for the 'man' question in international relations, in M. Zalewski and J. Parpart (eds) *The Man Question and International Politics*. Oxford: Westview Press.

Parsons, T. (1955) The American father: Its relation to personality and to social structure, in T. Parsons and R. F. Bales (eds) *Family Socialization and Interaction Process*. New York: The Free Press.

Parsons, T. and Bales, R. F. (eds) (1955) *Family Socialization and Interaction Process*. New York: The Free Press.

Pease, B. (2000) *Recreating Men: Postmodern Masculinity Politics*. London: Sage.

Peteet, J. (2000) Male gender and rituals in the Palestinian Intifada, in M. Ghoussoub and E. Sinclair-Webb (eds) *Imagined Masculinities*. London: Saqi Books.

Petersen, A. R. (1998) *Unmasking the Masculine: 'Men' and 'Identity' in a Sceptical Age*. London: Sage Publications.

Phillips, A. (ed.) (1998) *Feminism and Politics*. Oxford: Oxford University Press.

Phizacklea, A. (1990) *Unpacking the Fashion Industry*. London: Routledge.

Pleck, J. H. (1981) *The Myth of Masculinity*. Cambridge, MA: MIT Press.

Pleck, J. (1987) American fathering in historical perspective, in M. Kimmel (ed.) *Changing Men: New Directions in Research on Men and Masculinity*. London: Sage.

Plummer, K. (ed.) (1981) *The Making of the Modern Homosexual*. London: Hutchinson.

Plummer, K. (1992) *Modern Homosexualities*. London: Routledge.

Plummer, K. (1995) *Telling Sexual Stories: Power, Change, and Social Worlds*. London: Routledge.

Pollack, W. (1998) *Real Boys: Rescuing Our Sons from the Myths of Boyhood*. New York: Henry Holt and Company.

Pollert, A. (1981) *Girls, Wives, Factory Lives*. London: Macmillan.

Prieur, A. and Taksdal, A. (1993) Clients of prostitutes – Sick deviants or ordinary men? A discussion of the male role and cultural changes in masculinity. *Nora*, 1(2): 105–14.

Probyn, E. (1993) *Sexing the Self: Gendered Positions in Cultural Studies*. London: Routledge.

Pronger, B. (1990) *The Arena of Masculinity: Sports, Homosexuality and the Meaning of Sex*. London: Gay Men's Press.

Ramazanoglu, C. (1989) *Feminisms and the Contradictions of Oppression*. London: Routledge.

Ramazanoglu, C. (1992) On feminist methodology: Male reason versus female empowerment. *Sociology*, 26(2): 207–12.

Rapoport, R. N., Fogarty, M. and Rapoport, R. (1982) *Families in Britain*. London: Routledge and Kegan Paul.

Rattansi, A. (1992) Changing the subject? Racism, culture and education, in J. Donald and A. Rattansi (eds) *Race, Culture and Difference*. London: Sage.

Redman, P. (1994) Shifting ground: Rethinking sexuality education, in D. Epstein (ed.) *Challenging Lesbian and Gay Inequalities in Education*. Buckingham: Open University Press.

Redman, P. (2001) The discipline of love: Negotiation and regulation in boys' performance of a romance-based heterosexual masculinity. *Men and Masculinities*, 4(2): 186–200.

Redman, P. and Mac an Ghaill, M. (1996) Schooling sexualities: Heterosexual masculinities, schooling, and the unconscious. *Discourse*, 17(2): 243–56.

Renold, E. (2000) 'Coming out': Gender, (hetero)sexuality and the primary school. *Gender and Education*, 12(3): 309–27.

Reynand, E. (1983) *Holy Virility: The Social Construction of Masculinity*. London: Pluto Press.

Richards, M. (1987) Fatherhood, marriage and sexuality: Some speculations on the English middle-class family, in C. Lewis and M. O'Brien (eds) *Reassessing Fatherhood: New Observations on Fathers and the Modern Family*. London: Sage.

Riseborough, G. (1993) GBH – The 'Gobbo Barmy Harmy' – One day in the life of the YTS boys, in I. Bates and G. Riseborough (eds) *Youth and Inequality*. Buckingham: Open University Press.

Roberts, H. (ed.) (1981) *Doing Feminist Research*. London: Routledge.

Roberts, K. (1999) *Leisure in Contemporary Society*. Wallingford: CABI.

Robinson, B. E. and Barret, R. L. (1986) *The Developing Father. Emerging Roles in Contemporary Society*. New York: The Guilford Press.

Robinson, K. H. (1992) Classroom discipline: Power resistance and gender. A look at teacher perspectives. *Gender and Education*, 4(3): 273–87.

Roper, M. (1994) *Masculinity and the British Organization Man since 1945*. Oxford: Oxford University Press.

Rose, J. (1996) *States of Fantasy*. Oxford: Clarendon Press.

Rowan, J. (1987) *The Horned God*. London: Routledge and Kegan Paul.

Rowan, J. (1997) *Healing the Male Psyche: Therapy as Initiation*. London: Routledge.

Rowbotham, S. (1997) *A Century of Women: The History of Women in Britain and the US*. London: Viking.

Rubin, G. (1993) Thinking sex: Notes for a radical theory of politics of sexuality, in H. Abelove, M. A. Barale, and D. M. Halperin (eds) *The Lesbian and Gay Studies Reader*. London: Routledge.

Russell, G. (1983) *The Changing Role of Father*. London: University of Queensland Press.

Russell, H. (1999) Friends in low places: Gender, unemployment, and sociability, *Work, Employment and Society*, 13(2): 205–25.

Rutherford, J. (1990) A place called home: Identity and the cultural politics of difference, in J. Rutherford (ed.) *Identity, Community, Culture and Difference*. London: Lawrence and Wishart.

Rutherford, J. (1992) *Men's Silences: Predicaments in Masculinity*. London: Routledge.

Saco, D. (1992) Masculinity as signs: Post-structuralist feminist approaches to the study of gender, in S. Craig (ed.) *Men, Masculinity and the Media*. Newbury Park, CA: Sage Publications.

Salisbury, J. and Jackson, D. (1996) *Challenging Macho Values: Practical Ways of Working with Boys*. London: Falmer Press.

Savage, M. (2000) *Class Analysis and Social Transformation*. Buckingham: Open University Press.

Schacht, S. P. (1997) Feminist fieldwork in the misogynist setting of the rugby pitch: becoming a sylph to survive and personally grow. *Journal of Contemporary Ethnography*, 26: 332–63.

Scheurich, J. J. (1995) A postmodernist critique of interviewing. *International Journal of Qualitative Studies in Education*, 8(3): 239–52.

Schwalbe, M. (1996) *Unlocking the Iron Cage: The Men's Movement, Gender Politics, and American Culture*. Oxford: Oxford University Press.

Sedgwick, E. K. (1990) *Epistemology of the Closet*. Berkeley, CA: University of California Press.

Sedgwick, E. K. (1994) *Tendencies*. London: Routledge.

Segal, L. (1990) *Slow Motion: Changing Masculinities, Changing Men*. London: Virago.

Seidler, V. J. (1988) Fathering, authority and masculinity, in R. Chapman and J. Rutherford (eds) *Male Order: Unwrapping Masculinity*. London: Lawrence and Wishart.

Seidler, V. J. (1991) *Recreating Sexual Politics: Men, Feminism and Politics*. London: Routledge.

Seidler, V. J. (1992) *Men, Sex and Relationships: Writings from Achilles Heel*. London: Routledge.

Seidman, S. (1996) *Queer Theory/Sociology*. Cambridge, MA: Blackwell.

Shakespeare, T., Gillespie-Sells, K. and Davies, D. (1996) *The Sexual Politics of Disability: Untold Desires*. London: Cassell.

Sharp, S. (1996) Gendering nationhood: A feminist engagement with national identity, in N. Duncan (ed.) *Bodyspace*. London: Routledge.

Shire, C. (1994) Men don't go to the moon: Language, space and masculinities in Zimbabwe, in A. Cornwall and N. Lindisfarne (eds) *Dislocating Masculinity: Gender, Power and Anthropolgy*. Routledge: London.

Silva, E. B. and Smart, C. (eds) (1999a) *The 'New' Family?* London: Sage.

Silva, E. B. and Smart, C. (1999b) The 'new' practices and the politics of family life, in E. B. Silva and C. Smart (eds) *The 'New' Family?* London: Sage.

Simpson, M. (ed.) (1996) *Anti-gay*. London: Cassell.

Simpson, M. and Zeeland, S. (2001) *The Queen is Dead: A Story of Jarheads, Eggheads, Serial Killers and Bad Sex*. London: Arcadia.

Sinfield, A. (1994) *Cultural Politics: Queer Reader*. London: Routledge.

Skeggs, B. (1997) *Formations of Class and Gender: Becoming Respectable*. London: Sage.

Skelton, C. (1998) Feminism and research into masculinities and schooling. *Gender and Education*, 10(2): 217–27.

Skelton, C. (2001) *Schooling the Boys: Masculinities and Primary Education*. Buckingham: Open University Press.

Smith, D. (1987) *The Everyday World as Problematic: A Feminist Sociology*. Milton Keynes: Open University Press.

Snodgrass, J. (ed.) (1977) *For Men Against Sexism*. New York: Times Change Press.

Spradley, J. P. (1979) *The Ethnographic Interview*. New York: Holt, Rinehart and Winston.

Squires, J. (1999) *Gender in Political Theory*. Cambridge: Polity Press.

Stacey, J. (1991) Promoting normality; Section 28 and the regulation of sexuality, in S. Franklin, C. Lury and J. Stacey (eds) *Off-Centre: Feminism and Cultural Studies*. London: Routledge.

Stacey, J. (1996) *In the Name of the Family: Rethinking Family Values in the Postmodern Age*. Boston, MA: Beacon Press.

Stanley, L. and Wise, S. (1990) *Breaking Out: Feminist Consciousness and Feminist Research*. London: Routledge and Kegan Paul.

Stoller, R. (1968) *Sex and Gender*. New York: Science House.

Stoltenberg, J. (1989) *Refusing to be a Man*. New York: Meridian.

Sullivan, A. (ed.) (1997) *Same Sex Marriage: Pro and Con – A Reader*. New York: Vintage Books.

Sweetman, C. (1997) *Men and Masculinity*. Oxford: Oxfam.

Taylor, F. W. (1947) *Scientific Management*. New York: Harper and Row.

Taylor, I., Evans, K. and Fraser, P. (1996) *A Tale of Two Cities: Global Change, Local Feeling and Everyday Life in the North of England: A Study in Manchester and Sheffield*. London: Routledge.

Thomas, D. (1993) *Not Guilty: In Defence of the Modern Man*. London: Weidenfeld and Nicholson.

Thorne, B. (1993) *Gender Play: Girls and Boys in School*. Buckingham: Open University Press.

Tolson, A. (1977) *The Limits of Masculinity*. London: Tavistock.

Trotter, J. (1999) Subjects: Sexuality; education; gay and lesbian issues. *British Journal of Social Work*, 29: 955–61.

Tyler, S. A. (1991) A Post-modern In-stance, in L. Nencel and P. Pels (eds) *Constructing Knowledge: Authority and Critique in Social Science*. London: Sage.

Van Every, J. (1995) *Heterosexual Women Changing the Family: Refusing to be a Wife*. London: Taylor & Francis.

Velu, C. (1999) Faut-il 'practiser' avec l'universalisme? A short history of the PACS. *Modern and Contemporary France*, 7(4): 429–42.

Walby, S. (1986) *Patriarchy at Work: Patriarchal and Capitalist Relations in Employment*. Minneapolis, MN: University of Minnesota Press.

Walby, S. (1990) *Theorizing Patriarchy*. Oxford: Blackwell.

Walby, S. (1997) *Gendered Transformations*. London: Routledge.

Walby, S. (1999) *New Agendas for Women*. London: Macmillan.

Walkerdine, V. (1984) Developmental psychology and the child centered pedagogy: The insertion of Piaget into early education, in J. Henriques, W. Hollway, C. Urwin, C. Venn and V. Walkerdine (eds) *Changing the Subject: Psychology, Social Regulation and Subjectivity*. London: Methuen.

Walkerdine, V. (1990) *Schoolgirl Fictions*. London: Verso.

Walter, B. (1999) Gendered Irishness in Britain: changing Constructions, in C. Graham and R. Kirkham (eds) *Ireland and Cultural Theory: The Mechanics of Authenticity*. London: Macmillan.

Warner, M. (ed.) (1993) *Fear of a Queer Planet: Queer Politics and Social Theory*. Minneapolis, MN: University of Minnesota Press.

Warren, C. (1988) *Gender Issues in Field Research*. Newbury Park, CA: Sage.

Warren, H. (1984) *Talking about School*. London: Gay Teachers Project.

Watney, S. and Carter, E. (eds) (1989) *Taking Liberties: AIDS and Cultural Politics*. London: Serpent's Tail.

Weber, M. (1958) *The Protestant Ethic and the Spirit of Capitalism*. New York: Charles Schribner's Sons.

Weedon, C. (1987) *Feminist Practice and Poststructuralist Theory*. Oxford: Blackwell.

Weeks, J. (1977) *Coming Out: Homosexual Politics in Britain from the Nineteenth Century to the Present*. London: Quartet.

Weeks, J. (1981) *Sex, Politics and Desire*. London: Longman.

Weeks, J. (1989) *Sexuality and its Discontents: Meanings, Myths and Modern Sexualities*. London: Routledge.

Weeks, J. (1990) Post-modern AIDS? in T. Boffin and S. Gupta (eds) *Ecstatic Antibodies: Resisting the AIDS Mythology*. London: Rivers Oram Press.

Weeks, J. (1995) *Invented Moralities: Sexual Values in an Age of Uncertainty*. Cambridge: Polity Press.

Weeks, J., Heaphy, B. and Donovan, C. (1999) Families of choice: Autonomy and mutuality in non-heterosexual relationships, in S. McRae (ed.) *Changing Britain: Families and Households*. Oxford: Oxford University Press.

Weeks, J., Heaphy, B. and Donovan, C. (2001) *Same Sex Intimacies: Families of Choice and Other Life Experiments*. London: Routledge.

Westwood, S. (1996) 'Feckless fathers': Masculinities and the British state, in M. Mac an Ghaill (ed.) *Understanding Masculinities: Social Relations and Cultural Arenas*. Buckingham: Open University Press.

White, S. C. (1997) Men, masculinities and the politics of development, in C. Sweetman (ed.) *Men and Masculinity*. Oxford: Oxfam.

Williams, I. and Mac an Ghaill, M. (1998) *Older Irish Men: An Investigation of Health and Social Care Needs*. Birmingham: The Irish Government's Dion Fund and Focus Housing Group.

Willis, P. (1977) *Learning to Labour: How Working Class Kids Get Working Class Jobs*. Farnborough: Saxon House.

Willis, P. (1979) Shop-floor culture, masculinity and the wage form, in J. Clarke, C. Critcher and R. Johnson (eds) *Working Class Culture: Studies in History and Theory*. London: Hutchinson, in association with the CCCS, University of Birmingham.

Willis, P. (2000) *The Ethnographic Imagination*. Cambridge: Polity Press.

Willott, S. and Griffin, C. (1997) 'Wham Bam, am I a Man?': Unemployed men talk about masculinities. *Feminism and Psychology*, 7(1): 107–28.

Winnicott, D. W. (1993) *Talking to Parents*. Cambridge, MA: Perseus Press.

Wolpe, A. M. (1988) *Within School Walls: The Role of Discipline. Sexuality and the Curriculum*. London: Routledge.

World Trade Organization (2000) *International Trade Statistics*. Geneva: WTO Publications.

Young, B. (2000) Globalization and gender: A European perspective, in R. M. Kelly, J. Bayes and B. Young (eds) *Globalization, Democratization and Gender*. Oxford: Oxford University Press/Routledge.

Young, I. M. (1993) Together in difference: Transforming the logic of group political difference, in J. Squires (ed.) *Principled Positions: Postmodernism and the Rediscovery of Value*. London: Lawrence and Wishart.

Young, M. D. and Willmott, P. (1957) *Family and Kinship in East London*. London: Routledge and Kegan Paul.

Young, M. and Willmott, P. (1973) *The Symmetrical Family: A Study of Work and Leisure in the London Region*. London: Routledge and Kegan Paul.

AUTHOR INDEX

SUBJECT INDEX

African-Caribbean, 74–6
age, 32, 58, 70–3, 87, 89, 136, 140,
    141, 148–9
    see also generational specificity
AIDS/HIV, 4, 12, 13, 17, 58, 78–9, 99,
    137, 139, 142
androgyny, 10, 48–9
androcentrism, 103–4, 134
American men, 26–7, 38, 45, 51, 94,
    110, 126, 132
    academia, 103, 133
    context, 50, 134, 129, 149
    culture, 74, 97, 98
    military, 96
    politics, 128, 137, 143
Anglo-American, 77
Anglo ethnic majority, 74–5
Anglo gender majority, 14
anthropology, 13, 113, 118–19
anthropological stranger, 107
anti-feminism, 109, 110, 132, 133,
    134
anti-oppressive framework, 79, 108,
    112, 136
anti-racist politics, 64, 116, 136
anti-sexist politics, 64, 128–9,
    142

Australia
    context, 13, 50, 66, 129, 134, 149
    masculinities, 68

biological differences, 6, 9, 15–16, 22,
    44, 54, 57, 60, 86, 92, 129, 147–8
bisexuality, 131
black masculinity, 7–8, 28, 73–6, 87, 99
black men, 56, 120, 134, 136, 137
black politics, 137, 140
body, 12, 15–16, 20, 18–30, 36, 40,
    94–5, 99, 116, 147
boys, 7–8, 58, 65, 66, 69–73, 85–6, 89,
    91, 120, 129, 150
    Asian, 74–5
    black, 74–6
    gay, 79
    identity, 69, 72, 85–6
    underachieving, 41, 148
breadwinner, male, 21–2, 27, 30, 33,
    37–8, 44, 47–8, 54, 56
Britain, 93, 96–7
    as case study, 23, 45, 46, 105–6
    as context, 50, 55
British
    academia, 48–9, 58, 106, 129
    colonialism, 87–8